Ships' Graveyards

Published by The Society for Historical Archaeology

Ships' Graveyards

Abandoned Watercraft and
the Archaeological Site Formation Process

Nathan Richards

SOCIETY *for* HISTORICAL ARCHAEOLOGY

Second Edition
Copyright 2022 by The Society for Historical Archaeology
Printed in the United States of America

13 12 11 10 09 08   6 5 4 3 2 1

Library of Congress Cataloging-in-Publication Data
Richards, Nathan.
Ships' graveyards : abandoned watercraft and the archaeological site formation
process / Nathan Richards.
p. cm.
Includes bibliographical references and index.
ISBN 978-1-957402-00-0
1. Shipwrecks. 2. Shipwrecks—Australia. 3. Underwater archaeology.
4. Underwater archaeology—Australia. I. Title.
VK1259.R53 2008
930.1028'04—dc22   2008008249

Cover photo: Tangalooma breakwater, Tangalooma, Queensland (2001),
by Nathan Richards.

Dedicated to my parents, Robert and Raelene Richards

Contents

Tables

Figures

Preface

The historical importance and archaeological potential of deliberately discarded watercraft has not been a major feature of maritime archaeological enquiry. This book examines this undervalued resource, assessing the behaviors associated with deliberate discard in a maritime context. It considers a number of aspects of discard behaviors, examining many of the cultural processes that have contributed to the spatial patterns of discard areas; the historical, economic, and technological causes of abandonment; and archaeological remnants of such historic events and human activities. Its aim is to show that the remains of discarded vessels are significant cultural resources and have the potential to illuminate aspects of the past. This research aims to illustrate that when researchers use appropriate comparative methods, the importance and archaeological potential of many aspects of our hitherto undervalued maritime heritage may return considerable data, highlighting average working vessels and the lives of the people who worked on them.

Watercraft abandonment is a process almost as old as shipbuilding, and the discard of ships follows every aspect of maritime commerce. Hence, discarded vessels have the capability to communicate characteristics of technological change and diffusion, evolving economic conditions (especially in relation to ship owning and shipbuilding), and social history (the effect of changes within technology and economy). They are also objects imbued with cultural codes, rich with the evidence of the people who used, and disposed, of them.

This book also embraces the argument that the perspectives that predominate the study of shipwrecks (arguably the main subject of maritime archaeology) are generally not conducive to understanding abandoned watercraft. Moreover, this stance maintains that traditional views have negatively influenced the study of discarded watercraft and prejudiced maritime archaeologists against the significance of discard sites.

Many previous studies have acknowledged the scientific, experimental, and educational significance of discarded watercraft, and a select few have recognized the archaeological significance of this resource. However, there has been no appreciable attempt to understand the nature of discard in conjunction with the applied use of data from discarded watercraft. As a consequence, the subject has lacked thorough exploration. This is in part a problem arising from the particularist manner and site-specific methods in which these studies have proceeded, and the way that they have ignored the causal and behavioral attributes of this particular resource.

The research represented by this book is an attempt at a comparative/nomothetic approach to maritime archaeological material. It strives to demonstrate that comparative methods coupled with broad theoretical underpinnings have the potential to recontextualize undervalued categories of maritime heritage. It also endeavors to outline that such an approach is not simply a useful tool within maritime archaeology for behaviorally oriented studies; indeed, for some aspects of the maritime archaeological record, comparative approaches may be the only feasible way of assessing, or recasting, meaning and significance. I hope that this work may have some influence on future assessments of the significance of the undervalued abandoned watercraft resource and bring about further attempts at its analysis.

Acknowledgments

While researching and writing this study and previous, related papers, I had the pleasure to meet, work with, and be guided by a number of individuals and organizations that are owed not only recognition but also my earnest gratitude. First, my thanks must go to Mark Staniforth. Without his knowledge, advice, and guidance (and more than a little pushing) many of the great things in my life would have never occurred. I have no doubt that it would be hard to find a better role model, friend, and scholar.

In relation to actual research, there are a host of people the length and breadth of Australia who deserve credit and thanks. In the Northern Territory, I would like to thank David Steinberg, Silvano Jung, and Paul Clark. In northern Queensland, Brad Duncan, Grant Luckmann, Ewen McPhee, and Coleman Doyle, and in southern Queensland, Warren Delaney and David Bell. In Victoria, thanks goes to Ross Anderson, Peter Harvey, Peter Taylor, and Malcolm Venturoni. In Sydney, David Nutley, Tim Smith, Stirling Smith, Janis Winn, and John Riley; in Western Australia, Michael McCarthy, Jeremy Green, Corioli Souter, and Patrick Baker; and in Tasmania, Mike Nash and Harry McDermott. Additionally, I would like to thank Cosmos Coroneos, whose expertise and knowledge was not limited to New South Wales but veritably into the many corners of the country.

South Australian experts deserve special acknowledgment. I would like to thank Bill Jeffery, Terry Arnott, and Robyn Hartell of Heritage South Australia, whose extensive knowledge, patience, and expertise proved to be one of the major starting points for my foray into maritime archaeology. Heartfelt thanks is also owed to the staff and students of various maritime archaeology subjects and field excursions from first year to honors level at the Department of Archaeology, Flinders University whose work and fresh perspectives provided much food for thought. This goes double for Lis Janssen, whose help to graduate students can never truly be acknowledged enough. Additionally, I would like to thank the scores of individuals who over the years have helped in my fieldwork by trudging around in the mud and dealing with my continual musings and mutterings about the remains of "old boats." Related to this, special note is made of my friends and regular field crew experts Cassandra Philippou, Aara Welz, Chris Lewczak, Susan Briggs, Tim Owen, Jody Steele, Sally May, Chris Langeluddecke, and Kirsten Brett. Holgar, Maggie, and Niki Welz are also owed my gratitude for their assistance and hospitality during the Kangaroo Island phase of fieldwork.

I would also like to acknowledge the assistance gained from the Port Adelaide Historical Society, the Society for Historical Research, the Mortlock Library of South Australiana, and the South Australian Maritime Museum. Special thanks here to Tony Arbon, whose encyclopedic mind and extensive archives were never closed to me, and Daryl Metters of the National Tidal Facility, Flinders University.

All of the individuals mentioned above were enthusiastic in their support and generous with their advice and feedback during this research, providing me with much valued support and friendship.

I would also like to thank the four authors of the material that has to a large degree formed the core of this research: Ronald Parsons, Geoff Plunkett, Graeme Broxam, and the late Jack Loney. Without their voluminous knowledge and commitment to the publishing of maritime historical material, this research would simply not have been possible. Likewise, thanks are due to some people I feel are the "intellectual fathers" of my research: Michael B. Schiffer, Larry Murphy, Daniel Lenihan, Mark Staniforth, and, last but not least, Michael McCarthy.

Also, my heartfelt thanks to the people involved in the editing process: Martin Gibbs, Matt Russell, David Conlin, Sami Seeb, Michael McCarthy, and, especially, Michael B. Schiffer. Also thanks to Eli Bortz and John Byram at the University Press of Florida. I would especially like to thank the Society for Historical Archaeology for providing me with the opportunity and support to publish this work, as well as the South Australian Museum (Kevin Jones), Western Australian Museum (Michael McCarthy), State Library of Tasmania (Ian Morrison), and the Ron Blum Collection (Ron Blum) for permission to reprint images from their collections.

Finally, I would like to express my gratitude to my colleagues at East Carolina University, Michael Palmer, Bradley A. Rodgers, Carl Swanson, Annalies Corbin, David Stewart, Larry Babits, and Frank Cantelas, for their support.

Abbreviations

AHSD	Australian Historic Shipwrecks Database
ANAVD	Australian National Abandoned Vessel Database
ANMA	Australian National Maritime Association
ANMM	Australian National Maritime Museum
COIITC	Committee of Inquiry into Technological Change in Australia
DASETT	Department of the Arts, Sport, the Environment, Tourism and Territories
FAD	Fish aggregation device
GMT	Greenwich Mean Time
GRG	Government Record Group
GRT	Gross registered tons
IMO	International Maritime Organization
LASH	Lighter aboard ship
MAAQ	Maritime Archaeological Association of Queensland
MAAT	Maritime Archaeological Association of Tasmania
MAAV	Maritime Archaeological Association of Victoria
MAAWA	Maritime Archaeological Association of Western Australia
MAGNT	Museum and Art Gallery of the Northern Territory
NSW	New South Wales
MAS	Marine Archaeological Society
PAHS	Port Adelaide Historical Society
QLD	Queensland
SA	South Australia
SUHR	Society for Underwater Historical Research
NT	Northern Territory
UARG	Underwater Archaeological Research Group
VAS	Victoria Archaeological Survey
VIC	Victoria
WA	Western Australia

1

Introduction

The hulks especially are a forgotten group and instead of viewing them as they now appear . . . they can be a fascinating starting point for further study of history and archaeology.

—Michael McCarthy, *Jervoise Bay Shipwrecks*

Over time, people have built, used, and discarded an untold number of watercraft. Since humans first began building ships, they also have found value and meaning in the ways and means of discarding them. The catalysts and causes of this behavior are as diverse as the functions the vessels once served.

Similarly, since researchers first turned to the historical and archaeological record in the hope of rediscovering the past, they have stumbled across the accounts, remains, and residues of old, unwanted, and obsolete ships in all their varied forms. The knowledge that has emerged from the study of isolated discarded vessels, from the accumulations of dilapidated ship shells, as well as from the vessels' more ephemeral disarticulated remnants, is substantial.

This book is about how the deliberate abandonment of watercraft may contribute to understanding the behavior of past human societies. More specifically, it concerns the way that archaeologists and historians, through an engagement with the intangible histories and tangible remains of abandoned ships, may interact with themes of agency and human decision making.

The research presented within these pages is a result of the Abandoned Ships Project, an initiative of the Department of Archaeology at Flinders University in South Australia.[1] This research, carried out between 1997 and 2002, focused on understanding the nature and potential of the deliberately abandoned watercraft resource of Australia since its settlement by Europeans in the late eighteenth century. As a study set in Australia, this book will obviously have relevance to an Australian audience interested in maritime history and archaeology. Although providing context to the study, however, this historical background is both secondary and incidental. Rather, this research also should appeal to scholars of archaeological method and theory. In particular, one idea explored within these pages is that comparative approaches assist in the process of conceptualizing the cause-and-effect relationships between human historical processes and the formation of maritime archaeological sites. Resulting behavioral models may hold true in any region, irrespective of historical context. From this position, understanding that the history of ship technology, maritime commerce, and technological change in Australia is essentially a derivate of world trends, one may suggest that the potential for the extension of regional or national comparative research to global levels is significant. Here too this work may be of some use to scholars of the techno-economic aspects of human cultures from the late eighteenth century onward.

Additionally, this work may serve as a guide to the ever-growing library of the "signatures" of activities that appear on the vestiges of abandoned watercraft. Here, I hope that this book contributes to the already large body of work in behavioral archaeology, reinforcing the utility of this theoretical approach to the maritime archaeological community. It may be that the methods and findings of this work have their greatest application in the establishment of similar regional, national, or global studies of abandoned watercraft sites or sites like them—whether wet, intertidal, or "high and dry."

Research for the Abandoned Ships Project and this book involved the collection of historical and archaeological information about deliberately abandoned vessel remains. I collated historical data from a diverse array of published and unpublished sources, including online data, archives, maritime indexes, databases, journals, newspapers, books, manuscripts, and images.[2] This information came from a number of research institutions across the Australian continent.[3]

The project also involved the collation of data from the archaeological vestiges of watercraft sites. I chose candidates predominantly from references discovered in historical sources matching a previously defined definition of *deliberate discard* (outlined below). Suspicions of catastrophic or premature loss were the basis of exclusion from the study.

My intention in using this selection strategy was to engage in comparative analyses of the abandoned watercraft resource. I concentrated on the location and inspection of the remnant structures of the ships, as well as the analysis of their spatial arrangement. This focus included determining the location of ships' graveyards and vessel dumping sites and the investigation of the logistics of the abandonment act and salvage. To a lesser degree, I attempted to see sites as a component of the landscape in order to understand the evolution and use of places as abandonment areas, and to compare their location with associated infrastructure and other abandonment areas. The position of a vessel in relation to other aspects of its setting, such as navigable waterways and adjacent industry or land use, shed light on the reasons for the formation of ships' graveyards.

The focus of archaeological investigation was to visit as many sites as possible and to visit places that reflect the different types of abandoned vessels uncovered by historical research. I visited both collections (ships' graveyards) and isolated (individual) abandonment sites, as well as sites reflecting distinctive postabandonment uses. I examined a wide variety of environmental circumstances, ranging from intertidal situations to deepwater contexts, although, due to issues of access, the majority of sites I visited were in this first category.

Archival research in consultation with state cultural heritage management agencies ran parallel with the assessment of archaeological sites. In some instances, I discovered vessel remains not previously documented in the historical record, demonstrating the incompleteness of the historical record as well as the absence of a comprehensive history of many of the vessels discovered.

Site inspections included both diving on the archaeological remnants of watercraft and accessing them at low tide. In the case of beached vessels, site access normally required a combination of wading, snorkeling, and diving. In all scenarios, written observations, photographs, site measurement, and detailed site description formed the core of a diverse recording regimen. I also used a two-page standardized form, similar to that employed for recording abandoned watercraft on the Medway River in the United Kingdom, for compiling detailed information.[4] These detailed site inspections yielded many separate attributes of the archaeological remains, including spatial coordinates, environment description, dimensions, evidence of propulsion, construction details, scantling dimensions, exposure at tides, orientation, signatures of discard, description of salvage activities, and intactness. No archaeological deposits were disturbed during examination, and portable material culture was not analyzed. At the conclusion of the site inspection phase of research, I had visited more than 140 separate beached and submerged abandoned watercraft (true numbers are hard to determine due to the disarticulated nature of some remains).

Following creation of this archive of abandonment sites, I designed a relational database, the Australian National Abandoned Vessel Database (ANAVD), as an analytical tool.[5] Due to the correspondence of documentary materials concerning watercraft dimensions with site observations, it

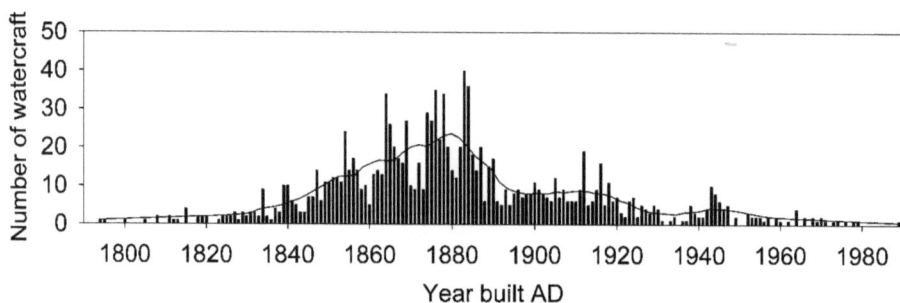

Figure 1. Temporal distribution of abandoned watercraft in ANAVD by year of build (1790–1990) (n = 1,254).

was possible to merge the historical and archaeological records. The database provided insight into a range of technological and economic issues and supplied evidence for describing cultural site formation processes. It also enabled analysis of the technological and economic causes and ramifications of deliberate abandonment.

At the conclusion of data collection in February 2002, this database included 6,082 individual historical sources attached to more than 1,500 records of deliberately discarded watercraft spanning the period 1806 to 2001 (see figure 1 for temporal distribution). Vessels previously engaged in commercial/merchant operations such as merchant shipping, passenger transport, resource exploitation (such as fishing), or the support of these activities (harbor support craft such as tugs, dredges, and barges) accounted for more than 98 percent of the database, with naval vessels present but underrepresented due to problems with access to military dumping records.

Abandoned Ships in Australian Maritime Archaeology

The Abandoned Ships Project was not the first investigation of discarded watercraft sites in Australia. In the 1970s, the Western Australian Maritime Museum carried out the first archaeological investigations of deliberately discarded watercraft in Australia. By 1983, researchers such as Mike McCarthy were writing that archaeologists could learn valuable lessons by studying the discarded watercraft within the ships' graveyards of Australia, New Zealand, and Southeast Asia.[6]

Despite this, it is clear from the lack of publication of abandonment-related research that the maritime archaeological community at the time generally continued to consider deliberately abandoned watercraft as a resource of negligible importance. This was largely due to preconceptions concerning archaeological significance, a focus on artifact assemblages, and the centrality of the image of the shipwreck within the mind of the subdiscipline. These views also concentrated on a number of aspects: the age of a ship, any association with famous individuals or events, and preoccupations with the condition or environmental setting of shipwreck sites.[7] The 1980s, however, saw a challenge to this position. A new perspective, arguing that more modern watercraft, representing unspectacular aspects of the past, irrespective of their degree of intactness or environmental conditions also had archaeological potential. To a large degree this mirrored changes in terrestrial archaeology, which had begun to reject the notions that "we must dig for our data, and that archaeological data must be old."[8] In particular, this change was justified through the work on intertidal and exposed vessel remains,[9] as well as the arguments against "celebrity ships" and the *shrine complex*, the latter a term used to define "an undue emphasis upon the excavation and restoration of relics associated with national heroes and historically famous accomplishments."[10] These works had an enormous impact on the way that abandoned watercraft (which are generally nonfamous vessels in intertidal contexts) have come to be perceived.

Another important factor was the growing argument concerning the significance of iron and steam shipwrecks. One publication representing this important development was the landmark publication *Iron Ships and Steam Shipwrecks: Papers from the First Australian Seminar on the Management of Iron Vessels and Steam Shipwrecks*,[11] which emerged from a conference hosted by the Western Australian Maritime Museum in Fremantle, Australia. This changing view of archaeological significance was largely the work of McCarthy, who advanced the view that the importance of the iron and steam vessel resource was attributable to multiple layers of historical, technical, and anthropological potential.[12] The end result was the growth of a "grudging support"[13] for the worth of this resource and the slow rise of a more inclusive view of significance. Publication of *Iron and Steam Shipwrecks* had two other implications for deliberately discarded watercraft. Ironically, four out of five of the most significant iron and steam shipwrecks noted in the study were also abandoned watercraft, and the text cited as evidence of the importance of iron and steam, Brouwer's *International Register of Historic Ships*,[14] also included many examples of discarded ships.[15] Although these developments had an undeniable role in the consideration of abandoned vessels as significant cultural resources, it did not lead to an immediate avalanche of archaeological investigations, or to any serious appraisal of their significance.

It did, however, spark the increased production of research by museums, cultural resource agencies, consultants, universities, and archaeological associations into abandoned ships. We see this in general heritage studies that include abandoned ships, historical and archaeological studies dealing specifically with discard of watercraft, and studies dedicated to collections of abandoned watercraft (ships' graveyards.)[16] These Australian case studies illustrated the movement toward comparative and thematic investigations of discarded watercraft. Additionally, they were significant for contributing to our understanding of how behaviors associated with activities such as salvage, demolition, and scuttling translate to the archaeological record. These studies also touched upon the scientific and experimental potential of discarded watercraft, the causal nature of discard activities, the spatial dimension of deliberate abandonment, and the changing nature of the disposal and postabandonment use of unwanted watercraft.[17] Despite these advancements, there continued to be a lingering suspicion about discarded vessels. The tendency to see their significance simply in relation to their educational potential, and the small number of them protected by legislation, are evidence of this. To a large degree, it was also attributable to a continued preoccupation with celebrity, age, and intactness. Nevertheless, by illuminating the range and diversity of the sites, these investigations became important preludes to the few behaviorally focused archaeological studies of the resource that would emerge later.[18]

In another way, these studies represent a significant difference in approach. This difference includes their tendency to be anthropological, thematic, and comparative because they are focused on *behavior*. Although some researchers had identified that there were semantic issues regarding the study of "abandoned vessels" because they were not "shipwrecks,"[19] it was never acknowledged that the differences in terminology were reflective of major behavioral differences. This in turn had consequences for the consideration of the significance and study of these ships. In essence, there was a continued trend to assess and investigate abandoned watercraft as if they were the product of catastrophic processes. The behavioral studies sought to explicitly examine and rigorously define the terms *shipwreck* and *abandonment* in order to illuminate the many differences between these two categories of archaeological site.

Shipwreck and Abandonment: A Dichotomy

Shipwreck is a popularly used term that can evoke many meanings. The *Oxford English Dictionary* defines a shipwreck as "what is cast up from a wreck; the remains of a wrecked vessel; wreckage" and the "destruction or loss of a ship by its being sunk or broken up by the violence of the sea, or by its striking or stranding upon a rock or shoal."[20] At the heart of these definitions it is clear that catastrophic events are what turn ships to shipwrecks. From such categorization, it also follows that discarded vessels, those ships deliberately thrown away or disposed of by their owners, do not fit the traditional definition of a shipwreck. These semantic differentiations are pivotal for understanding the nature of abandonment processes, discard activities, and, most important, the role of behavior in the creation of certain types of archaeological sites.

The term *abandonment* also has many meanings. In relation to shipping and marine insurance terms, it has a specific connotation that refers to the giving up of control of a vessel upon its *constructive total loss*. These definitions are also predominantly concerned with wrecked watercraft.[21] Within normal use, however, this term is more synonymous with phrases like "to relinquish," "to throw away," and "to reject." From this perspective, the word *abandonment* represents a variety of behaviors that include the accidental and catastrophic as well as the deliberate and well rehearsed. To take this a step further, all watercraft, irrespective of their fate, have historically come to be abandoned in some way by the people who used them, whether the abandonment involved people scurrying to leave a sinking ship or merchants seeking to dispose of their unwanted craft.

From a behavioral perspective, it is clear that catastrophes and deliberately determined acts will induce different responses in human beings. Nevertheless, many maritime historians, when writing the histories of ships, have tended to consider deliberately discarded vessels simply as shipwrecks missing the drama of the wrecking. Maritime archaeologists have also largely overlooked this major distinction, despite believing that when we examine the archaeological record, we are not reading things but reading people with all of their varied experiences and behaviors. Also largely ignored is the fact that where the traces of a shipwreck represent the powerlessness of humans within a hostile natural world, the remains of discarded vessels represent the nature of the power that humans have within the landscape of their own construction, *the cultural environment.*

Some researchers, however, have commented upon this shipwreck-abandonment dichotomy. Donald Shomette, for instance considers abandoned vessels an "important variation of the shipwreck category."[22] This view focuses on the role of behavior in order to classify archaeological site types. It pays more attention to the role of human agency as a historical force and a significant influence on altering both the landscape and the archaeological record. As a consequence of taking this approach, Shomette touches on many of the issues concerning watercraft discard discussed in this book. His distinction between "abandonments at sea," which emerge from catastrophic events, and "old or useless wrecks," which are often disposed of due to their obsolescence and condition, is one that allows for the behavioral aspects of the archaeological remains of watercraft to be better understood. Additionally, he examines the abandonment of unwanted vessels from the perspective of their representativeness, while also considering that discarded vessels represent an amalgam of industrial, technological, economic, and regulatory developments in human society. Finally, he touches upon the processes that are involved in their abandonment, such as the location of discard and their use as recyclable materials and structures after abandonment.

The direction of this work acknowledges Shomette but differs subtly. This book does not maintain that abandoned vessels are a variation of shipwreck; rather, it considers shipwrecks and abandoned watercraft as two related but discrete aspects of the maritime archaeological record. This is an important distinction in justifying the generalist/nomothetic analyses (designed to study or discover general scientific laws) within this study. This study also suggests that the processes interacting with a ship on its journey from its life of use to its integration as a component of the archaeological record are not just many and diverse but also have major ramifications for how we read the archaeological record and how we use archaeological resources in research. Moreover, these distinctions are significant because they demonstrate the relationship between abandonment activities and cultural processes.

The dichotomous relationship between wrecked ships and discarded ships is also important because both categories of maritime archaeological site exist at the extremes of a behavioral spectrum concerned with the nature of human decision-making processes (agency). Within this continuum, there are essentially three major classifications of abandonment behavior, each illustrating a range of cultural behaviors associated with the loss and discard of watercraft.

Catastrophic abandonment takes place when the desertion of a ship becomes a prerequisite in the preservation of life. For example, the passenger steamer RMS *Titanic* (1912) was abandoned when it hit an iceberg, the English naval frigate, HMS *Pandora* (1791), when it struck the Great Barrier Reef, and the English flagship of the Virginia Company, *Sea Venture* (1609), when it collided with the islands of Bermuda.[23] In other instances, crew may abandon a vessel because of perception of an *impending* disaster, allowing the vessel to become derelict.[24] In both instances ships invariably become shipwrecks and *abandonment* becomes synonymous with *escape*. The decision to abandon occurs without consideration of the value of the vessel undergoing abandonment, and the end product is a bone fide *shipwreck.*

Consequential abandonment occurs when there is a need to ruin a ship in order to protect lives, cargo, and other structures from damage or destruction. One example of this was the burning of the merchantman *General Knox* in August 1894 while it was alongside a New York wharf. A threat to all surrounding it, the vessel was scuttled in order to extinguish the flames.[25] Also included in this category are cases of the nonaccidental wrecking of vessels after mishaps at sea where the deliberate destruction of the ship is needed in order to create better circumstances for the preservation of life and cargo. One such occurrence was the wrecking of the "country" trade merchantman *Sydney Cove* near Preservation Island, Tasmania, in 1797. In this case, the threat of losing cargo due to prevailing natural forces impelled the captain to deliberately run the vessel aground on the closest shoreline.[26]

Despite catastrophic circumstances leading to the destruction of these ships, it is clear that the act of abandonment in all cases occurred because inaction would create a more substantial tragedy. Within this definition, the loss of the watercraft is always a consequence of actual or imminent catastrophe, but decisions occur with some thought concerning value and the potential losses and gains that would culminate with the act of abandonment. In this light, the term *consequential abandonment* becomes synonymous with the term *deliberate wrecking.*

With both catastrophic and consequential abandonment, some degree of human decision making plays a role in the way events pan out. When deliberately running a vessel aground in order to save crew and cargo, for instance, a captain will have some time to make choices regarding the location for the ship's abandonment. Indeed, research regarding wreck patterning strongly suggests that even in the worst catastrophic circumstance, the route taken on a journey already reflects a large degree of decision making concerning potential risks to ship, lives, and merchandise.[27] It is important to remember, however, that the decisions are not being made at the leisure of individuals but are instead being forced upon them, and their options are normally limited. Hence, both types of abandonment are examples of *premature loss.*

Whether deliberately or catastrophically wrecked, the occurrence of loss through an element of surprise is the reason definitions of abandonment within marine insurance exist. If a vessel is lost unintentionally, for reasons not attributable to the owner or operator, the ship will remain covered by insurance. Any captain or owner not seeking to reduce their loss or choosing to abandon their ship under such circumstances will be legally negligent.

This is not the case with *deliberate abandonment*, which occurs when the act of abandonment involves premeditation in every sense. In these cases abandonment under marine insurance definitions do not apply, as the act of disposal is a planned one, without urgency, and without genuine threat to life or cargo. Here the act of destruction or discard is in every way intentional. Deliberately abandoned vessels are significantly different from catastrophically or deliberately wrecked watercraft because their final resting place, the intactness of their hull, and the inclusion of any material within their hull is totally determined by human intentions, decision-making processes, and actions. The only exception to this is when a vessel befalls catastrophe en route to its location of discard, or where there are accidents during preparations for its disposal. For example, the barkentine *City of Adelaide* was wrecked on Magnetic Island, Queensland, before the proposed time for disposal and one bay from its intended destination.[28] In another case, the iron screw steamer *Glaucus* had its flotation compromised while undergoing salvage activities in the lead up to its final discard in Adelaide, South Australia. So to avoid the creation of a navigation hazard, the ship breaker towed the vessel to a nearby ships' graveyard and beached it.[29] With *deliberate abandonment*, the location of discard is not the most crucial factor in the process. It is normally the facilitation of the loss of the vessel that drives its owner, irrespective of the location and circumstances of abandonment. Of more importance are the decisions to abandon and the implementation of the processes that prepare the ship for its integration into the archaeological record. Exceptions only occur when people repair and refloat an abandoned vessel for further use, where it remains until it is somehow lost to human use a second time.

There is one last thing to say about abandonment. This study stresses that although the term may often imply a relinquishing of mercantile, support, and/or postdiscard function, it does not imply a loss of cultural value. Although the abandonment of vessels occurs because they are unwanted (refuse), sometimes the act of discard occurs with the intention of creating a new function for the vessel following its deposition. Subsequently, all abandoned watercraft (whatever the category) often retain cultural, economic, and technological value.

Researching Deliberate Discard

Variations in behavior and classification are not the only differences between wrecked and abandoned ships. When researching deliberately discarded watercraft there are many methodological hurdles for those accustomed to shipwreck research, as well as variations in historiography. In particular, the process of compiling historical data concerning abandoned vessels is significantly different from that for shipwrecks. This is principally because abandoned vessels are usually less visible in documentary sources. The reasons for this are many. It may be because the abandonment of ships is not often newsworthy, that newspapers only rarely reported on acts of discard, or because owners discarded their vessels secretly in order to avoid the attention of port authorities, environmental protection agencies, and other assorted government entities. As one researcher has commented:

> Unlike the fanfare of their launch, the disposal of ships at the end of their working lives was often gradual and received little public attention. If not completely broken up, they were stripped of machinery, scuttled in deep water, whether alone or in marine graveyards. Invariably they faded from sight, their disappearance easily forgotten, unlike memorable shipwrecks.[30]

Even in cases where ship abandonment occurred in shallow water, in places within the view of the public, the perception of their remains were never far from that of "eyesore"—and their history rarely spectacular enough for reflection.

It cannot be overstated what ramifications these facts have on the study of deliberately abandoned watercraft. On the simplest level, it may be difficult, or impossible, to locate documents pinpointing exact details of the discard date of a ship. Where times of abandonment are concerned, however, there are other complications. Whereas all watercraft that are wrecked are lost at a particular, definite point in time (whether or not this is defined in historical literature), abandonment is rarely an *event* (an exception being deliberate sinking, or "scuttling"). Rather, abandonment is frequently a *process* in which a vessel may undergo salvage or, sitting exposed to the elements, may slowly deteriorate over the years. With these vessels, refloating and reuse may also occur at any given time. Where this occurs, it becomes unclear just when the act of discard occurs, and if it can actually be determined accurately. This is even more difficult in the case of demolition, where a vessel may be discarded and salvaged to such a degree that little or nothing representing the vessel may exist. On the other hand, following their discard, abandoned vessels may remain untouched, dissolving into the archaeological record, have components reintegrated into use, or be refloated and refurbished many years into the future. Here again we see the human mind at work.

Yes, there is much room for confusion when defining a time of abandonment, and questions abound. Is abandonment the time a vessel becomes derelict, the date it is "laid up" at a slip or dock while not in use? Or is it the time of final disposal? This is a particular hurdle to the comparative method used in this study, which is largely dependant on defining dates of build and loss in order to analyze change through time. Effectively, this period between the "laying up" of vessels and their actual discard illustrates the role of human decision making in the transformation of a once-functional ship into an archaeological site.

Another problem involved with data collection involves the process of collecting information about abandoned vessels and the ambiguous nature of the historical record. Vague descriptions of vessel fate within historical records are a major problem when trying to determine a vessel's status as a deliberate abandonment or catastrophic loss. The terms *demolished* and *broken up* are two examples of this. Both imply the dismantling of a vessel to such a degree that it may no longer remain discernible in the archaeological record. Historical and archaeological research, however, suggests that these terms do not necessarily reflect this, and many ships listed as dismantled may still have substantial archaeological remnants at the location of their salvage. Michael Richards, for instance, noted that *broken up* actually refers to the removal of useful equipment. He also maintained that in 1907 it was not possible to "cut up an iron hull."[31]

Unclear language also often makes it difficult to extract examples of discarded ships from historical records. Vessels "abandoned as a wreck" are normally examples of cataclysmic or accidental loss and may be disregarded due to possible catastrophic implications in their fate.[32] A vessel "burned at sea," on the other hand, may refer to an accident or mishap that culminates in catastrophic loss, or may indicate the deliberate burning of a vessel. Such language, which provides no insight into the "accidental or deliberate," is common. An even more complex notation in the records is "allowed to sink."[33] When this terminology is used, an obvious question concerns whether the abandonment date is the date of sinking or the date from which the vessel "was allowed" to sink.

In other cases, authors have particular definitions for terms that may not, at first glance, correspond with the preconceptions of the researcher. For instance, an author may define "abandonment" in a way that includes vessels that were forsaken after a catastrophic occurrence or accident, a definition adhering to one outlined as a "consequential abandonment" and therefore not representing the full range of human decision making processes present in "deliberate abandonment."[34] In other cases, historical documents may simply be wrong or incomplete. In some cases, watercraft listed as "wrecked" or "no longer in existence" may indeed exist within the context of deliberate discard.[35] In such cases, only thorough historical and archaeological legwork may resolve whether the vestiges of a ship remain.

For the archaeologist, these facts make it difficult to decide which particular historical records represent good leads for locating the archaeological remains of deliberately discarded watercraft. Some researchers, for instance, have made reference to inconsistencies where the word *dismantled* is concerned. In one example, Nutley and Smith noted that according to oral history, rampaging youths burnt the vessel *Myall River*, despite alternative citations regarding its complete dismantling.[36] Ambiguities in relation to the method of disposal also appear to indicate deliberate abandonment, but in the absence of other corroborating evidence they can equally describe the aftermath of shipwreck.[37] This is also the case with the notation "ashore," which may refer to the beached remains of a ship as much as it may indicate a catastrophic wrecking event.

The restoration and reuse of previously abandoned watercraft is another problem faced when collecting data. In isolated cases, this has occurred in conjunction with trends of incorporating historic vessel remains into new tourist vessels.[38] Similarly, preserved vessels pose a problem. Although the original purposes of these ships have been abandoned, the possibility of future restoration remains.

From Shipyard to Graveyard

The lifespan of a vessel is invariably the foundation upon which researchers must build models of watercraft abandonment. The task of measuring the trajectory of a ship, from its building to its discard, may be a tool for better understanding some of the behavioral attributes of maritime cultures. Such an assignment, however, is impossible without examining the ways in which maritime cultures have interacted with their craft from shipyard to graveyard. Consequently, chapter 2 presents a literature review of international examples concerning the study of abandoned vessels spanning many thousands of years. These international case studies illustrate that discarded watercraft have a long and significant history and demonstrate that abandoned vessels are amongst some of the oldest and most intact specimens of craft encountered by maritime archaeologists to date. Similarly, they have also played a role in the many aspects of the developing discipline of maritime archaeology. These range from redefining our understanding of ancient Egyptian shipbuilding to shedding light on the evolution of watercraft in northern Europe or providing insight into the sailing characteristics of ancient Saxon ships.[39] Some examinations of deliberately abandoned watercraft have also contributed to shifts in our thinking. Studies of watercraft such as the HMS *Vixen* have been at the forefront of recent changes in the approaches of maritime archaeologists to material culture as well as the transition to relying on in situ investigation and nondisturbance techniques.[40] Nevertheless, it seems that although most of these studies have succeeded in communicating the richness of the abandoned watercraft resource, few have contributed to archaeological theory. This is largely because they have concentrated on the remains of "significant" or famous watercraft at the expense of those that are more representative of human behavior and behavioral processes.

Chapter 3 is an outline of the theories about abandonment used in this study. This communicates the diverse theoretical background to this study and examines the theoretical underpinnings of the Abandoned Ships Project. The chapter also extends an argument endorsing the benefits of comparative approaches to the remains of watercraft with specific reference to site formation processes and the systematic analysis of discard activities. Although historical particularist approaches, which tend to focus on data from discrete archaeological sites, are an acknowledged and important part of the theoretical toolkit available to maritime archaeologists, this research instead represents a nomothetic/generalist study that proposes that deliberately abandoned watercraft are *deep structures*. Borrowed from anthropological structuralism, this term refers to the linguistic expression of a theoretical construct, analogous in this study to the way we may interpret abandoned ships as expressions of underlying technological and economic change in human communities.[41]

Although it is not the intention to cast this approach as the antithesis to historical particularist approaches in maritime archaeology, I have specifically sought to exclude detailed case studies in order to illustrate that comparative methods have the potential to make significant contributions to archaeological theory and the reappraisal of history through archaeological investigation. This view maintains that these sites have important archaeological, social, and historical layers,[42] and that they have the potential to illuminate and bring about a reappraisal of the consequences of technological and economic development and change on maritime trades.

This argument contends that in order to understand this resource, and to draw meaningful evidence from it, an approach rather different from some of the traditional methods and perspectives of maritime archaeology is required. This approach is as broadly comparative as it is anthropologically oriented. Such an approach enables the examination of economic and technological trends in association with documented discard activities. It additionally allows for the creation of generalizing statements about developments within maritime history while contributing to our understanding of the archaeological signatures of cultural site formation processes. Another consequence of the use of a comparative methodology is that whether we see abandoned vessels as sites, structures, or artifacts (or all three simultaneously), they are deeply layered with social, technological, economic, and archaeological meaning. Finally, it is using an explicit theoretical approach that a study such as this one concerning the abandoned watercraft of Australia has relevance to other regions and nations.

Chapters 4 and 5 concentrate on the examination of historical correlations between the tendency to discard watercraft (the discard trend) and a number of historical events and processes. This includes a comparison of abandonment data with environmental change, economic recession and boom, war and its aftermath, changes to regulatory and legislative frameworks, port development, and the role of these factors on the location and use of official and unofficial dumping areas. Because abandoned watercraft come to the end of their mercantile and support functions noncatastrophically after their use, they may represent a microcosm of trade and changing commercial conditions.

Australia is an island, and one of the most urbanized countries in the world, but it also has an extremely low population density. For these reasons, it has always been very dependent upon maritime transport to traverse the large distances between its few large centers of population.[43] Consequently, the abandonment of watercraft can be seen as an indication of general economic health and as an index of the economic effects of certain regional, national, and global events.

A range of diachronic analyses illustrating the correlation of significant national and regional events with changes in discard trends may expose the connection between discard activities and the ebb and flow of economic conditions throughout Australian history. Additionally, indications of the distinct economic consequences particular types of economic events, such as depression and war, have on the shipping industry and the economy in general may be visible within the discard trend. Abandoned watercraft data can, for instance, add substance to the assertions of authors such as John

Bach, who has stated that there were "major dislocations of shipping econo-mies caused by the two world wars"[44] by showing such disorder in relation to real case studies.

Chapters 6 and 7 are concerned with the use-life of watercraft and the many site formation processes that they go through on their journey through initial functions, possible support roles, and postabandonment utilization, as well as their transition into archaeological contexts. These chapters pro-gressively transition from historical analyses to an examination of the ar-chaeological signatures of discard activities. Additionally, these chapters concentrate on the use, modification, and discard of watercraft and their status as documents of the site formation processes of these activities.

Chapter 6 discusses the archaeological signatures of use and modification that may have ramifications for the time of discard, position of abandon-ment, and condition of remains upon disposal. The signatures representing these functions and modifications tell us much about the technologies that were often at their pinnacle at the time of a vessel's manufacture, and a ship's "flexibility" in changing to new economic, social, and technological conditions over time. In this way, the type of vessel constructed and the events that bring about its transformation within systemic (use) contexts are directly relatable to subsequent discard processes and are important predepositional cultural site formation processes. Legislative and regula-tory frameworks as defined by bureaucracy also act as forms of cultural constraint. These restrictions are often the direct cause of the creation of designated dumping areas and ships' graveyards.

Chapter 7, on the other hand, examines the archaeological signatures of discard leading up to and following the discard event. These signatures are relics of the processes that act upon a vessel and signs of transitions between systemic and archaeological contexts. This chapter concentrates on a number of the discernible postabandonment archaeological formation processes representing actual discard events, such as structure minimiza-tion, hull reduction, and placement assurance strategies.

It is important to point out that because this was the first known dedi-cated comparative study of abandoned watercraft, and because it was na-tional in scope, the potential range of questions posed by the Abandoned Ships Project was huge. For this reason, I exercised some degree of judg-ment in order to keep the original study, and this book, within practical limits. Indeed, most of the analyses undertaken in this research have the potential to become dedicated studies in their own right. This is particularly the case in relation to economic analyses, and especially correct when refer-ring to regional economic analyses. It is also true in relation to a dedicated study of the role of technology and technological change in directing discard trends. Likewise, many of the archaeological aspects of this research warrant expansion.

The last chapter summarizes the findings of the research and brings together the common threads within preceding chapters. These linked arguments reinforce the contention that the many discard remnants of beached hulks and scuttled ships dotted all around the coasts and waterways of all nations are important tools for the creation of theoretical models, particularly when concerning cultural site formation processes in the maritime archaeological record. Moreover, as reminders of the commencement and culmination of maritime trade over many generations, they are a resource for researchers in the reassessment of historical trends. The study of these collected sites seeks to expose the interconnected political, technological, economic, and policy-driven processes that drove their discard. As will be shown, one of the consequences of using general comparative methods is that many of the nonshipwreck components of our maritime heritage have substantial, but hitherto untapped, potential.

2

Abandoned Watercraft in History and Archaeology

Ships abandoned in harbors and waterways sometimes become eyesores, nuisances, or even hazards to navigation, and were removed; others provided the basis for landfill and other marine engineering works, as rudimentary piers, wharves and breakwaters.

—Alan Moore, *Last Days of Mast and Sail*

Ships are not simply the tools of commerce, industry, and warfare, they are also objects replete with the qualities of particular cultures. Their creation, retention, and destruction tell us much about the circumstances of social, technological, and economic change through time and illuminate the changing role and importance of aquatic transportation across human history. Understanding how and why owners abandon ships is not a simple matter of augmenting history. As the final phase in the life of tried and tested technologies, we may find clues to the catalysts and consequences of other changes within human societies.

On the most basic level, the discard of watercraft is the abandonment of one function for the adoption of another. In more detail, these changes may require a transformation of structures or functions or may constitute a symbolic reuse. The decision to create, retain, and destroy a vessel may also often relate to it matching criteria emerging from the consequences of economic and technological change. These transitions reflect the changing needs and desires of maritime people and are representative of technological, economic, and social issues.

Over the past four decades, maritime researchers have learned this and much more from the study of the varied yet ultimately connected topics within the subject of ship abandonment. The watercraft representative of this theme have proven to be as diverse and dispersed as their shipwrecked counterparts. So, too, these unwanted vessels exist within an extended temporal span corresponding to other categories of archaeological sites, from examples many thousands of years old to the continuing, present-day use of the sea as a dumping ground and ships as reusable objects.

Discard sites are also representative of carefully planned decision-making processes. Understanding this, their study has facilitated insight into the social, economic, and technological realities of the past. Such archaeological sites represent the unfolding story of the history of deliberate watercraft abandonment and the continuity and evolution of human behavior. We may see the changing role and importance of watercraft within society in the clues gleaned from the diverse themes, site types, and perspectives represented in previous examinations of the history and archaeology of discarded vessels.

Abandonment as Theme

Archaeological studies of abandoned watercraft exist within three major site types: isolated ship finds, discarded and recycled disarticulated vessel components, and accumulations of watercraft known popularly as ships' graveyards, marine bone-yards, and rotten rows. Running throughout these site types are a number of concurrent themes representing many extinct or rare behavioral traits as well as ones that continue to thrive.

Ritualistic Discard

One such theme is the concept of sacrificial and ritualistic discard, best seen in the votive offering of vessels (an offering of personal property to fulfill a religious vow) and the reuse of ship hulls as graves. Since at least the seventeenth century, there have been reports of the reuse of ships as tombs in Scandinavia. Poetic works, dating to many hundreds of years before this, also describe this activity, and researchers believe that many hundreds of such sites exist. Five sites, extensively recorded and published—the Snape boat grave, the Sutton Hoo vessels, the Oseberg ship, the Tune ship, and the Gokstad ship, dating to between the seventh and tenth centuries—best exemplify this site type.[1]

There is a close relationship between the intentional discard and symbolic reuse of boats for inhumation and the abandonment of ships as votive offerings. Documentary sources concerning votive offerings are particularly old in Europe. Johnstone cites the Roman historian Tacitus (A.D. 55–120) in reference to votive offerings made by Germanic tribes: "When they meet in battle, they generally promise the spoils of war to the God of War. After the victory, captured materials are sacrificed to him and the rest of the booty is put in the same place."[2] This behavior is illustrated in the case of the Hjortspring boat (c. 350 B.C.) and other possible sites found in Danish bogs.[3]

Often there is some difficulty in defining sites as boat inhumations due to the lack of in situ human remains. Research has suggested that certain identifications concerning boat burial sites such as Sutton Hoo could be mistaken because the ships may also represent cenotaphs or monuments.[4] This would put them in the category of votive offering rather than within their current classification as ship burials. Additionally, the existence of stone ship settings, as described by Klavs Randsborg, is important because of the evidence they provide concerning the symbolic status of watercraft as grave monuments.[5] Meaney and Fenwick have also listed similar "pseudo-ship burials" at Caister-on-Sea, Norfolk, where graves had not been filled but were instead covered with a piece of the side of a vessel.[6]

Many examples of "boat graves" discovered in Egypt are often actually votive offerings. The difference is due to the symbolic association of the abandoned craft with the afterlife rather than as a receptacle for human remains. Egyptian boat graves show up in the archaic period (First and Second Dynasties) as illustrated by the royal monuments at Abydos, in the necropolis of the nobles at Helwan, and in the Fourth Dynasty at Giza.[7] Votive sites in Egypt are represented by a number of well-known studies, such as the Cheops ships (c. 2600 B.C.) and Dahshur boats (c. 1850 B.C.), as well as other archaeological work indicating that other pyramids had pits once holding ceremonial watercraft.[8] There are two dominant theories regarding the reasons for the burial of the boats, both concerning the use and symbolism of the boats in the pharaoh's journey to the afterlife and in funeral rituals. These theories, which relate mainly to whether the vessel was functional or purely symbolic, will not be discussed here, but they fundamentally relate to the deliberate, votive abandonment of the vessels.[9]

Structural Adaptation

In comparison to studies of the symbolic reuse of watercraft, studies of vessels reflecting functional and structural adaptation are much more common. In particular, the use of intact, articulated hulls as buildings or foundations is a subject well represented in archaeological literature. There are three variations on this theme of abandoned vessel as building, relating to the types of postabandonment functions that watercraft often serve: reclamation schemes, foundations, and buildings. What binds all three is their dependence, to a large degree, on the articulation of the extant hull.

The reclamation of ground adjacent to waterways for creating more secure foundations for built structures is a common use for abandoned watercraft. Notable examples of this are located at Portus Augusti (Ostia, Italy), the B&W Engine Factory site (Christianshavn, Denmark), and a number of sites in the ancient port of London, including the New Guy's House boat (second century A.D.) and the County Hall ship (190–225 A.D.).[10]

The investigations of the County Hall ship are particularly notable because they provide us with an insight into the benefits of incorporating discard hypotheses into the archaeological investigation of vessel fate. Peter Marsden's account of the County Hall ship attributes the loss of the vessel to an act of abandonment before 300 A.D.[11] Marsden believes that the evidence of few repairs to the vessel suggests that it was relatively new when eventually disposed of. An alternative to this abandonment hypothesis is that the vessel was catastrophically lost during a battle about 296 A.D.[12] Although research notes that there is no evidence of burning or other disposal activity associated with the ship, Marsden supports an abandonment theory due to its location in the marshy southern bank of the Thames, the same kind of area used for the disposal of unwanted vessels in more modern times. Other proof, such as the vessel's position close to shore and away from areas of major port activity, may also indicate deliberate disposal. Both Merrifield and Marsden make the analogy between ship abandonment in the region around the 1920s and the time of the abandonment of the County Hall ship.[13] Merrifield's discussion of the vessel contributes an additional piece of information to the debate on the fate of the County Hall ship. He states that a block of stone was "thrown from a considerable height" and deposited within the hull of the vessel and considers the possibility that the vessel had been used as target practice, the stone shot from a catapult.[14] The use of derelict or outmoded ships for target practice is an activity still practiced today, and the use of various projectiles to ensure that vessel's hull is adequately breached during deliberate sinking is well attested to in the historical record for ensuring loss. Understanding these behaviors are important clues in determining the method of loss of watercraft in the archaeological record, something all too often forgotten in the rush to assign catastrophic events to the archaeological remains of watercraft.

Two other sites, Blackfriars Wrecks 1 and 3, are representative of the different perspective Marsden brings to the analysis of ancient boat remains by incorporating theories of abandonment into his interpretation of sites.

In both cases, initial hypothetical considerations included abandonment scenarios as the reasons for their loss. In the case of Blackfriars Wreck 1, the rejection of this hypothesis occurred following observation of the ship's pronounced list and general lack of structural support. Marsden interpreted the substantial lateral tilt of the vessel as an argument against the use of the ship in reclamation or as construction material. Likewise, the absence of holes in the bottom of Wreck 3 discounted a theory of deliberate discard.[15] It is significant in both cases that Marsden asked questions regarding the method of vessel loss. His analytical framework also considers the location of the vessels as a hazardous impediment to navigation, something normally taken into account when discarding a ship.

Related to reclamation, discarded watercraft may also provide solid foundations for buildings. Probably the most famous case of the use of an articulated hull for this purpose is the Ronson ship.[16] The Ronson ship was used in the reclamation of land along New York's East River sometime the mid-eighteenth century, when it was stripped, deliberately sunk, spiked through its hull with a set of piles, and filled with sand and rocks for use as a caisson or "crib hulk." By the conclusion of reclamation, the vessel was under meters of debris and was two street blocks from the waterfront. Before that, evidence illustrates postabandonment functions of the vessel as a harbor wharf or quay prior to its end as landfill material in the form of a crude rock fireplace, a bow-mounted capstan, a small loading crane, and excessive wear to the upper deck.

The reuse of ship hulls as above-ground structures also has a long history and is well represented in historical and archaeological literature. There are many examples of watercraft being converted into terrestrial structures in the archaeological literature, such as the various hulks of Port Stanley in the Falkland Islands; an unidentified nineteenth-century vessel at the Royal Navy Dockyard, Bermuda (believed to be either the *Dotterel, La Tourterelle,* or *Antelope*); the unfortunate *Arkansas, Niantic,* and *Apollo,* abandoned at the San Francisco waterfront during the California Gold Rush; and two wooden ships abandoned in New Zealand, the *Edwin Fox,* and *Inconstant.* These watercraft served a variety of functions, from victualing stores and slave dwellings to warehouses, barns, taverns, hotels, restaurants, offices, jails, churches, landing stages, and wharves.[17] Such activities also continue in the present day, albeit infrequently. Ships and boats, for example, can still be found in a variety of reuse functions, such as old herring boats from Lindisfarne, England, halved and boarded up for use as fishing sheds.[18]

The cases of the *Niantic* and *Edwin Fox* are especially interesting because of the methods used in their disposal. In particular, these sites illustrate that people employed *placement assurance strategies* intended to ensure that ships remained abandoned following disposal. Such strategies include removing masts and ballast for beaching as well as driving piles for stabilization.[19]

Salvage and Recycling

In many ancient and modern cultures, Christoffersen notes, an "unknown number of boats, including wrecks, have been broken up and used for building or other purposes, or simply as firewood."[20] The act of abandoning and dismantling watercraft for the salvage and use of their component parts is another common activity demonstrating the many ways that unwanted vessels may retain value. As Basil Greenhill has noted, all watercraft, irrespective of their hull material, are inherently biodegradable and destined to be condemned.[21] This virtually unknowable "use-by date" is an idea that can also play an important part in our perception of the archaeological potential of vessel remains. Even before a ship is constructed, its owner considers a number of contingencies for it, including its potential retirement or replacement. Even in the case of replica ships and preserved historic vessels, only extensive, complicated, and expensive overhauls will hamper any inherent biodegradability, ensure seaworthiness, and preserve any heritage value that may exist. Indeed, this continuing requirement for maintenance is a central issue for shipowners who opt for the abandonment and/or breaking up of their vessels. In most cases, watercraft will come to a stage where the costs to maintain or repair them will exceed the benefits of their use or the cost of a new vessel. Preservation activity associated with the salvage and transformation of vessel elements into other objects (such as the transformation of timbers from Sir Francis Drakes's *Golden Hind* into a number of historic keepsakes in the 1660s) are the only exception to this rule.[22] Such cases are rare, however, and vessels are normally broken down for more pragmatic, economically derived reasons.

The perception that economic benefits gained from salvage (mainly from the subsequent use or sale of hull material and fixtures) will be greater than any costs (such as wages or wharfage dues) is what inevitably guides ship breaking. Often the burden of having a derelict vessel, which continues to accrue fees and is in danger of sinking where it floats (causing further economic burdens due to removal and cleanup), may also guide the decisions to finally dispose of it.

Demolition, an act involving the systematic separation of vessel components, is a different form of abandonment because the versatility of its component parts has become more important than the hull structure. Recycling nevertheless has connection to human decision- making processes concerned with the assessment of the suitability of watercraft components for other applications. The transformation of an object as large as a vessel from its initial use to another function is evidence of certain behavioral traits, from the ability to take risks in new markets to the ability to think ingeniously in times of economic stress and find new uses for unused watercraft.

Other than as fuel, another incentive in the dismantling and breaking down of wooden vessels is their value and suitability for the manufacture of other structures. Although components of wrecked vessels may become significant features in terrestrial constructions, this is unlikely. Locating and salvaging the remains of a wrecked vessel is normally difficult and has little economic justification (especially in the prediving era). Old or unwanted vessels, no longer suitable for their original function, are more likely to have their components used as building material, simply because of their proximity or transportability to ship breakers. The recycling of ship's timbers allows for some economic reimbursement to the shipowner and may reduce costs for the construction of new ships. Acts of salvage tend to occur when dismantled vessel remnants would have been the major source of raw materials, especially in regions largely devoid of timber suitable for the assembly of large structures.

There are two site types representative of the reuse of disarticulated watercraft timbers—actual ship-breaking industry sites and the sites where humans reused the salvaged timbers. There are few locations currently known that represent ship-breaking industries and activities in antiquity. Such places are difficult to identify due to the problems in distinguishing between the archaeological signatures of ship breaking and those of shipbuilding. Indeed, the likelihood of both shipbuilding and ship-breaking activities existing at the same site poses a major challenge to maritime archaeological research.

The remains of nine late Roman Rhine boats (c. fourth century A.D.) found in an ancient Roman harbor at Mainz, Germany, in 1967 are probably the best known sites believed to exhibit ship-breaking activities.[23] The large number of vessels located in one main area, the type of surrounding structures, and the instance of one vessel "hacked" in half lengthways strongly suggests that the area was a ship-breaking yard.[24] One other example is work undertaken by Christoffersen on the island of Funen (Fyn) in Denmark, where he identified a presixteenth-century ship-breaking or shipbuilder's yard in association with material culture from the Scandinavian Iron Age.[25]

Similarly, ships' timbers found reused as decking at a site on the Thames foreshore in London in 1995 were interpreted as evidence of a ship-breaking yard.[26] These timbers, reassembled as a grid, created a platform on which ships needing repair would lie. The site dates from at least 1838, when the vessel *Temeraire* was broken up in the vicinity.[27] Individual ship breaking and timber reuse has also been noted in a number of sites. These include the third century B.C. Kyrenia ship (deck built from previously used timbers), the Sea of Galilee/Kinneret boat (also partially constructed from used timbers and interpreted as a working vessel subsequently used for spare parts), and numerous medieval Viking boats.[28]

The recycling of timber salvaged from watercraft is a very different process from the structural reuse of entire vessels. Salvagers choose timbers from unwanted vessels for their shape, even when vessel components, such as large sections of planking, are relatively complete. With the odd exception, the selection strategy in the reuse of ships' timbers has been to choose "flat planking of fairly constant width."[29] In certain cases, researchers have been able to make identifications of vessel types from the discovery of non-planking components in archaeological deposits, observations of treenail hole spacing, and the dimensions of planks and fastenings. In this context, an uncharacteristic modification to (usually) complete ship components is an indication of reuse. Heal and Hutchinson used this reasoning to show the intentional structural reduction and reuse of an incomplete log boat found at Tamworth, Shropshire.[30] Another clear example of modification for subsequent use were the existence of holes and tool markings on the boat. Damian Goodburn has also used the existence of similar markings to suggest that fragments of a severely damaged ancient ship were those of a wrecked vessel and not from a structure using reused watercraft elements.[31]

The existence of recycled ships' timbers in shipwrecks, abandoned vessels, or waterside structures can tell us about a range of behaviors associated with the tendency to retain, destroy, or improve ageing ships. They may even inform us about the changing costs of ship production over time.

Other signatures on disarticulated timbers indicate the possible use of fire in a hull-reduction context. Traces of burns on planking from a medieval revetment (dating to c. A.D. 1501–71) found in 1987 along a section of river between Hays Wharf and Abbotts Lane in Southwark, London, could conceivably predate the reuse of the planks and plausibly represent abandonment or salvage activity.

Evidence of the reuse of dismantled ship timbers also comes from Lisht, Egypt, around the early Twelfth Dynasty Middle Kingdom pyramid of Senwosret I (1959–1914 B.C.) and is believed to be from watercraft associated with monumental structures in the area.[32] Other evidence of the reuse of ships' timbers in the context of subsequent building activity comes much later (between the tenth and seventeenth centuries A.D.) in western and northern Europe. Archaeologists have found these types of sites in medieval period waterfronts from Dublin, Ireland, to Bergen, Norway. In particular, a number of British studies have extensively documented timber reuse at a number of locations around London, York, Bristol, Hartlepool, Newport, and Newcastle.[33]

These studies are important for what they tell us about the condition of the vessels before salvage (reused timbers were often old or had been repaired) and illustrate the process of watercraft abandonment in the past. They give some insight into the nature of trade and technology in antiquity and inform us about the changing nature of the use of particular ships. Such comparisons are useful in our assessment of similar behaviors evident in the reuse of watercraft or parts of watercraft in more modern times, such as in the Falkland Islands.[34]

In the era of iron and steel vessels, the use of salvaged materials from abandoned ships takes on a new characteristic due to the dominant role that ferrous-hulled vessels and their salvage play in relation to watercraft abandonment. Wooden ship scantlings can only be used according to the soundness and suitability of their physical form in a compatible usage in a new structure or object. Iron and steel, however, can be melted down and reformed. Here, the shape, condition, and size of the material salvaged from the dismantled vessel became unimportant due to the transformable features of the ferrous materials. Large groups of unwanted ships became refined veins of iron and steel, ready for mining.

Ships' Graveyards

The term *ships' graveyard* is often used by researchers for all collections of ships, such as at Yassiada (in the Sea of Marmara) and the region popularly known as the "Graveyard of the Atlantic" (along the Outer Banks of North Carolina).[35] These sites, however, contain a high concentration of wrecked vessels rather than deliberately discarded watercraft and are thus more appropriately called *ship traps*. True ships' graveyards represent the gamut of modern watercraft abandonment behaviors.

These graveyards are accumulations of watercraft retired and abandoned by their owners following a decision that their vessels are ineffective or inadequate for their intended purpose. The following criteria serve as a basis for the determination of whether a region or location is indeed a ships' graveyard: one discarded vessel lies in close proximity to other abandoned watercraft, watercraft are discarded due to decisions regarding their suitability for use, and the location of abandonment is determined due to the consensus of a group of people. Ships end up in ships' graveyards because their owners see more benefit in their discard and destruction than in their use and care.

Such sites are the culmination of many of the behaviors linked with carrying out the sacrifice, adaptation, and reuse outlined above. Woven into the fabric of the everyday occurrence of vessel abandonment in the modern world are the same behaviors and ideals that constituted the discard of watercraft in ages gone by. Even watercraft deliberately abandoned today provide a record of the circumstances of their working lives and operating environments. They are also representations of the continuation of traditions inextricably linked with the economic and technological transitions of human societies and are documents of such changes themselves.

There are two types of ships' graveyards. In the first, vessels are deliberately abandoned in the context of war. This often involves the strategic use of watercraft as barriers against the enemy penetration of navigable waterways or strategic shorelines. The second type is a more general accumulation due to the dumping of unwanted vessels. This distinction is important for two reasons. The dumping of vessels within conflict-related graveyards often occurs at one given time, or at least over a very short period. The vessels are often disposed of due to imminent enemy capture, the perception that the vessel might be used against its owner, or as a defensive measure intended to slow the advance of an adversary. Due to the relatively short period for planning and implementation in this scenario, these sites may have rich artifact assemblages. These graveyards are widespread geographically and, in many cases, incorporate large numbers of watercraft.

Within the second type of ships' graveyard, vessels are disposed of over an extended period. These dumping areas, often described with much flowery prose as the places where ships "are retired," accumulate a large number of diverse types of vessels. In a romantic fashion, historians and sailors alike have tended to see these locations as miserable places, not worthy of more than a passing comment, or as eyesores, nuisances, or hazards to navigation, a veritable hell for "once glorious ships."[36] Nevertheless, researchers may find many examples of ships' graveyards in the historical record, and in some cases documents have prompted maritime archaeologists to examine these conflict and obsolescence-laden sites.

Discard, Strategy, and Conflict

The history of conflict-inspired abandonment is at least as old as the European Nydam boat finds (A.D. 350–400) and is represented by many case studies, from the late Saxon Clapton logboat (Great Britain) and the sixteenth-century Mukran Wreck (Germany) to the large post–thirteenth century assemblages of vessels in Kalmar Harbor (Sweden) and eleventh-century block ships at Skuldelev, Jydedybet, and Skane (Denmark).[37] Abandonment in the context of conflict tends to follow a number of themes related to the strategic use of watercraft.

By far the most common strategies of abandonment during conflict entail the scuttling of one's own vessel or fleet, the demolition of incomplete vessels, or the destruction of a vessel by its captor, usually to evade vessel capture and avoid the transfer of useful goods to an enemy. Such events occurred often. In Europe, these activities date from at least the seventeenth century; the English destroyed their ships during the Second Anglo-Dutch War (1662–67), the English and Dutch committing similar acts against their own fleets in 1690, and the French scuttled ships in 1704 during the English attack on Toulon.[38] In North America, similar events occurred in connection with the French and Indian War (1754–63) and Seven Years' War (1756–63), in the prelude to and during the American War of Independence (1776–83), during the War of 1812 (1812–15), and during the American Civil War (1861–65).

They are represented in investigations of the Wiawaka and James River bateaux sites, the French frigates *Machault, Marquis de Malauze,* and *Bienfaisant,* the British sloop *Boscawen* (all lost in the French and Indian War), the privateer *Defence,* and the remains of the HMS *Betsy* and Cornwallis Cave Wreck at Yorktown (American Revolutionary War).[39]

Naval scuttling strategies have persisted to the twentieth century, and there were many instances of deliberate vessel destruction during the World War I and World War II. For example, the largest conflict-related destruction of naval vessels in history occurred on 21 June 1919, when the German navy destroyed seventy-four of its own vessels at Scapa Flow (Orkney Islands, Great Britain) to prevent British capture.[40]

In other situations, navies may abandon their vessels in a manner that transforms them into devastating weapons. Many terms apply to the strategic abandonment of vessels used in this way. These terms fall within two categories: vessels modified for aggression in war and vessels modified for defense in war.

A *block ship* is scuttled as a wartime defensive measure designed to block passage into a waterway—one of the oldest naval tactics on record. Block ships date from at least the pre- Roman Iron Age in Scandinavia and are believed to stretch much further back.[41] Navies have employed block ships for centuries, from their use at Skuldelev beginning around the eleventh century, in the nineteenth century during the American Civil War, and into the twentieth century when the British sank vessels at Scapa Flow to protect an anchorage from submarine attack.[42] One other case of a deliberate blockage is documented in an account titled "Visit to India, China and Japan in 1853," written aboard the American clipper ship *Sea Serpent* during a visit to Asia. It reads, "We passed the first bar, which was created by the Chinese sinking junks to prevent the English from reaching Canton."[43]

Fire ships are vessels filled with flammable materials for the purposes of deliberate ramming or attachment to enemy ships. Examples of this tactic date to at least the seventh century A.D. The best-known examples are associated with Spanish and English conflicts from 1587, when the Spanish used fire ships to force Francis Drake out of Cadiz and the English used them in the defeat of the Spanish Armada in 1588.[44]

In 1672, the Dutch sent fire ships against the English, and the Turkish fleet used them in 1788, during the last Austro-Turkish War (1788–91).[45] The British also used fire ships against the French during the American Revolutionary War (1775–83), sailing five ships into a French fleet blockading the mouth of the York River.[46] In the American Civil War, Confederate forces used *fire rafts*, long, flat boats filled with combustible materials in their military campaigns.

Despite a relationship between these strategies of naval engagement and catastrophic abandonment, many of these ships provide clues about the behaviors that brought about their abandonment. For instance, the Skuldelev vessels are important because evidence has shown that at least one vessel (Skuldelev 5) was of advanced age, had been regularly patched up, had been built or repaired with recycled materials, and at the time of deposition was probably bordering on unseaworthy.[47] This illustrates the persistent economic angle associated with discard events of all varieties.

Likewise, the manner in which the British navy scuttled HMS *Betsy* in 1781 during the battle of Yorktown illustrates the methods used to ensure its destruction. Archaeological investigation of the vessel showed that the

Betsy was sunk with the use of a "scuttle-hole": The inner starboard planking of the vessel had been cut carefully with hammer and chisel to facilitate the sinking of the vessel.[48]

These cases are also important because they tell us about the perceived artifact sterility of deliberately abandoned watercraft. In particular, the case of HMS *Boscawen*, a sloop abandoned after the French and Indian War at Ticonderoga, Lake Champlain, is significant in the analysis of the archaeology of the deliberately abandoned ship because of what it indicates about the possible artifact richness of deliberately discarded vessels:

> The excavation of the *Boscawen* produced many surprises, not the least of which was the quantity and quality of artifacts contained within the hull. Prior to excavation we assumed that the sloop had been thoroughly stripped of equipment before abandonment, and that finds would consist of buttons, glass and ceramic shards, musket shot and other minor debris.[49]

Archaeologists Kevin Crisman and Arthur Cohn discovered a rich assemblage of artifacts, including an array of rigging, tools, clothing, armament, faunal remains, seed, and plant materials. All provide some insight into life on board the vessel.[50]

In another case, the Royal Navy strategically scuttled the ironclad HMS *Vixen* in order to block the Chubb Cut Channel off Daniel's Head in Bermuda as a part of defense preparations for shore batteries.[51] The purpose of the vessel's abandonment was to restrict navigation and ensure that any enemy approaching the Royal Navy's dockyard would have to come within close range of shore batteries. Richard Gould's work on this ship is important, because he considers the cultural catalysts for abandonment as well as the act of abandonment itself, and his research considers both crucial aspects of archaeological site formation. Gould sees historical sources such as the Daniel's Head Channel Act (1887) as important factors facilitating the process of discard. He considers predisposal salvage an important part of a sequence of events leading to the final abandonment of the *Vixen*, as well as something that may be deduced from its archaeological remains.[52] Although the historical record was an important part of understanding the nature of the archaeological remains, it was the structural remains themselves that provided insight into the methods used to remove boilers and engines and explained the cultural elements of the site. Evidence related to the use of explosive charges in the scuttling process was also examined.[53] At the conclusion of the project, by considering how human behavior left signatures of discard procedures, it was possible to create an enlightened interpretation of the remains that did not rely on understanding natural disintegration processes.

Another variation on the theme of conflict-inspired abandonment relates to the aftermath of war. The changing economic conditions that emerge after conflict often have a marked effect on the tendency to abandon watercraft. As Daniel Lenihan has commented, "It is typical for societies to discard the tools of war when the conflict has ended. War weary nations focus on rebuilding . . . actively forgetting the carnage recently experienced."[54] Although a tendency to abandon may be attributable to economic transitions in a burgeoning postwar world, it is also often due to the decreased need for warships and to costs associated in retarding their eventual deterioration.[55]

In other circumstances, a victorious military force may compel defeated groups to discard their fleets. Here, discard activities are colored by undeniable political meaning. It is noteworthy, for instance, that Allied forces scuttled or scrapped most of Japan's remaining naval fleet in the aftermath of World War II, despite the technological advancement of many ships, such as the Japanese battleship *Nagato* (1920–46).[56]

The phenomenon of sinking target ships is another example of conflict-inspired deliberate abandonment. This occurs largely outside of times of war, when nations test the effectiveness of weapons on naval targets. One example of an early target vessel was the steel-hulled USS *Katahdin*, sunk during gunnery practice as "Ballistic Experimental Target A" in Virginia after its decommissioning in 1898.[57] Although target ships are normally isolated, sometimes military weapons testing has created extensive ship-discard sites. The ships associated with the Operation Crossroads atomic tests in the Kwajalein and Bikini Atolls in the Marshall Islands in 1946 are the best example of this. These tests emerged from American fears that the advent of atomic warfare at Hiroshima had made the world's navies fortresses of redundant scrap. The tests involved the destruction of former U.S. Navy combat vessels struck off the active list and German and Japanese war prizes.[58] Reminders to the world of the power of the United States, these test were the first shots in the Cold War. Instead of the intended overawing of other nations, the tests created a security need as nations strove to demonstrate their own nuclear capacity. The fact that five submarines used in this operation were not redundant at the time of their use in the tests further illuminates the arm-flexing intentions of these activities.[59]

Discard, Trade, and Technology

When we refer to the dumping of unwanted vessels within the context of mercantile obsolescence and economic redundancy there are two kinds of sites. First, there are isolated abandonment sites. Here, watercraft are dumped in solitary locations along the coasts and waterways of any number of maritime nations. There are many examples in historical and archaeological literature of such vessels.[60] Second, there are major collections of ships, mirrors of the changing circumstance of local trades and global mercantilism.

One of the clearest examples of an isolated abandonment site representing mercantile obsolescence is also one of the oldest. In the case of the Graveney boat (A.D. 893–974), a combination of an absence of artifacts and beds of branches beneath the boat contributed to an hypothesis concerning its manner of loss. The branches, interpreted as a "hard," an artificial surface built to stabilize a stretch of coastline or river edge, was evidence that the vessel's owners had deliberately placed it on the shore. A trace of rope tied to the sternpost of the vessel was further evidence of discard, suggesting that at the time of abandonment it may have been on the shore for repair, supported when replaced frames and fastenings were detected. Alternatively, axe cuts on the extremities of some planking were potential indicators of dismantling for recycling and reuse.[61]

Another study of an abandoned vessel is the nineteenth-century schooner *Annabella* at Cape Neddick, Maine, a once-derelict vessel, apparently beached due to the expenses involved in its repair and excavated by a group of archaeologists from the United Kingdom with assistance from Texas A&M University in May 1995. Researchers saw the location of the vessel, as well as its orientation, as telltale signs of discard.[62]

Ann Merriman's study of a North Carolina sail flat also discovered piles in association with structural remains. Merriman considers piles a major piece of diagnostic evidence suggesting the flat's intentional disposal for use as a breakwater.[63]

Irrespective of how such sites are reflected in the literature, the nature of shipping and ship owning suggest that the number of vessels abandoned over time simply because they are of no further use has to be immense. The frequency of this abandonment behavior in relation to the use of the sea and other waterways as a dumping ground is nowhere better illustrated than by the number and scale of watercraft disposal sites littered in and around the shorelines of almost every maritime nation.

For instance, archaeologists discovered eighteenth-century bateaux (shallow-draft river vessels) in 1974 and 1984 at the Musée de la Civilisation

(Quebec City), further illustrating the tendency of humans to use vessels in waterside construction (they had been used as temporary dams).[64] Another, more recent Canadian ships' graveyard is located at the southern end of the Great Cataraqui River in the inner harbor of the city of Kingston, Ontario. This collection includes many vastly different vessels, from unnamed barges discarded in the 1860s to the screw steamer *C.D. 110*, abandoned in 1965. Many such vessels underwent conversion for postabandonment uses as breakwaters and pier extensions, drastically altering the shape of the coastline.[65]

In the United Kingdom, abandoned ship surveys at places such as Whitewall Creek (River Medway), Kidwell (Dyfed), the River Tamar, and Shropshire Union Canal have added substantially to archaeological methodology.[66] One standout project is the Maritime Fife Project. Its initial findings concerning one of the study areas dating to World War I have indicated that "there is some evidence to suggest that craft may have been stockpiled in anticipation of periods of more favorable trading conditions that never came."[67] The existence of ship stockpiles illustrates the underlying economic reasons that guide abandonment behavior and shows how curatorial and reuse behaviors can exist concurrently at abandoned watercraft sites.

Other investigations of ships' graveyards expose the environmental factors that direct the location of ships' graveyards. Environmental damage, caused by cultural activities in the landscape, is something that Somasiri Devendra cites as a catalyst for the discard of watercraft in Sri Lanka.[68] Here, alterations in the landscape were noticeable in changes along rivers and at river mouths that had been brought about by deforestation connected with plantations. This resulted in alteration to the water levels of rivers, the erosion of riverbanks, and the transformation of streams into mere trickles of water. Environmental ruin resulted, as well as the destruction of the networks used by waterborne transport. The other inevitable effect was the eventual abandonment and concealment by encroaching silt of large river craft, which could no longer travel the waterways.

In another case, Mark Leone examines environmental changes brought about by vessel abandonment in the Patuxent River at Chesapeake Bay.[69] On an even larger scale, environmental change on the fringe of the Sahara in the late 1980s was a cause for the abandonment of boats, with drought causing Lake Chad to shrink to such an extent that boats could be thirty-two miles inland of the new shoreline.[70]

Ships' graveyards also tell us about the way humans structure their use of bodies of water. Geographical factors also played a role in the abandonment of watercraft at Port Stanley in the Falkland Islands. In this case, vessel abandonment occurred due to the island's strategic position close to notoriously dangerous Cape Horn and its importance as a location for ship repair or abandonment.[71] In a similar case, a ships' graveyard at Quail Island (Otamahua, New Zealand) was placed on the west side of Lyttelton Harbour "because of its distance from shipping routes" and, for some unknown reason, "its isolation from . . . the leper and animal quarantine stations."[72]

The sites at Port Stanley, extensively documented by historians and archeologists alike, are additionally important because of what they tell us about the techniques people used in abandoning and reusing the ships.[73] In particular, Stammers and Kearon have suggested that local quarried stone was dumped into the hold of the abandoned nineteenth-century merchantman *Jhelum* to prevent it from floating off.[74] At the proposed Cypress Landing Marina Complex site in Chocowinity Bay, North Carolina, Merriman also noted that an abandoned vessel had been haphazardly filled with deposited debris and discarded half brick.[75] Although there was no extended discussion of why these bricks were in the hull, Merriman considered paved areas at the stern of the vessel as an indication of cargo—but it is also possible the brick served to ensure final abandonment of the vessel.

Port Stanley is also significant because it has a history of abandoned structures such as storage hulks and jetties constructed from unwanted vessels. Each company trading in the Falklands built

> a jetty running out into the harbor, at the end of which were one or more hulks broadside on, some of which were partly disassembled for their lumber and used as working platforms for more complete hulks which were moored beside them. Tunnels were often cut through the 'tween deck of the end hulk so that cargo could be carried through to a waiting ship.[76]

In the process of constructing these jetties, many vessels were connected together, and many required that piles be driven through them for stability and support. These ships were used for storage purposes almost to the present day.[77] Other vessels, such as the *Fennia*, were salvaged, and their components were then used in dockside structures—in the case of the *Fennia*, as jetties joining two other ships, the *Actaeon* and *Charles Cooper*.[78] In other cases, vessels became makeshift coal bunkers.[79] In the specific case of the American clipper ship *Snow Squall*,

> the Company strengthened the jetty in the 20th century by driving piles through the *Snow Squall*'s hull and crushing her middle section with tons of rock fill. A barge sank on what was left of her stern, and warehouses were built atop the jetty.[80]

Such amendments to the hull of the vessel often have major implications for the structural integrity and long-term survival of the vessel. This is another important factor in the cultural aspects of the site formation process. Mensun Bound noted this modification on *Jhelum* in particular:

> An access way has been cut through the hulk at 'tween deck level. Unfortunately, this, on her port side, has severed the top timbers, waterways, shelves and clamps, or, in other words, those very timbers on which she most depended for her longitudinal strength and integrity.[81]

Most individuals making modifications would not have been ignorant of shipbuilding and would have understood the ramifications of the modification. They saw the new function of the vessel, reflected in the structural changes, as more important than the ship's long-term survivability.

One of the most relevant projects that relates closely to this study concerns Shomette's investigations into a large ships' graveyard at Mallow's Bay, Maryland.[82] Shomette makes a number of observations with repercussions for how we perceive the logistics of abandonment and the cultural site formation processes at discard sites. This includes observations about the time taken to burn wooden vessels and the tendency to fill abandoned watercraft with sand, gravel, stone, or dredge spoil to ensure its sinking.[83] Shomette also uses the ships' graveyard to discuss the lucrative (but risky) nature of the scrap-metal industry, identify a relationship between scrap-metal prices and wartime economies, chart the growth of subsistence salvage during economic depression, and chronicle pre–World War II fluctuations in metal prices due to Japanese demand for scrap.[84] Ships at the Mallow's Bay site also indicate the persistence of many of the placement assurance strategies already listed, having had piles driven through their hulls to stop them from floating into navigation channels.[85]

All of these studies reinforce the fact that shipowners do not simply abandon unwanted vessels when they are worn out. The reasons for abandonment vary from a combination of processes associated with general economic and technological change to more specific, regional developments, such as changes to port infrastructure, the development of alternative modes of transportation, and vessel age and condition. The effects of changing networks of transportation themselves seem to change with circumstance, and there is some divergence of opinion regarding the growth of alternative transportation, the redirection of resources into alternative transport infrastructure, and its effects on economic growth (which directly relates to discard trends). For instance, William Peterson cites railroads as both the stimulus for growth and the catalyst for failure in Mississippian trade as well as the well-being of river cities.[86] The growth of railroads in the Mississippi Valley and the westward movements of immigrants between 1850 and 1870 augmented river trade because the railroads were not constructed north-south along the river banks but perpendicular to them. The later construction of the railroad to cities such as St. Paul became the "death-knell" of steamboating for this port due to falling rates of steamboat passenger and freight services and the "general indifference to the opening of navigation."[87]

In the case of the western rivers of the United States, Louis Hunter outlines the devastating effect of railroad development in creating competition between railroad and riverine transportation, as well as the detrimental competition between steamboat owners. Another limiting factor here, however, was the physical characteristics of the rivers. Although the rivers had a huge effect on the design of vessels, they were also the cause of their decline because of the inability to predetermine the route of commerce despite attempts to construct expensive canal systems.[88]

Other evidence from the United States attributes the death of regional coastal trade to railroads. Lincoln Paine writes that around the 1870s, the state of Maine put great efforts into the development of its railroads.[89] In particular, the state focused its efforts at redirecting the coastal north-south axis of their railroad infrastructure to an inward west-east axis in order to harness the interior. Instead of enhancing the state through the better transportation of goods to and from the sea, and hence boosting maritime trades, it moved the population west. Maine in many ways became a place one went through on the way to somewhere else, and commerce followed.

Conclusion

Humans abandon watercraft for many reasons. What connect these motives are the deliberate acts that bring about the transformation of usable ships into archaeological sites. The site formation processes, and the archaeological signatures left in the wake of these planned acts of destruction, are important clues in extracting intention from the archaeological record. The way these signatures shed light on the psychological framework that defines abandonment behavior and illustrates the technological, political, economic, and social aspects of discard activities will be a subject of later discussion.

The identification of discard and reuse mechanisms in the material record and the archaeological signatures that accompany them has the potential to illuminate many aspects of the past. The particularistic case studies discussed above are important because they describe the behaviors and the physical clues found at similar sites from many periods from around the world.

The following chapter discusses alternative theoretical approaches to the study of watercraft discard. This other perspective, in stark contrast to the case studies described here, represents a nonparticularistic, non-artifact-focused, broadly comparative methodology that allows for the assessment of reuse, salvage, and postabandonment processes.

3

The Abandonment Process
and Archaeological Theory

Viable maritime archaeology should aim to provide insights into the past that are not necessarily available through other means, such as archival sources. At the very least it should act as an independent test of histories created through other sources. It should have its own status as a reconstructable science.

—Peter Veth and Michael McCarthy, "Types of Explanation in Maritime Archaeology"

The theoretical framework and methods of analysis outlined in this book are unlike the traditional orientation of maritime archaeology, called *historical particularism*. A school of thought originally created by cultural anthropologist Franz Boas (1858–1942) as an antigeneralist critique of *cultural evolutionism* and *diffusionism*, this paradigm considers individual cultures as products of distinctive historical circumstances. Accordingly, because of the special circumstances associated with cultural development, anthropologists should study cultures as unique and consider "the impossibility of general theories."[1]

In maritime archaeology, the definition of historical particularism and its practitioners is somewhat different:

Historical particularists are artifact oriented and are concerned with artifacts and their functions. This approach is particularly appropriate for the archaeology of shipwrecks, because, being a new field of study, the material artifacts are often not well understood. It is important, therefore, to build up a clear understanding of the material before constructing deeper hypotheses.[2]

The maritime version of historical particularism is a matter of debate. One perspective is that it simply outlines a deductive approach that endorses the ownership of data before you build theory from that information. Another explanation maintains that the definition varies from Boasian anthropological meaning because instead of saying that we *cannot* or *should not* generalize about cultural change, it simply says that we *do not.* In this light, it is arguable whether some forms of historical particularism in maritime archaeology actually refer to a theoretical framework or are largely atheoretical antiquarian methodologies focused on the collection of facts and the creation of typologies. Nevertheless, historical particularism has played a pivotal role in the subdiscipline and, consequently, has an important place in maritime archaeology.[3]

Historical particularism should not be dismissed as irrelevant; researchers should understand what it is yet be open to other approaches. There is a need for a broadened thematic basis to studies, whereby the investigations of larger, germane questions in history and archaeology guide the process of site selection and investigation and by default there is increased attention to the comparative aspects of research.

Arguably, a continued adherence to historical particularist approaches will not facilitate this. A "3-stage approach" advocated by Babits and Van Tilburg illustrates the need for a movement toward postparticularist perspectives and comparative archaeological studies:

> First, . . . sites . . . must be exploited to the fullest informational extent possible; second, sites of a given locality or type must be interrelated with each other to provide both interpretations and predictive modeling; finally sites must be presented within interdisciplinary and regional, if not global, perspectives to allow determinations of importance and provide better understanding of each individual site.[4]

Generally, work within maritime archaeology today still constitutes a site-based, particularist mindset lacking what Mark Staniforth has termed "theoretical sophistication."[5] There has been some recent commentary regarding the benefits of combined approaches. Veth and McCarthy, for instance, have asserted that

> maritime archaeology may well be served by research which aims to create both general and predictive models about nautical behavior (i.e. functional/systemic processual approach) and to characterize the motivation and meaning behind strategies adopted by maritime societies and individuals (i.e. a critical deconstructionist post-processual approach).[6]

Likewise, Michael McCarthy and Colin Martin have endorsed a combination of particularist and generalist approaches.[7] For Martin, however, this is for "de-particularizing the particular."[8] He maintains that because ship-wrecks in the postmedieval period are often rich with archaeological and documentary evidence, they tend to be "over-particularized."

Theoretical Evolution

Despite many decades of publication by social theorists in the terrestrially inclined areas of archaeological research, nonparticularist, anthropological, and behaviorally focused studies have been relatively scarce in maritime ar-chaeology. This is also the case within the Australian traditions of maritime archaeological research, which heavily influence this study.

Australian commentators on the directions of the subdiscipline have generally only credited the work of Richard Gould and Keith Muckelroy as representing such approaches.[9] But recently this has begun to change, as is demonstrated in a number of publications.[10] Nevertheless, the impe-tus to pursue generalist studies in maritime archaeology is a phenomenon predominantly from outside Australia and is especially the result of work undertaken in the United States. Muckelroy's and Gould's works do indeed represent these perspectives, but other important recent works, such as that of Donna Souza and Annalies Corbin, have also made significant con-tributions.[11]

There have, however, been some examples of an increasing attentive-ness to comparative, behaviorally focused work in Australia predating these examples. Work undertaken by Leonie Foster on behalf of the Victorian Archaeological Survey (VAS) culminated in one of the first, and most ex-tensive, comparative studies in Australian maritime archaeology, and it in-fluenced later, similar studies.[12] Foster's reports concerning regions within Port Phillip Bay (adjacent to Melbourne) included 280 vessels wrecked and abandoned between 1835 and 1985. Although the study presented ship-wrecks in a site-by-site format, it also attempted to analyze the degree to which they represent a microcosm of state history.

In 1989, William Jeffery published a study concentrating on the examina-tion of aspects of shipbuilding using a comparative approach.[13] The study compared the design attributes of 84 coastal vessels wrecked in South Aus-tralian waters from 1840 to 1900. Jeffery's comparisons allowed for the test-ing of historically based assumptions concerning the Tasmanian origins of wooden coastal sailing ships and the provenance of the timbers used in their construction. Jeffery's main comparative method was his use of length to breadth, and breadth to depth, ratios, and the coefficient of underdeck tonnage that allowed for comparison of design elements. Although Jeffery considered his archaeological conclusions speculative, his approaches went some way toward making general and predictive statements about the maritime archaeological record. He followed this study with an examination of Australian-built coastal shipwrecks in South Australia.[14] Both studies were able to contribute to a definition of the typical watercraft in operation and wrecked in South Australia during the nineteenth century.

In 1991, Cos Coroneos published an interpretation for the short working lives of early Australian wooden sailing vessels in Victorian waters presented along similar lines as Jeffery's 1989 study.[15] Although Coroneos stated that his intention was not to undertake comparative analysis in the same way as had Jeffery, his study was able to make conclusions about the relationship between wrecking events in Victoria and the construction quality of vessels between 1836 and 1845 using comparative methods.[16] Coroneos carried this comparative methodology to later work, especially the analysis and discussion of the shipwreck resource in regions of South Australia.[17]

Rebecca O'Reilly's 1999 thesis is another example of comparative archaeological research.[18] Her study concentrated on the materials and ship construction methods of vessels built between 1850 and 1899 operating the South Australian intrastate trade. It compared the material remains of wooden sailing vessels in an assessment of cultural continuity and cultural adaptation in ship design and construction.

James Cook University has also produced two large comparative studies: Brad Duncan's examination of shipwreck patterning and cultural seascapes in the Gippsland region of Victoria and Coleman Doyle's examination of loss and discard correlates in the vicinity of Townsville (Queensland) between 1865 and 1981.[19] Although Duncan's study was by far the larger of the two (with about 130 shipwrecks in a larger geographical area), Doyle's study (41 wrecked and discarded watercraft) has particular importance to this research because many of the perspectives he outlined are similar to those expounded here. His comparative approach was highly successful in describing the causes of loss, and it illuminated relationships among increased tonnage, increased trade, and increased catastrophic loss.[20]

These studies are some of the examples of the evolution and development of new theoretical and methodological tools in Australian maritime archaeology. Such studies illustrate a movement toward an "opening up" of approaches to more comparative studies set within much wider geographical and thematic environments. There is still much room for expansion of thematic studies to a national level.[21]

Theoretical Approaches

It is difficult to see any expansion of maritime archaeological scholarship occurring without a commitment by researchers to explore and embrace new theoretical tools for the subdiscipline. I agree with Ian Hodder's assertion that "we need to move towards the recognition that there is not only one right way to do archaeology. There are many right ways."[22] Thus there are a number of underlying theoretical perspectives evident in this research drawn from a diverse array of theoretical traditions both within and outside of archaeology. This array of perspectives owes much to the work of Staniforth, in particular, his assertion of the value of "diverse, complex and ambiguous" archaeological theory within the discipline.[23]

Consequently, there are a number of theoretical assumptions in this book, ranging from my views concerning the practical nature of the planning of discard events concerning watercraft to assumptions that artifacts (here represented by watercraft of different design) are expressions of cultural ideas and norms that are definable temporally, spatially, and ethnically. Also of central importance is the author's adoption of a belief borrowed directly from Larry Murphy's observation that the

> archaeology of shipwrecks should not merely [be] the embellishment of the maritime historical record, but the elucidation of otherwise unattainable aspects of human behavior. The combination of shipwreck archaeology with the methodologies of other disciplines will result in the authentic reconstruction of behavior patterns, and will permit the formulation of generalities regarding maritime life-ways and social processes.[24]

In order to do this, this study leans heavily toward processual approaches. Much of this investigation entails the testing of statistical data against propositions evident from analyzing the nature and effect of events in history. The tendency of processual methods to produce generalizing statements concerning cultural processes must also, however, be tempered with the admission that it will concurrently reduce the role of individual agency in the creation of archaeological sites.[25] However, this study does not embrace, or strive toward, the idea of creating universal and global theories. Its findings are an attempt to contribute to the understanding of the interaction between national and regional events and archaeological phenomena that exist in relation to highly specific historical contexts. This postprocessual perspective is reenforced with the questioning of evolutionary assumptions that are evident in technological paradigms. The manner in which I have viewed historical data as information for scientific correlation is not an attempt at creating absolute scientific truths. As Veth and McCarthy have stated:

> One vital component of any maritime archaeological reconstruction of the past must be clear and explicit statements of how specific nautical behaviors and belief systems can be reliably correlated with patterns in the material record; regardless of whether we are dealing with assemblages of artifacts, vessels, or indeed, coastal ports and settlements.[26]

Gauging and assessing social change through a joint reading of the rich historical and archaeological record is the major interpretive aspect of this study, something equivalent to what Hodder has communicated as a movement from *testing theory* to *fitting theory* in order to accommodate a scientific component into archaeological analysis while staying true to the research goals within the humanities.[27] The incorporation of the diverse historical contexts and the meaning behind such events illustrate the influence of postprocessual ideas on the analyses undertaken.[28]

Furthermore, the potential for the maritime archaeological record to allow creative generalizations about the maritime past is a central aspect of this work. The creation of broad anthropological accounts regarding human behavior is pivotal to the argument made throughout this book concerning the usefulness and significance of the abandoned watercraft resource and the worth of broad comparative studies within maritime archaeology. The tendency for comparative studies to be preoccupied with process and to draw archaeological inference toward anthropology is deliberate. As Richard Gould has noted, "Anthropology has been a useful source for generalizations about human behavior."[29] This is also a reflection of my views regarding the social relevance of the study in understanding the past in order to plan the present and predict the future, another attested theme in early processual theory.[30]

Conceptual Hurdles, Theoretical Tensions

Excluding historical factors, comparative maritime archaeological studies have not been popular due to a number of conceptual hurdles and theoretical tensions. Patty Jo Watson explains the resistance to generalist archaeological studies:

> A final sobering and complicating factor is that, at the present moment in the real world of shipwreck archaeology, the only thoroughly and comprehensively published work is idiographic; the generalists

have yet to prove themselves by designing projects, carrying them out, and publishing them in detail so the results can be evaluated and used by interested experts and scholars of all kinds.[31]

To some degree, the resistance to pursue comparative aspects of research is also the result of the tendency to view individual shipwreck sites as isolated time capsules. As Gould has commented, "The drama of a shipwreck focuses attention on the event, but the conditions that produced the wreck and the consequences arising from it are as significant as the event itself."[32] In light of this comment it is understandable that what Watson calls the "perpetual tension between the idiographic (particularist) and nomothetic (generalist) approaches" is also fundamentally a tension between the notion of the event and the notion of process.[33] Additionally, Gould has commented on the problems associated with event-based studies in comparison with what process oriented approaches can achieve:

> If archaeological events derived from assumptions about Pompeii-like or "time-capsule" associations are illusory, so, too, are historical events such as the wrecking, scuttling, and even construction of ships. Upon close examination, these so-called events are embedded in ongoing processes linked to social, economic, and even symbolic activities.[34]

By deemphasizing the importance of events, and by thinking about process, archaeologists have come to see ships as more than just the paraphernalia of human activity. Indeed, researchers have come to see watercraft from a range of creative perspectives. In terms of design, some researchers have recognized the richness of watercraft as documents with ethnic origins:

> Broad and narrow, deep or shoal, bluff or fine, high or low-wooded, square or fore and aft rigged, each type of ship had been, over centuries fashioned for a particular role that had, in broad terms, been created by her country's special characteristics.[35]

Similarly, other researchers have understood watercraft as objects imbued with technological meaning:

> When analyzing technological change in the merchant marine, there are a number of peculiarities that must be taken into account. Perhaps the most important is that the sector in question is a consumer of technology: a ship is an "artifact" with its technology already incorporated, and the skill required to manipulate it is much less complex than that needed to construct it.[36]

Likewise, there have been many changes in the perception of shipwrecks and ship remains throughout the development of maritime archaeology. In the 1970s, Keith Muckelroy was at the head of a major paradigmatic shift within maritime archaeology away from the purely descriptive with the proposal that ships could be seen to represent "machines" and "closed communities."[37] Since this time, there have been many other subtle transitions, all of which have had ramifications for the way that watercraft are incorporated into theoretical frameworks. Researchers such as Daniel Lenihan have seen them as "the material expression of more generalized cultural dynamics,"[38] and others have commented that ships "are conceived and designed according to the influence of various mental templates and ideologies."[39]

Of major importance is the idea that a ship or shipwreck is an "artifact" as well as a site. Just as maritime archaeologists endeavor to consider material culture in relation to shipwrecks, or terrestrial sites in spatial and temporal ways, they can view watercraft as artifacts existing on a less easily defined but larger scale. A ship is a composite artifact in many ways. There are variations not only in materials but also in the sources of materials, the types of components of vessels, the manufacturers of those components, and how it is all put together. For these reasons, we can see watercraft as artifacts from many different perspectives. The statement by Murphy that "the life of a ship and its use will be reflected in material remains" is pivotal to comparative watercraft research.[40] As McCarthy has asserted, this statement brings to light the fact that a ship is not a monochronic unit but is diachronic, spread out in time, a snapshot of a dynamic process.[41] This makes ships objects highly sensitive not only to the cultural conditions of the time of their creation (as reflected in elements of their design) but also to cultural transformation (that may eventually be reflected in the form of archaeological signatures). Peter Throckmorton was probably the first to outline such a view:

> A sailing ship, seen as an artifact, is one of the most interesting and beautiful of human creations. In it is concentrated the accumulated knowledge of half a dozen crafts through many generations. Like public buildings, ships are expressions of the societies that create them.[42]

Since Throckmorton's statement, many authors have commented along similar lines.[43] This concept is important to consider because it links method and theory when carrying out generalist studies on the structural remains of watercraft. As Watson has proposed, "Logically speaking . . . the empirical data from shipwrecks can be recorded and recovered for any purpose or set of purposes from the highly idiographic to the highly no-mothetic."[44] Of more relevance to this study, Martin has written, "Set into wider contexts . . . shipwrecks can be regarded as wide-ranging paradigms of the societies to which they belong."[45] For this reason, this study takes a multilayered approach that sees ships simultaneously as composite arti-fact, structure, and site (a structure containing artifacts); the differences are largely perceptual.

What can we learn from such a vast resource? By considering elements in design, build, and technology in ship construction as well as particular historical documentation concerning each vessel, we can identify diagnos-tic features. We can allude to or explain certain trends in technology, see quite clearly the effect of economic or historical change, and understand why certain incidental historical changes had wide repercussions in legisla-tion and bureaucracy. We also may be able to demonstrate the effects of technological change on society and the effect of societal change on tech-nological development and innovation. When we examine certain elements quantitatively, many trends and developments become obvious. All of these ideas can be seen in the evolution and diversification of theory in the field of maritime archaeology. The perception of such a multifaceted resource like a ship as either artifact, structure, *or* site tend to limit conceptualization of watercraft, as well as the choices that a researcher may make regarding the utility of various theoretical approaches.

Technology and Theory

Theoretical debates and the changing consideration of how we view wa-tercraft are also tied to theories of technology. Despite an apparent declin-ing belief in technological progress among technological theorists, tech-nology has traditionally played a major role in archaeological theory. This has occurred even though assumptions about technology and technologi-cal progress are not always made explicit within research.[46] To some de-gree, this is attributable to a common view that culture is comprised of three interrelated subsystems: technology, social organization, and ideol-ogy. From another perspective, culture is composed of techno-economic, social, and ideological components.[47] Consequently, technology features prominently in theories of cultural development, and some studies border on the techno-environmentally deterministic because of their perception of change in technological terms.[48] This is because diffusion, as a force of cultural change, is a pivotal aspect of unilinear evolutionary concepts that enable broad economic trends to be easily discussed.[49] Even where the technological aspects of society are only one important catalyst of societal change, researchers have often used technological notions to explain cultural differences. Trigger has commented on this in relation to the early work of V. Gordon Childe, noting that

> instead of interpreting cultural change as the result of technological innovation, he saw broader economic and political contexts influencing the uses that were made of innovations. This allowed him to explain how the same technological innovations could produce very different types of societies in Europe and the Near East.[50]

There have been many archaeological studies focused on describing social change in relation to technological transitions. Indeed, technological change features prominently in empirical studies outlining social change.[51] Gould has also noted the

> materialist-Marxist assumption that human behavior and history are structured primarily by the relations of production—that is, the technological and economic factors involved in the development of human institutions coincides nicely with the remains found in the archaeological record.[52]

Alternatively, the dominance of technological paradigms in archaeological theory is attributable to the view that the formation of the archaeological record is a continuous process that has occurred over the entire duration of the human past and continues to occur. From this, we may be able to test and challenge the history of human development (often based on economic and technological assumptions) through our observations of the archaeological record.[53]

Many studies of technology, especially those concerning maritime technologies, also contemplate the role of consumer choice in the adoption of new technology. Owing to this, they are also related to studies of consumer choice in historical archaeology.[54] Additionally, some models of consumer behavior include considerations of loss, abandonment, and discard processes.[55]

The idea of technology and technological progress is pivotal to maritime archaeology. The nineteenth and twentieth centuries have been important in the history of technology. Whereas the nineteenth century is credited as a "revolution in the history of seafaring, a turning point upon worldwide cultural, economic and technological development,"[56] the twentieth century has been cited as the century within which "every aspect of trans-port—speed, convenience, comfort, availability—has undergone dramatic development."[57] As one author has noted:

> Waterborne craft have been basic human tools since prehistoric times. Many societies rose or declined as a direct result of whether they successfully utilized ships for subsistence, transport, and protection. Ship production and deployment have been the focus of intense human cooperation and organizational efforts for several millennia. Ships have been, and still are, the largest and most complex mobile structures produced.[58]

Although this book does not seek to specifically comment on or discuss the many factors and historic events that have constituted the processes for and against technological innovation, diffusion, and change, it nevertheless discusses many issues associated with technology.[59]

Technological change also comes about via cultural imperatives and advances in scientific knowledge, engineering expertise, or managerial processes. These aspects of technological change concern processes such as production, methods of design and maintenance, and the establishment of successful markets for product.[60] Technology and the nature of technological change is a complex subject, and it is generally accepted that it is not possible to estimate general rates of technological change due to major differences between technologies.[61] A central aspect of the history of transport and maritime trade is the impact of technological change. It is additionally important because researchers often cite it as one of the main factors in economic growth, due to the ability of new technologies to lower costs; increase output, competition, wages, and living conditions; and implement product improvement.[62] Technological change, as one source notes, "has been linked to economic growth so closely that within the long-term growth trend one can identify recurrent accelerations and decelerations related to various technological changes."[63] A "kondratieff cycle" is the term used for these fifty-year periods of growth.[64] The connectedness of economic and technological issues is evident from the beginnings of the use-life of watercraft, as mentioned by one author:

> The economic factor is of prime importance in designing a ship. An owner requires a ship which will give him the best possible returns for his initial investment and running costs. This means that the final design should be arrived at taking into account not only present eco-

nomic considerations, but also those likely to develop within the life of the ship.[65]

It is almost impossible to separate the technological and economic aspects of any aspect of history. This is because economic development is often dependent on technological innovation and diffusion, and these processes themselves are dependent on economic development. There have been many studies on the connection between technological change and economic growth. Noted research includes Jari Ojala's study of technological change and economic growth in eighteenth- and nineteenth-century sea transport in Finland and Henning and Henning's study on the transition from sail to steam in the export lumber shipments of the Pacific Northwest, 1898–1913.[66]

Studying the process of technological change may also relate important notions that shed light on the historical and economic processes that underlie such transitions. There has been a traditional acceptance that at many times in history certain events have pitted technology against technology, culminating in revolution. Such "revolutions" are described as turning points in history and are credited as times of cataclysmic and almost overnight change, bringing about the acceptance of a new technological status quo. There are many examples of this, from the Neolithic era to the Industrial Revolution.[67] In other cases certain historical events, such as the opening of the Suez Canal, or conflicts, such as the Crimean War and World War II, have been regarded as revolutions.[68] Often-cited revolutionary events in naval history of significance to general technological change include the defeat of the Spanish Armada (1588), the battle of Trafalgar (1805), the standoff between the USS *Monitor* and the CSS *Virginia* (1862), and the creation of the HMS *Dreadnought* (1906).[69] The notion of "technological revolution," however, is problematic because it erroneously implies overnight change. But technological change is a prolonged process accompanied by complimentary theoretical breakthroughs. In light of this, the "rude test of war" can be better viewed as a catalyst for drastic technological transformations as well as a vehicle for dramatic economic change.[70]

Maritime archaeologists have traditionally been interested in a range of issues concerning technology, and it has played a fundamental role in the interpretation of the past. Early examinations, however, tended to focus on the nature of, and relationship among, commerce, distribution, and shipbuilding. Studies also tended to fixate on debates concerning opposing "evolutionist" or "diffusionist" theories.[71] In some instances, this may be concerned with the correlation of individual shipwrecks to technological progress or the nature of technological change itself. Studies replete with technological facts, figures, and theories are common within the subdiscipline, and many of them are often theoretically inclined.[72] In other cases, archaeologists have attempted to use archaeological data to reassess technological adaptation, as communicated by Lenihan:

> Adaptive change in design is far from the rational, step-by-step, upward evolution implied in many works on marine history. Industrial archaeologists on land have demonstrated the anxiety that using new materials causes in structural engineering.[73]

Indeed, watercraft are perfect for such assessment because they are catalysts of change in many ways. Murphy's work, for instance, is replete with technological notions. Ships are "vectors of the spread of technology," and ship design (a reflection of technological norms at one time) is a major component in the assessment of social organization, the exchange of ideas, the flow of influence, and understanding national identity.[74] Likewise, Gould has commented on the nature of technological obsolescence and the accidental nature of technological innovation.[75]

Another important aspect of maritime archaeological investigations of technology is associated with the role of archaeological enquiry in reassessing and augmenting the history of maritime technology. This is best summed up by Murphy, who maintains that the "developmental history of the design and construction of vessels, is not complete, and often the only means of study is the archaeological record."[76]

Additionally, maritime archaeologists can understand changes in the technology represented by watercraft design in relation to environmental adaptation and socioeconomic adaptation.[77] Considerations of technological change play two important roles in this research. They play a major part in the economic analyses of subsequent chapters and underlie theories of archaeological site formation.

Archaeological Site Formation

Central to the study of any maritime archaeological resource are the site formation processes involved in the creation of the archaeological record. As already stated, the main distinction between "shipwreck" and "abandoned vessel" is the level of accidental or deliberate, natural or cultural, and catastrophic or predetermined aspects of the site formation process.

A processual/behavioral approach to material culture in the form of site formation theory is central to the theoretical work in this research and is the predominant middle-range method used in this study.[78] Site formation studies have a particular view of archaeological evidence:

> Archaeological evidence results from two processes—initial human behavior (i.e. the phenomenon of a shipwreck which is a culturally-derived event) and subsequent transformational actions (effect of natural processes and subsequent human activities).[79]

Ian Oxley has described formation processes as "how archaeological evidence (in the form of artifacts, structures etc) came to be buried, and what events distorted or destroyed it subsequently, regardless of whether those events were of human or natural origin."[80] Formation processes are the causal mechanisms that facilitate the movement of artifacts from their systemic or use context (where an artifact is participating in a behavioral system) to their archaeological context (where an artifact is only interacting with the natural environment). Previous studies on abandonment and abandonment processes (such as the ethno-archaeological work done by Catherine Cameron and Steve Tomka on domestic and prehistoric sites in African villages) have made much use of site formation theory.[81]

Site formation theory is best represented by Michael B. Schiffer's and Keith Muckelroy's studies, which are similar to a degree.[82] Muckelroy's "extractive filters," for example, resemble Schiffer's "transformation processes,"[83] and both researchers describe processes that are factors involved in the creation of the historic and archaeological record.

Maritime archaeologists most often cite Muckelroy's work on shipwreck disintegration as site formation theory. His work, built on by various researchers, outlines processes that are comparable with many of the aspects of Schiffer's site formation theory.[84] However, because Muckelroy's site formation theories concentrate on the natural aspects of shipwreck site degeneration and are not as developed or universal as Schiffer's concepts, the latter is increasingly preferred.[85] Likewise, Schiffer's version of site formation theory is preferred in this research because of its compatibility with other behavioral theories and case studies, and also because of the greater attention Schifferian site formation places on cultural processes.[86]

There are two major categories of transformation process: noncultural/natural (or n-) processes, which represent all natural factors that impinge on and affect archaeological material, and cultural (or c-) processes, which are represented by a diverse array of human behavioral practices that affect and modify material culture after their initial use for a particular function.[87]

The uses of n-transformation processes in archaeology are well known.[88]

They are also prominent in maritime archaeology, mainly because of the preoccupation with the role of environmental variables in the shipwreck site disintegration processes. The uses of site formation processes in maritime archaeology have, however, largely been used in a particular manner. As Gould has noted, "Much of contemporary archaeological theory is aimed at recognizing postdepositional processes and measuring their relative effects on the archaeological record."[89] These postdepositional (i.e., post-wrecking event) processes have characteristically focused on the natural aspects of site formation (wrecking processes and wreck disintegration).[90] Generally, this is because the "cultural aspect of formation process concepts has not been appreciably developed."[91] Moreover, this is because researchers rarely perceive shipwrecks as being the result of human intent, usually viewing them as entirely accidental. Lenihan and Murphy make particular reference to the work of Lucien Basch and Keith Muckelroy in propagating this view.[92] Despite this, Murphy has also highlighted the cultural aspects of the wrecking event: "Although it is frequently asserted that the final location of a wrecked vessel is an accident; in a more general sense wreck concentrations represent patterns of human activity in an area over time."[93] Gould also refers to the sociocultural processes of wrecking events in relation to the poor maintenance of the twentieth-century tanker and bulk carrier *Marine Electric* and potential criminal activity on the nineteenth-century barque *North Carolina*.[94]

Other than acknowledging that noncultural formation processes act on cultural materials at all times and are relevant in relation to salvage because of the decision-making processes focused on the degree of natural attrition on salvageable materials, this book predominantly concentrates on c-transformation processes. This is because of the major role cultural factors such as human decision making plays in adopting technology, determining obsolescence, choosing discard locations, and undertaking salvage activities on unwanted vessels.

Although site formation and the investigation of culturally derived archaeological signatures have been the subject of many studies, such as Gould's examination of the archaeology of war, cultural site formation is a neglected aspect of maritime archaeological scholarship.[95] Where researchers have considered cultural factors, however, the depth of our understanding of archaeological sites invariably increases.

In the case of the Bird Key wreck, an unidentified nineteenth-century steamer lost in the Dry Tortugas, Florida, Gould also made a range of behavioral inferences from the articulation and orientation of structural remains. These inferences pertained to the deposition of the ship, which may have been deliberately run aground.[96] Of particular interest is the analysis of the ships' propeller, which suggested that the vessel had been running in reverse (with propeller moving in a counterclockwise fashion) just before grounding, supporting the notion of an accidental wrecking.[97] This is a major departure from the usual investigation of shipwreck sites, where researchers usually interpret the absence and position of structural and diagnostic vessel elements as a product of natural attrition on the hull. The Bird Key wreck is also a case study that takes into account site formation events, such as the use of explosives on the vessel, and how this contributed to its disintegration.[98]

McCarthy's investigation of the steamship *Xantho* is one of the best examples of the representation of cultural transformation processes occurring in one vessel. It is also important because it links site formation theory, technological notions, and the perception of watercraft as artifact. Additionally, McCarthy explicitly considers disposal or abandonment behavior in his discussion of these processes:

> Through this particular transformation process, a redundant artifact (the *Xantho*) was modified and re-used, rather than being broken up in order to retrieve useful materials before deliberate scuttling or abandonment, as was the norm.[99]

McCarthy's statement embodies not just an admission that abandonment was a behavior associated with ship owning but also that such an act of abandonment is common and wrapped up in notions of salvage and technological obsolescence. It also communicates that objects are replete with signatures of use that can illustrate the way they interact with humans while being used.

Combining ideas about abandonment and redundancy with site formation theory can also lead to the distinction between, and analysis of, predepositional and postdepositional processes caused by cultural activities. Indeed, the assessment of site formation processes is important in the examination of all watercraft remains, as Babits and Corbin-Kjorness indicate:

> Site formation processes are relevant because they affect information potential and site condition. Was the vessel present at the site because it was a derelict, wrecked or abandoned; accidentally or deliberately grounded, stripped or burnt before ultimately being examined as an archaeological site.[100]

Although this study is concerned with c-transformation processes in the archaeological record, it is important to acknowledge the fundamental distinctions between c- and n-transformation processes. Whereas n-transformation processes are concerned with the interaction of the natural environment on artificial constructions, their effects are universal, constant, and therefore highly deducible by scientific methods.[101] On the other hand, c-transforms are borne out of behavioral processes. As Hodder suggests, "We cannot generalize easily nor can we construct universal c-transforms about human behavior because human intentionality intervenes."[102] To argue against such a statement is impossible. This does not mean, however, that we should not attempt to find and describe these processes. Additionally, it does not suggest that c-transforms cannot be determined from the archaeological record and are not important signatures of the behaviors represented in archaeological remains. Furthermore, the understanding of cultural site formation is pivotal to the understanding of discard behaviors. As Bruce Trigger has noted, "The realization that large numbers of artifacts are found in contexts of disposal rather than those of manufacture or use has stimulated much ethno-archaeological research that aims to discover regularities in patterns of the disposal of refuse."[103] Indeed, it seems increasingly obvious that when archaeologists have historical records they can make many correlations between historical events and the archaeological record that signify such events. Hence, c-transformation processes are an important part of interpreting the archaeological record.

Another reason for the consideration of cultural site formation theory in ship-abandonment studies is cited by Oxley, who writes, "Reviewing the formation of shipwreck sites in relation to other marine sites (e.g. drowned landscapes) and the consideration of 'ship traps' and 'ship graveyards,' has potential for the future study of shipwreck site formation processes."[104] Additionally, ships' graveyard sites are characteristically diverse in vessel types. As Schiffer notes, "Artifact diversity is a characteristic of deposits particularly sensitive to cultural formation processes."[105] This is another indication of the utility of site formation theory in understanding the complexities of the behaviorally defined aspects of sites.

Types of C-Transformation Processes

Schiffer discusses many cultural transformation processes at length, including reuse, discard, loss, abandonment, reclamation, and disturbance processes. Most of these are relevant to the study of watercraft abandonment.[106] Site formation studies rest on the fundamental principle that after use, humans either reuse or deposit artifacts in some manner.[107] Fundamentally, there are three general perspectives of formation processes concerning watercraft abandonment, those that are evidence of activities during use, those that are evidence of the process of abandonment, and those that are evidence of activities after abandonment.

Reuse Processes

Evidence of reuse processes, detected on watercraft-abandonment sites, survive in the archaeological record. Generally, reuse processes are behaviors that see a change to the user, use, or form of a particular artifact.[108] Different reuse mechanisms, however, are associated with distinct behaviors.

Lateral cycling occurs where there is a change in the user or the transfer of the ownership of an artifact without a change in the form and use of the object. In relation to maritime commerce, the transfer of a vessel from one owner to another while maintaining its use as a tool for trade represents this process.[109] The object remains in a systemic context.

Recycling entails the reintroduction of cultural material into an industrial process that transforms an object's fabric into some other form and/or function.[110] The salvage of objects, including the dismantling of watercraft, is an example of this process.

Secondary use is a term that refers to changes in the function of cultural material without substantial alteration to the form of that material. This usually occurs in objects that have undergone extensive wear.[111] Within the context of this study, an example is the conversion of vessels into secondary support roles, such as hulks and lighters, or other more specific and distinctive functions.

Conservatory processes constitute the transition of an object from its techno-function (related to use) to socio- or ideo-function.[112] Such processes are not common within this study and are only represented when vessels cease to serve primary or secondary functions in relation to trade and are conserved due to a perception of their historical value (such as tourist ships).

Discard Processes

Schiffer describes the term *abandonment* as "the process whereby a place— an activity area, structure, or entire settlement—is transformed to archaeological context."[113] As abandonment is a form of cultural deposition, it is also a discard process. Whereas reuse mechanisms describe the transformation of cultural remains through a range of systemic functions, discard processes are concerned more with the transformation of objects from systemic contexts to archaeological contexts. This activity normally occurs because of the failure of an artifact to fulfill any kind of use role (techno-function). Examples include unrepairable damage or mechanical ineffectiveness because of breakage, use-wear, or deterioration.[114]

Discard processes are also particularly relevant to the analysis of space, and the location of abandonment areas. As noted by Schiffer, the spatial dimension of archaeological evidence may inform the researcher about site formation processes:

> In the field, artifact locations are recorded with reference to grid systems, but locations can also be described in terms of behaviorally significant divisions of space, such as activity areas and the domains of various cultural units.[115]

Schiffer's statement also contributes to how we understand the reasons for the location of watercraft-abandonment sites, and it is important in interpreting why major ship-discard sites (such as ships' graveyards) exist where they do. The cultural context of discard is also explained by the observation that "people tend to dump trash where others have previously dumped trash; thus concentrations arise."[116] This leads to another distinction in the types of discard sites: those that are *primary refuse sites* and those that are *secondary refuse sites*. Primary refuse sites occur where artifacts/watercraft are discarded at the location of their use or salvage; at secondary refuse sites, these activities occur at a place specifically used for disposal activities—salvage and use has happened elsewhere.[117] Both types inform us about the complexities of salvage activities and distinguish variations in behavior. Often, secondary refuse sites are indicative of *maintenance processes* or *waste streams*. These activities occur when a site accumulates so much refuse that a periodic complete or partial removal of waste to other locations has to take place. Such a behavior is known as the *Schlepp effect*, a reference to the transportation and discard of material from large game animals as represented in the faunal assemblages found at kill sites.[118] These are the reasons, largely, for the creation of watercraft-abandonment sites as secondary refuse sites. Due to the large amount of material retrieved during salvage, and because of the logistical aspects of vessel deconstruction, ship breakers often abandon watercraft remains away from their location of salvage following some initial dismantling.

Similarly, Schiffer's notion of the *relational dimension* is associated with the spatial dimension of archaeological evidence because watercraft-abandonment sites can be seen as locations of *singular association* where two or more watercraft are located in close proximity to each other. On a larger scale, discarded ships are examples of *recurrent associations* because they exist within the same spatial and behavioral contexts from region to region.[119]

In direct contrast to catastrophic and consequential abandonment, geographical constraints on the disposal of vessels are linked to the expenses involved in their removal and the limitations imposed by regulation.

Abandonment Processes

Abandonment processes bear some resemblance to discard behaviors. One major distinction, however, is that they are more specifically related to the abandonment of entire sites. Within the context of this research, abandonment processes are analogous to the discontinued use of entire regions (ship-breaking yards and ships' graveyards) for the abandonment of watercraft. The terms *de facto refuse* and *curate behaviors* are also part of abandonment processes. Schiffer describes de facto refuse as "tools, facilities, structures, and other cultural materials that, although still usable (or reusable), are left behind when an activity area is abandoned."[120] In the context of watercraft abandonment, this is most relevant when people cease to use abandoned vessels for the purposes of material procurement and when they discontinue using established ships' graveyards for dumping their unwanted watercraft. A number of variables—the rate of abandonment, the degree to which abandonment is planned, the available transport for access to the site, the season of abandonment, the distance to the closest populated area, and the size of the local community—are linked with the formation of de facto refuse sites.[121]

In the context of watercraft discard, de facto refuse sites relate to salvage behavior and the interaction between spatial and logistic factors in the procurement of raw materials for recycling. Schiffer defined curate behavior as "the process of removing and transporting still-usable or repairable items from the abandoned activity area for continued use elsewhere."[122] In this way, curate behaviors are forces working against the creation of de facto refuse. At the extreme end of this activity, curate behaviors may see humans completely strip sites of usable materials for recycling and eventual reintegration into systemic contexts. Both processes exist in the planning phases of abandonment activities, and they tell us whether there is an expectation of a return to the site.[123] We can see this especially at intertidal ships' graveyards, where the highly exposed remains of unwanted watercraft sites of repeated return for the purposes of salvaging materials.

Reclamation Processes

Reclamation processes can be seen as reuse mechanisms where recycling occurs. They take place where human agents transform artifacts from an archaeological context back into a systemic context.[124] Such behaviors are more likely to occur at archaeological sites that are recurrently occupied, although these practices may also occur in conjunction with curate behaviors that see sites (such as ships' graveyards) visited periodically over an extended period of time during which cultural materials are removed.[125] Salvage and scavenging processes are the most common reclamation mechanisms in this research. This is reflected in two behaviors—the salvage of objects or structures (de facto refuse items) for reuse and the salvage/scavenging of structures for raw materials.

Scavenging is a generic term related to the exploitation of objects following their discard. Scavenging also has a socioeconomic context related to the unsanctioned, illegal, and often clandestine salvage of material from watercraft-abandonment sites for profit.[126] More specifically, scavenging activities in ships' graveyard sites (which tend to be secondary refuse sites) are *gleaning behaviors* associated with *resource-use strategies*.[127] The reintroduction of de facto refuse items (such as watercraft) into some kind of systemic context is an example of scavenging. The assessment of de facto refuse items for continued use is a basis for this behavior. As Schiffer explains:

> Several variables influence the likelihood that particular artifacts will be scavenged. For example, all other variables being constant, intact artifacts and those with greater remnant uselives have a higher probability of being scavenged. One also expects replacement cost to directly influence scavenging probabilities.[128]

Another case where reclamation processes occur in the archaeological record is associated with in-filling procedures where humans use refuse in the transformation of once nonfunctional areas into land for use.[129] Such material is termed *displaced refuse*, something abandoned watercraft, from antiquity to the present day were often used for.

Conclusion

The recorded, deconstructed elements of a vessel are not just historically interesting. When examined diachronically and comparatively, they also are significant clues to changing technological and economic circumstances.

Similarly, the archaeological signatures of use, modification, reuse, and discard are opportunities to see historical processes reflected in archaeological remains.

In the words of Lenihan, "Shipwrecks are an extraordinary database for anthropologically oriented archaeologists."[130] Abandoned ships are also an "extraordinary database," and a comparative approach can provide the framework for understanding this database. Additionally, the development of comparative approaches to maritime archaeological materials is important for other reasons. As Murphy has noted, "The shift from considering ships as discrete time capsules to viewing them as integral aspects of a larger parent culture can produce methodological and theoretical developments heretofore not readily apparent."[131] He has also stated that shipwrecks "can properly contribute much to the study of human behavior in many areas, and the only limits are imposed by the nature and scope of the questions developed by researchers."[132] It is within this framework that this study finds meaning. The following chapters outline the results of the application of behaviorally focused investigation based on a comparative framework.

4

Watercraft Abandonment in Australia

National Perspectives

The ships have gone, their age is past. The sea has taken most of them herself. In some quiet by-way of the sea's waters we may find a hulk careened on a bank by the tide which has deserted her, and find, despite all infirmity of age, a beauty of form and line that holds us and constrains us to search, to spell at last from letters nigh effaced by tide and by wind, and by the relentless erosion of time, a name once famous in a hundred ports.

—Thomas Cunningham, "About Docks that Are Closed and Ships that Have Gone"

From the initial moment of the settlement of the Australian landmass by non-indigenous peoples, abandonment was inevitable for many of the watercraft that would shape embryonic colonies into an island nation. Guided by undulations within global economic circumstances and the fortunes of empire, the need to dispose of unwanted ships would mirror the health and vigor of an unfolding mercantile experiment in the Southern Hemisphere.

This chapter is about gazing into this mirror. Its intention is to illuminate the connections between discard and Australian economic development. The discussion that follows is a synopsis of research from the broadest geographical and temporal views—perceptions that concentrate on the degree of correlation between nationally significant economic and historical events and trends in watercraft abandonment.

Events have the ability to blind our understanding of the *conditions* that catalyze human behavioral responses. This is especially applicable in the case of the scholarly treatment of ship discard behavior, which largely has been blind to the processes that catalyze discard behavior. For instance, researchers may explain why vessel discard occurs via a simple notation that a vessel either "outlived its economic life" or was "replaced by a more modern vessel."[1] It is a common assumption that the main reason a vessel is abandoned is that it has become "nail sick" (worn out), economically redundant, or technologically obsolete. Often, the assertion that owners abandon their vessels for any one of these reasons becomes sufficient cause to discontinue further investigation into the reason for their discard. Similarly, researchers place the dumping of vessels in ships' graveyards to three main categories: vessels that had outlived their economic life, vessels that were not worth repairing, or vessels that were replaceable with more modern examples.[2] All three categories are reasonable, but they do not tell us the full story. Indeed, one may ask, what are the factors that lead shipowners to make the decision that they no longer require their vessels?

Economic Correlates

Abandonment trends are an amalgam of interconnected preconditions and historical agents. The following is an examination of economic and histori-cal events and their effect on the tendency to abandon watercraft in Austra-lia. A number of "national" economic events (those spanning the Australian continent and Tasmania) related to trends in ship abandonment have been extracted from historical sources. Due to the varied affects of these events on different colonies and states, only a select few case studies will be ex-amined. The next chapter is concerned with a more in-depth analysis of localized regional economic events.

The database compiled for this study shows that at least 1,542 vessels— watercraft built between the late eighteenth and late twentieth century— have been deliberately discarded in Australia (fig. 1). Historical sources document these vessels as discarded in Australian waters between 1806 and 2001. We cannot incorporate all of these vessels into economic analyses because not all of them have a date of abandonment recorded and in some cases their tonnage value could not be determined. Figures 2 and 3 repre-sent the abandonment of watercraft in Australia between 1802 and 2001. Figure 2 depicts the number of vessels abandoned by year (1,246 vessels), and Figure 3 shows the accumulated gross tonnage of vessels abandoned

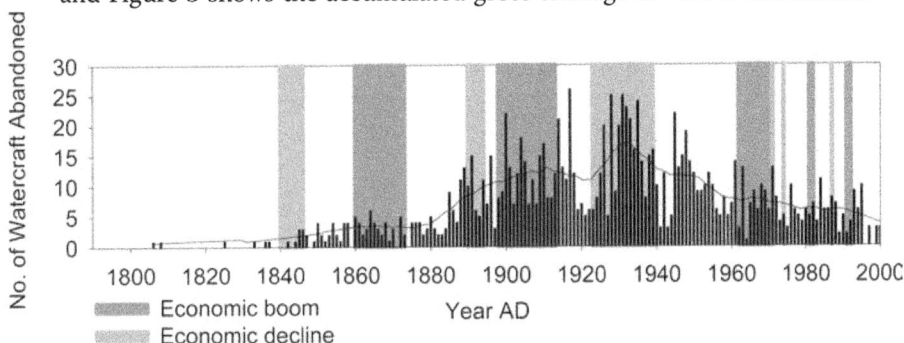

Figure 2. Watercraft abandoned in Australia (1800–2000) by number of watercraft (n = 1,246 watercraft).

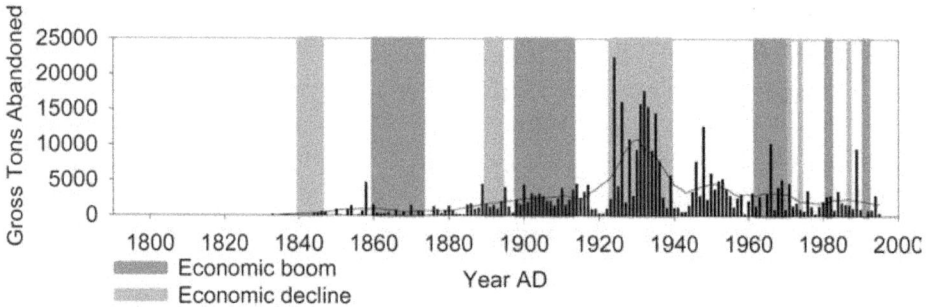

Figure 3. Watercraft abandoned in Australia (1800–2000) by gross tonnage (n = 1,235 watercraft, 413,950.1 GRT).

each year (1,235 vessels representing 413,950.1 GRT). Both graphs have periods of economic depression and boom superimposed on them to illustrate correlations between abandonment trends and nationally significant economic conditions. These figures are based on all vessels in the ANAVD irrespective of location (vessels of unknown location are included).

Economic Aspects of Ship Abandonment

From the early nineteenth century to the present day, only a small number of events have had discernible influence on ship abandonment in Australia: periods of economic expansion, periods of economic decline (recession, depression), times of war, and the aftermath of war (the transition to peacetime economy and economic reconstruction).

Wars, as events that bring about drastic technological change, are a special case study. Rapid technological changes, although having long-term benefits, also are normally associated with many social and economic disruptions during the process of transition.[3] Consequently, warfare, and the technological repercussions of war, is not only a catalyst for social and economic growth, decline, and change but also an important phase in the development of new technologies, which have their own economic ramifications. Mel Davies suggests that there were four major economic events between the 1840s and the 1870s.[4] Other than the Australian gold rushes of the 1850s, three of these were wars: the Crimean War (1854–56), the Indian Mutiny (1857–58), and the Second Opium War (1856–60).

There are many possible scenarios when we consider the economic background of watercraft abandonment. For instance, the abandonment of watercraft could be a consequence of business bankruptcy. Behind such an event, however, is the likelihood that the bankruptcy was the consequence of the economic climate of the time. Depression within a particular trade or business enterprise, or an endemic national recession or depression, also may be a cause.

A number of economic events have had direct influences on the predisposition of shipowners to abandon their watercraft. As Broxam has noted, Australia has experienced recessions and depressions approximately every forty to fifty years beginning in the 1840s (in the early 1890s, early 1930s, and early 1990s). All of these periods have come after a time of marked economic growth.[5] Likewise, other events, such as "rushes" and wars, although more often seen for their social or political ramifications, are also economic events of major magnitude. It is against this undulating economic climate that ship abandonment makes most sense.

R. G. Gregory outlines that the three primary indices against which we may analyze the effects of depression in individual nations are unemployment, employment, and output.[6] To some degree, we can ask whether the archaeological and historical data attached to the abandonment of watercraft may also be an index for appraising the results of economic change. For this reason, it may be possible to check information from the abandonment resource against other economic indices or use data pertaining to the abandonment of watercraft as an economic index itself.

There is some precedent for using aggregate data from historical documents to assess and reappraise aspects of history. For instance, Graeme Broxam suggests that the tonnage of vessels coming to trade in a particular port may be an indication of that port's prosperity. He also claims, in the specific case of Van Diemen's Land (present day Tasmania), that

> another indicator of the colony's maritime prosperity can be seen in the number and tonnage of ships built during the period 1843–1850. It will be seen that after a mini-boom in the late 1830s, [shipyard output] dwindled away to next to nothing by 1845, . . . largely due to the "lag-time" between ordering new vessels at the height of the depression (1842/3) and their completion. However, the recovery was swift and the resultant boom of the late 1840s was not repeated in Tasmania for nearly a century.[7]

Broxam also explains that a "dip" of some magnitude in 1849 was apparently the result of several large vessels ordered in 1847–48 but incomplete until 1850. The massive influx of overseas ships on the market as a result of the gold rushes caused the almost total collapse of the industry, which was not revived again to any appreciable extent until the 1860s.[8]

Although Broxam's implications that shipping arrivals may be a way of assessing local economic prosperity and that shipbuilding output may be a mirror of local economic boom-and-bust cycles remain largely un-tested, his use of this data as economic correlate is an alluring premise for researchers looking at economic maritime history. Arguably, Broxam's view also insinuates that the examination of watercraft abandonment trends may similarly become an interesting reflection of economic development. This is reinforced by the understanding that watercraft are often abandoned due to technological and economic issues (and not catastrophic circumstances). This view maintains that the incidence of discard, and the types of ves-sels discarded (because of the willingness of owners to repair or buy newer vessels), are potentially useful litmus tests of technological and economic change.

We must acknowledge, however, that the process of discard is a com-plicated one, and that economic and technological events do not often manifest themselves immediately in increased or decreased rates of water-craft discard. In essence, it is important to factor in lag-times. For example, Broxam notes that a so-called miniboom in shipbuilding in Tasmania in the 1830s had dwindled away by 1845 due to "the ordering of vessels at the height of the depression (1842/3) and their completion." If this is the case, then trends in discard may also be subject to lag-times.[9] The best example of a lag-time in watercraft abandonment is when a shipowner "lays up" a vessel during periods of economic downturn, often prolonging the process of abandonment just in case economic conditions improve. There are many important considerations to make when attempting discard analyses.

Periods of General Economic Boom

Historians have not documented periods of economic boom as well as peri-ods of economic decline, mainly due to the general lack of major (and often drastic) social upheaval. As a rule, Australian economic health, stability, and progress has to some degree been dependent on influences and de-velopments in international commerce. Furthermore, Australian overseas shipping has been traditionally owned by overseas interests.[10] In particular, British maritime supremacy, which had been in force since Waterloo (1815) has historically been the major influence on Australian trade, shipbuilding, and ship-buying trends. From the early days of the Australian colonies, Brit-ish control of global trade dominated the volume of imports and exports

Table 1. Abandoned Watercraft by Nationality of Build, Showing Number, Proportion of Total ANAVD, and Proportion of Vessels of Known Origin

Nation	No. Watercraft	% of Total	% Known
Australia	694	45.01	54.82
United Kingdom	391	25.36	30.88
Unknown	276	17.90	N/A
United States	48	3.11	3.79
Canada	39	2.53	3.08
Netherlands	15	0.97	1.18
Indonesia	14	0.91	1.11
New Zealand	14	0.91	1.11
Germany	8	0.52	0.63
Vietnam	8	0.52	0.63
Norway	6	0.39	0.47
France	5	0.32	0.39
India	5	0.32	0.39
China	4	0.26	0.32
Sweden	3	0.19	0.24
Ireland	2	0.13	0.16
Hong Kong	1	0.06	0.08
Seychelles	1	0.06	0.08
Spain	1	0.06	0.08
Finland	1	0.06	0.08
Denmark	1	0.06	0.08
Taiwan	1	0.06	0.08
Thailand	1	0.06	0.08
Burma/Myanmar	1	0.06	0.08
Austria	1	0.06	0.08
Italy	1	0.06	0.08
Total	1,542	100.00	100.00

into the country.[11] This domination was reinforced by the lack of competition from other nations, and by the 1850s Britain was "the workshop of the world."[12] In the period before 1850, Australian maritime trade was plagued with problems arising through the inability of Australian exports to fill the ships arriving from Britain. Consequently, many ships sought freight elsewhere and in doing so established trade links with China and India.[13] After the 1850s, the Australian colonies experienced an increase in economic activity, particularly in the ports of the southeastern colonies, that sparked further development.[14]

Table 1 shows the distribution of the 1,542 vessels in the ANAVD by their nation of build. These watercraft predominantly belong to three categories: Australian built, British built, and unknown location of build (88.27 percent of ANAVD). If we exclude watercraft in the "unknown" category, we can see that vessels were predominantly Australian, British, and from the United

States and Canada (92.57 percent of vessels of known origin). Vessels built in other nations account for only about 7 percent of vessels of known origin, or approximately 6 percent of the entire database.

Figures 4 to 7 show the proportion of British-, Australian-, North American–(the United States and Canada combined), and "other"-built vessels (all other nations) in the abandoned watercraft record by year of build. These analyses tell us much about changing economic circumstances in Australia between the 1790s and the 1990s. In particular, the large percentage of British-built ships within the assemblage of Australian abandoned watercraft as seen in figure 4 illustrates that Australia was part of an economic maritime mercantile system that was subject to the economic hegemony of Britain.[15]

Over the period 1860 to 1914, British trade went through a period of growth, partially facilitated through the opening of the Suez Canal in 1869.[16] This was interspersed with two major boom periods: 1860 to 1873 (known as "the age of affluence") and 1898 to 1913 (with the period 1873 to 1898 being a period of stagnation and depression in some regions). The period between 1860 and 1914 is also important because of the dramatic increase in the British portion of world shipping from its major share of 26.3 percent in 1860 to 60.2 percent in 1890, and its decline to 41.1 percent in 1914.[17] These figures were also reflected in British shipbuilding, with Britain building and launching more than 50 percent of the world's oceangoing tonnage by 1851, an estimated 75 percent by 1880, on average 60 percent before World War I, 41 percent between the wars, one-third between 1935 and 1939, and 20 percent by 1958.[18] Although these values do not coincide exactly with the numbers depicted in figure 4, we nevertheless see a notable dependence on British ships throughout the period covered.

Figure 5 shows why these figures are not as high as those cited in trade values and shipbuilding trends. This depicts the percentage of Australian ships in the abandonment record and reflects the large role that the Australian shipbuilding industry had in national economic development, especially around the 1880s, when domestic shipbuilding was at its peak.[19] Also reflected is the effect of the development of naval construction during the two world wars, which stimulated the postconflict Australian shipbuilding industry.[20] The dip in Australian-built ships and increase in British- and American-made vessels around World War I is also probably a reflection of the purchasing trends of Prime Minister William Hughes's government for the Commonwealth Government Line of Steamers from 1916 due to an "an acute shortage of tonnage space and power."[21] The reinstitution of the bounty (government subsidy) system (after its introduction in 1940 and re-

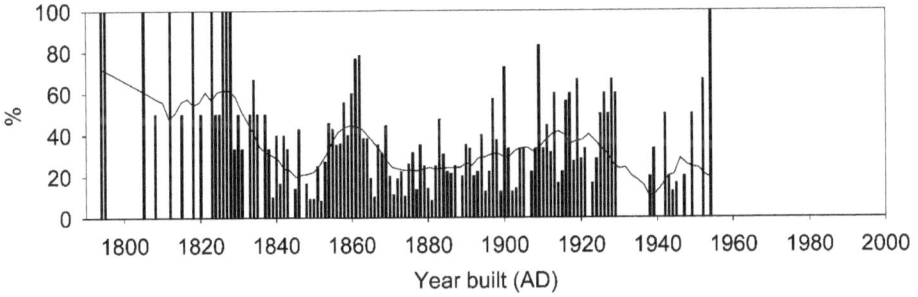

Figure 4. Percentage of British-built vessels by year of build (1790–1990) (n = 387 watercraft).

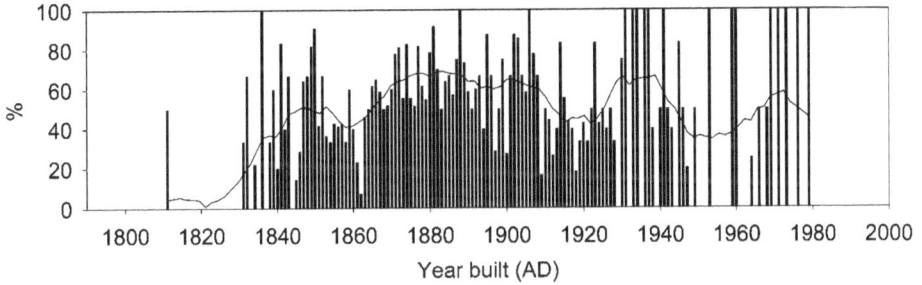

Figure 5. Percentage of Australian-built vessels by year of build (1790–1990) (n = 671 watercraft).

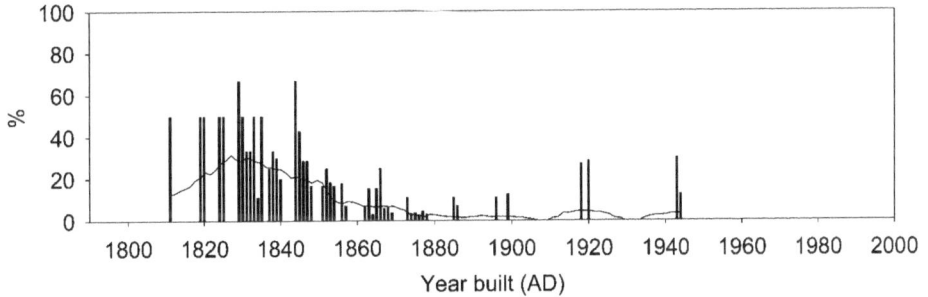

Figure 6. Percentage of North American–built vessels by year of build (1790–1990) (n = 83 watercraft).

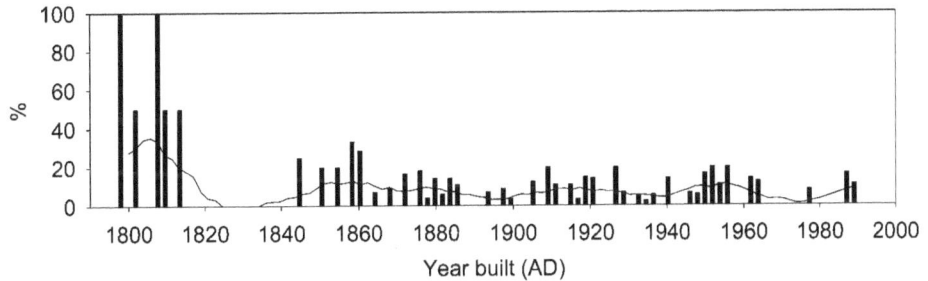

Figure 7. Percentage of non-Australian, British, or North American vessels by year of build (1790–1990) (n = 123 watercraft).

moval in 1943) may be one of the reasons for the abrupt end to the decline in Australian-built ships in the late 1940s.[22]

Figures 6 and 7 illustrate the relatively low representation of vessels built in all other nations. Figure 6 also clearly correlates historical literature concerning the challenge to British shipbuilding by the North American industry before the American Civil War (and its considerable decline thereafter), with two slight increases in the construction of North American ships around the time of World War I and World War II.[23] The historical record also supports this increase in North American ships around the wars. Indeed, James Culliton credits the American shipbuilding industry as at its highest capacity during times of war, citing World War I in particular as favorable to American owners.[24] During World War II, the American percentage of global shipping rose from 16 to 62 percent.[25] In light of this, it is surprising that we do not see an even larger percentage in the Australian abandonment record.

One consideration with the assessment of economic boom times is that they often coincide with the periods leading up to and following major wars. This is the story for much of the twentieth century. During World War II, trade operated at 75 percent of the level it had in 1939. By 1948, this level was at 94 percent of the prewar figure, in 1960 it was at 200 percent, and by 1973 it was at 250 percent (with a boom period between 1967 and 1970). A boom in 1951 and 1952 is also associated with the Korean War.[26]

The 1960s saw an agricultural boom, commencing in 1962, which ran into the next decade (and became a rural crisis in 1971).[27] The only military skirmishes of the 1980s and the 1990s, however, had either no impact or a positive effect, and different states of Australia went through boom periods. This was the case in most of Australia (but mainly Western Australia, Queensland, and the Northern Territory) in 1981–82 and 1991–92.[28] These booms occurred for a variety of reasons, according to international and local developments. Malcolm Tull, for instance, suggests that the economic growth in Western Australia during these periods was attributable to population increases and the expansion of agricultural and mining exports.[29]

Some regional economic booms, however, were actually detrimental to the shipping of the region in question, as well as to the shipping of other regions. The Victorian gold rushes of the 1850s, for instance, greatly influenced the economies of the Australian colonies. Although not the first discovery of gold, the finds in Bendigo and Ballarat in Victoria in 1851 were the first in Australia to develop into a "rush."[30] They were also the first historic events to have truly continent-wide economic ramifications. Indeed, its implications were so varied that it has been held responsible for many of the transitions in the Australian economy after 1850.[31]

The effects of rushes, however, are different for particular regions. Richard Cotter, for example, suggests that the effect of the Californian and Australian gold rushes were much wider than their respective regions, and despite vast geographical detachment they would impact the economies of Great Britain and Europe.[32] This was mainly due to the timing of the rushes during a period when there was a general world depression. In the context of the Victorian gold rush, the influence on Victoria itself was not surprisingly one of a major phase of development and the primary cause for the drastic expansion of trade.[33] As Manning Clark has stated, "Gold would attract so much of the commerce of the world to Australian shores, that the world would witness a change in the system of maritime commerce greater than that effected by the voyages of Columbus and Vasco da Gama."[34]

Indeed, Clark credits the rushes for establishing Victoria.[35] This economic boom, however, was not a catalyst of any drastic decrease in the deliberate abandonment of watercraft in Victoria. Surprisingly, quite the opposite occurred, with many more vessels destroyed under suspicious circumstances, as Jack Loney describes:

> The history of the Port of Melbourne contains many accounts of fires on ships. . . . Most of the early fires could have been started by seamen determined their ship would not set sail again and deprive them of an opportunity to join the thousands streaming to the Victorian goldfields.[36]

It appears that the early 1850s was a time of decreased or steady abandonment in all states of Australia, with the exception of Victoria. During this decade, records suggest that only six ships were discarded in total, two in 1853 and four in 1854. Indeed, 1854 saw the fourth highest peak in abandonment throughout Victorian history, and the vessels discarded from 1853 were the first abandoned watercraft in that state. Taking into consideration that acts of marine insurance fraud are very difficult to prove, it can be reasonably inferred that these are the minimum number of vessels abandoned or deliberately sunk during the rushes. The real numbers are likely considerably larger.

The negative affects of the drain in labor best describe the impact of these rushes on other colonies and on other industries in Victoria. This drain was similar to what occurred in 1848 because of the great California rush, which had already impacted the Australian economy.[37] Before 1851, the main basis of Australian wealth lay in the pastoral industry. Although the Victorian gold discoveries initially stimulated this industry, they eventually inflicted severe damage due to the migration of labor from this already understaffed sector.[38] Indeed, this migration was so great that New South Wales reportedly lost a quarter of its population, Tasmania a third, and South Australia lost up to one hundred workers a day.[39] We can learn many things from reading about the effects of the Victorian gold rush on the colony of South Australia. Whereas Castles and Harris, along with Clark, credit the rush with debilitating the colony, Stephen Roberts cites that for the farming industry, "the gold discoveries . . . caused a boom which lasted for eighteen years."[40] The effect on the South Australian maritime industry may not have been as pronounced as in the island of Tasmania, with the option for land transportation available to people wishing to make their way to the goldfields.

Indeed, the Victorian gold rush had as much of a negative effect on Tasmania as it did a positive effect on Victoria.[41] Broxam notes that in 1850 Van Diemen's Land was seemingly on the verge of "unprecedented prosperity" but was stopped by the commencement of gold fever on the Victorian gold fields in 1851.[42] This economic disruption not only sealed the colony's fate as an economic backwater for the ensuing decades but also was an event from which it is reputed to have never fully recovered. The gold rush would be further compounded by the cessation of the transportation of convicts to the island, an associated increase in labor costs, and increased migration to the mainland.

The analysis of national abandonment data shows that this example of a regional economic event is significantly different from the global ones discussed later. The rush in Victoria appears to have caused no increase whatsoever in ship abandonment in Tasmania, probably due to the movement of those ships to Victoria for the rushes. Indeed, the phenomenon of ship desertion appears to have only occurred in Victoria.[43] An analysis of vessel type and vessel ownership shows that many of the ships abandoned during the Victorian gold rush had once been operating in Tasmania. In this case, a regional economic boom not only created a migratory incentive and depleted the population of adjacent regions but also decreased the tendency to abandon ships by changing the dynamics of trade in the depleted colony. This trend is also married with an increase in the abandonment of vessels at the place of economic boom—apparently the only instance of such a reversal. Shipowners, having no crews due to desertion, were placed at great disadvantage.

Periods of General Economic Downturn

There have been many economic recessions and depressions throughout Australian history, and various factors such as wage issues and union strikes have marked affects on the profitability of shipping prosperity and the material wealth of the nation.[44] We can see many of these periods of economic decline reflected in the discard trend outlined in figures 2 and 3. A financial depression occurred in the four-year period between 1840 and 1844, causing the drastic decline of prices across the board and major increases in unemployment and destitution.[45] Indeed, historians have described 1841–46 as a time of "administrative and economic chaos."[46] The depression (which mainly was focused in commercial and agricultural sectors) was blamed on many things—the banking practices, the cessation of convict transportation, drought, land prices, and a decline in the demand for Australian wool by English manufacturers.[47] Although the period from the mid-1840s does coincide with an apparent increase in the regularity of abandonment events in Australia, the discard trends do not correlate well with the economic declines of this period of Australian history. This may be due to the economic immaturity of the relatively new colonies of South Australia, Victoria, and Western Australia. Hence, we may understand the early national trend better as a composite of trends in New South Wales and Tasmania.

The period after 1870 shows a more defined correlation. Bach has written that "between 1870 and 1914 the bad years are said to have outnumbered the good years two to one."[48] He further notes that an extremely low rate of expansion within Australia, Britain, and the world between 1873 and 1898 had a depressive effect on the economy. This is the period known generally as the "first great depression."[49] The 1890s were a watershed in Australian history, defined by debilitating economic depression, collapsing financial institutions, widespread labor strikes, increased unemployment, and amplified social tension and division throughout the colonies.[50] The depressions and strikes of the 1890s also impaired the low-profit Australian shipbuilding industry.[51] Historians trace this economic crisis to a financial crash in Argentina around August 1890, followed by the failure of Barings Bank in London. This depression was at its worst between 1890 and 1893 (1893 is known as the year of the Australian "Bank Smash") before the first signs of recovery around 1894.[52]

The British shipping industry, which was depressed in 1894, would improve, but it would not be a long-lived recovery.[53] Bach has noted that the "sufferings of the industry after 1900 seem to have been self-inflicted rather than as a result of depressed world trade; the great 45 percent increase in world tonnage between 1900 and 1910 was made more dangerous by the technological improvements that permitted greater carrying power for a given tonnage."[54] By 1902, 80 percent of British shipping is reputed to have been running at a loss, and by 1908, "shipping of every nationality was being laid up, there being nearly 2 million gross tons lying idle at the end of 1908, of which half was British."[55] The discard trend, with particular reference to the number of watercraft discarded between 1873 and 1908 (fig. 2), is in stark contrast with earlier periods. During this time, abandonment events became more common, with vessels discarded in substantially larger numbers than before.

Australian historians have written relatively little with regard to the interwar period, the Great Depression of the 1930s, and the decline in shipping. As Louis and Turner have noted, "Although the depression was—along with the crisis of the 1890s and the two world wars—one of the great traumatic experiences of Australian history, it has as yet attracted little attention from Australian historians."[56] Researchers have written even less on the effects of the Great Depression on maritime transport, even though writers such as Gazeley and Rice have commented that "shipbuilding epitomizes the chronically depressed industry of the 1930s."[57] Moreover, general accounts of this Great Depression from international and national perspectives neglect to mention its impact on maritime trades, despite the fact that overseas and interstate shipping was the dominant mode of transport and possibly even an important indicator of the true impact of the event.

The Great Depression of the 1930s was one of the pivotal turning points in the history of the twentieth century; its effects were many and varied. Between 1929 and 1933, world trade plummeted by 20 percent, freight prices dropped to prewar levels, one in five of the world's merchant fleet was laid up and out of use, and between 1929 and 1931 the volume of world exports fell by 30 percent.[58] In response to economic decline, most nations worsened conditions by instituting prohibitions and increasing tariffs on imports, thereby simultaneously inadvertently crippling export trades; this culminated in less need for the shipping of goods.[59] For global maritime trade, the Depression was particularly important because of the changes it brought about to the commercial conditions of the time, and it had particular ramifications for the position and power of the United Kingdom.

Britain is said to have been on shaky economic foundations before 1914 due to its industrial dominance and competitive advantages in a limited number of industries, such as coal, iron, and steel production and machinery, vehicle, ship, and textile manufacturing.[60] Likewise, the British shipping industry was in decline well before the crash of 1929, with some suggestions that there was a general depression in shipbuilding between 1922 and 1928.[61] To some degree, the economic problems of Britain were the same ones felt the world over in shipping in the 1930s, and they were as much about the aftermath of World War I, as they were about the Great Depression. The postwar boom went hand-in-hand with a reduction in the need for ships.[62] The artificially heightened demand for ships for service during the war was the cause of this. Another factor was an oversupply of tonnage. Often vessels were not needed or there was a preference for the larger, newer, and more-economical ones.[63] Dyos and Aldcroft, however, claim that after 1934 this overtonnage crisis stabilized, and by 1937 was in a balanced state.[64] The ships of this new era were, however, the harbingers of the new technological environment, being technically superior in efficiency (being mainly oil-fired or diesel propelled) and design. They were also larger and faster.[65]

Nations disposed of their obsolete watercraft in stages. First, shipowners put them on the market at high prices. Second, they sold them en masse and at cheap prices. Where merchants could not sell their ships, disuse and dereliction became their only other alternatives. The aftermath of the Great Depression stretched well beyond the early 1930s. For example, in the early 1940s, *Star 4* and *Star 5*, two whale chasers once operating out of Kaipipi, were demolished on the Bluff waterfront in New Zealand.[66] This same process occurred in Australia. In 1928, there was an initial decline in trade, by 1930, 58 percent of Australian merchant vessels were laid up, and some two years later, 40 percent of them were still out of service. The ships that emerged from the financial crisis were in most cases from the new generation of motor vessels; their economic advantages assumed them a place within a new technological status quo.[67]

For nations like the United Kingdom, these new vessels increasingly tended to be foreign built and owned, which exacerbated economic hardship and would eventually erode British prewar maritime and economic dominance. This new technological circumstance had come about partly because of the propensity for non-British (mainly northern European) nations to adopt the diesel engine, turbo-electric drive, and latest generation of geared steam turbine engine in their new vessels.[68] Additionally, by 1926, well before the onset of the Depression, German vessels were 28 percent cheaper than their British equivalent, and by 1938, Swedish vessels were 20–25 percent cheaper. Consequently, the British market share of shipbuilding fell from supplying 25–30 percent of this market before World War I to about 7.4 percent of the market by 1934. At the peak of the problem, between 1930 and 1935, 80 percent of the nation's shipbuilding berths lay idle, and a sterilization scheme was enacted that saw the destruction of 1.4 million tons of shipping capacity. Although this was partly due to the weakened demand for naval construction, it was also due to the weakening demand from all prospective ship buyers the world over (including the British) for British-built ships.[69]

All of these factors, coupled with Britain's dependence on, and over-achievement in, various export industries culminated in the decrease in the use of British vessels to the tune of 25 percent between 1913 and 1937. Subsequently, Britain lost major portions of its total market share.[70] Through such economic devastation, Britain would never again regain its dominant position in global trade.

From the viewpoint of the effect of the Depression of the 1930s on Australia, all of these factors are important. At this time, Australia was reliant on the economic fortunes of the United Kingdom. In particular, Australian reliance on Great Britain to supply ships ensured trade dependency.

As has already been shown, the Great Depression of the 1930s was not the first economic depression that Australia had known, yet it was undeniably the worst in its history. Additionally, it would become an important turning point in the nation's economic and technological evolution. During this period, a range of factors were to cause major economic disruption and social hardship. The Depression hit every sector of the Australian economy, causing a rise in unemployment to unsurpassed levels, stunting development, and ceasing a decline in the prices of staple goods such as wool and wheat. Increased foreign competition and an almost overnight decline in primary industry were to have dramatic effects.[71] Ships ordered before the Depression hit soon found that they had insufficient freight once built.[72]

The Australian heavy industrial sector, however, fared differently. For example, although steel production was one of the first, and hardest hit, industries on a global scale, Daniel Horne claims that "from the beginning of the First World War to the Depression manufacturing production went up by 70 per cent; and in the Thirties, despite the Depression, it more than doubled."[73] Historians also note that Australia suffered earlier and more severely than many other nations due to its dependence on exporting primary produce and the falling price of these commodities from the mid-1920s.[74]

The Great Depression of the 1930s was similarly the single most important event in the history of vessel abandonment in Australia. The experience of each Australian state was different to some degree. The analysis of abandoned-vessel data may indeed allow for the redefinition of this event from an Australian perspective, one that clearly shows that Australia was already in a significant economic depression before 29 October 1929.[75] Indeed, much of the problem with Australian perspectives on the Great Depression is the tendency to analyze the event from the date of the New York Stock Market crash. The inclination of many works on the Great Depression of the 1930s (even in Australia) is to consider 1929 as the year the Depression commenced and 1932 its nadir.[76] As one commentator has asserted, "The 1930s take much of their character from the great depression. Unlike a war, a depression is a catastrophe of which beginning and end can never be pinpointed to the day nor, perhaps, even the year."[77]

Some researchers have sought to better define the Great Depression of the 1930s.[78] In an Australian context, major downturns in trade not dictated by the stock market crash of 1929 preceded the Great Depression of the 1930s. Richard Morris's economic data from the pre-Depression era shows that by the mid-1920s wool was in decline, dropping 11 percent from 1925 to 1926, tonnage levels coming into Australian ports were in serious decline, and, by 1928, some notable Australian shipping companies were showing substantial losses.[79] An examination of the discard trend (as seen in figures 2 and 3) may even suggest that the depression in Australian maritime trades may have started to emerge as early as 1923 and continued until around 1939.

Leonie Foster, in the case of the number of shipwrecks in Port Phillip, states, "Gradually the numbers dropped until the period 1921–1940, when six of the nine vessels wrecked during the period were deliberately beached, sunk or dismantled."[80] Although it is not clear whether Foster refers to "deliberately beached" as "deliberately abandoned," or, rather, abandonment arising through crisis, this potentially supports national data showing that deliberate abandonment increases dramatically in the 1920s.

Over the period of the economic depression, many economic factors came into play that not only affected the economic health of the nation but also redefined the nature of trade and the technologies used to engage in commerce. Garry Kerr, for instance, has commented that the Great Depression was the single most important factor contributing to the cessation of the building and use of sail vessels engaged in various carting trades (especially the "barge trade").[81] Indeed, the building and abandonment of sailing vessels may be a good litmus test for the economic health of regions across time.

In many cases, the Great Depression simply brought on a period when shipowners could not meet any of the expenses needed to carry out trade. One such example was the four-masted, steel-hulled barque *Hougomont* (2,378 gross tons) built by the Scott Shipbuilding and Engineering Company of Greenock in 1897. In April 1932, the vessel was 530 miles west-southwest of Kangaroo Island bound to Port Lincoln from London when a gale took most of its masts and rigging. After reaching Port Adelaide, the owners decided that they could not afford twenty-five hundred pounds to fix a vessel valued at only one thousand pounds, and they opted to dispose of the barque. Authorities stripped the vessel of its fittings and took it to Stenhouse Bay, South Australia. On 8 January 1933, they positioned it southwest of the jetty and sank it with explosives to provide a breakwater for vessels loading gypsum.[82]

As for other detrimental economic events in the later twentieth century, the Middle East oil crisis of 1974 and the stock market crash of 1987 coincide with increases in ship abandonment in the mid-1970s and late 1980s.

Another reason for the overall increase in ship abandonment around this time can be attributed to the dramatic rise in refugee vessels and illegal fishing boats entering the Northern Territory, as well as the steady rise in the formation of artificial reefs.[83]

The Effect of War

Conflict is a special economic case study when referring to trends in the discard of watercraft. This is because war often has economic origins, and to a large degree the causes of war lie in economic conditions borne in times of peace or economic damage inflicted during previous wars.[84] To define these periods as mutually exclusive events denies their true cause.

The nation of Australia, along with the individual colonies before federation, were involved in many conflicts.[85] Historians have noted that wars before Australian federation, such as the Crimean War, had a substantial economic influence on the colonies because of their effect on world trade. Despite Clark's assertion that "the war in the Crimea threatened to upset those conditions of peace deemed essential for world commerce,"[86] the war is said to have had "an immediate effect" on the world's shipbuilding. In particular, the war increased the demand for ships. British shipping grew 70 percent between 1850 and 1860, and great profits were reaped.[87] Under these circumstances, we should note no increase in the abandonment of watercraft, and indeed, the abandonment trend (figs. 2 and 3) shows that there was no appreciable increase. However, we must remember two things. First, Australia as a nation was not actively engaged in this conflict, and second, the economic effects of many of these other conflicts in which Australians were active combatants (the Sudan War, Boer War, and Boxer Rebellion) have not been well documented. The years of these events (1885,

1899–1902, and 1901, respectively) do not, however, seem to coincide with any marked increase or decrease in ship abandonment. The first conflict to have had an effect on the Australian economy and subsequent reflections in abandonment trends was World War I. Yet World War I does not appear to have had as drastic and effect as later wars.

Nevertheless, historians credit the war for speeding up the economic development of many Western nations, such as the United States and Australia, and for being the catalyst for the production of many new industries.[88] World War II, however, was a time of massive upheavals in the maritime world. In the north of Australia, for example, the duration of the war saw the forced seizure and destruction of an unknown number of vessels to avoid their potential capture by Japanese invaders.[89]

Tull cites that the conditions during both great wars were significantly different.[90] He declares that the Australian economy stagnated during the first war, but in the second war expanded and experienced an accelerated growth of the industrial sector.[91] He also points out that although there was a national boom, it was concentrated in the eastern states, and other states, such as Western Australia, underwent the same economic stagnation of previous conflicts. We may also see this in a marked drop in exports from Fremantle. The economic boom created in the aftermath of World War II lasted to the 1970s.

The effects of subsequent conflicts, such as the Malayan Emergency (1950–60), Indonesian Confrontation (1964–66), and the Vietnam War (1962–72), are less certain. The Korean War (1950–53) differs from any other conflict discussed here because it caused an economic boom brought about by an increased demand for Australian primary produce.[92]

Target Ships

The use of target ships also relates to warfare. At least twenty-nine vessels (about 2 percent of the ANAVD) are listed as having been used in military-related maneuvers that saw them scuttled via military ordnance between 1887 and 1994 (see fig. 8). Of these, the military sank twenty-five vessels in strafing exercises and four during bombing practice. To this number we can add the destruction of the HMAS *Torrens* (1965–2001) off the coast of Western Australia.

There are other variations. Sources suggest that the steel steamer *Psyche* (1900–1940s), sunk in Salamander Bay, Port Stephens (New South Wales) sometime during World War II was both bombed and strafed during the scuttling process. Additionally, the military was involved in the deliberate

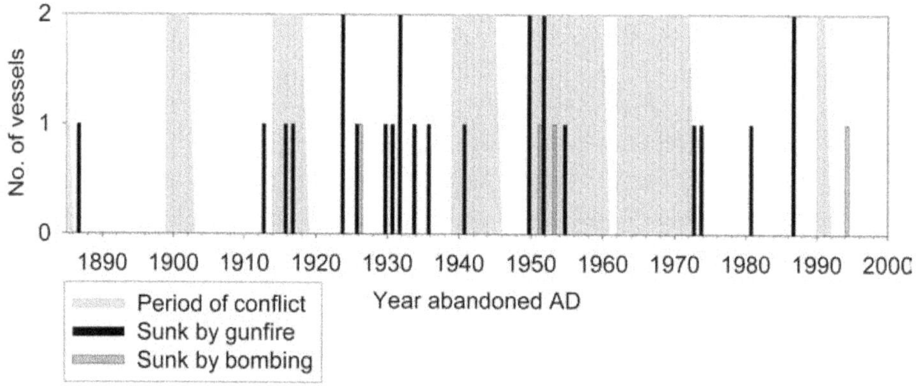

Figure 8. Watercraft abandoned or sunk in military maneuvers in Australia, 1885–2000 (n = 28 events).

sinking of the vessel HMAS *Adroit* (1967–94) in an unspecified naval exercise in 1994. In some cases, such as in the case of the *Moltke* (1870–1913), the armed forces also used vessels for target practice at a time substantially after its initial scuttling. This is well-established behavior, as there are many examples of the Royal Australian Air Force strafing wrecks in the state of Victoria. Examples of this are the wrecks of the *Riverina* (1887–90) and *Orungal* (1923–40).

This activity has occurred in all of the states and territories of Australia except Tasmania (table 2). The vast majority of this activity, however, occurred in the Sydney Heads ship-disposal area, a designated deepwater graveyard (also known as Commonwealth Area 1) eighteen miles off the coast of New South Wales. Also, surprisingly, only two-thirds of the vessels had at some stage been owned by an Australian defense agency (in most cases the Royal Australian Navy or the Royal Australian Air Force, but in one case the Victorian Colonial Navy). The remaining third were ships seized by the armed forces as opportunities to carry out military maneuvers and could reflect some degree of urgency to test new weaponry.

What is interesting about the times of the destruction of these target vessels is that only nine out of the twenty-four vessels (33 percent) listed as sunk by gunfire and two out of the four vessels (50 percent) listed as sunk in bombing practice were sunk during actual periods of conflict (approximately 36 percent overall). Although no complete list of discarded military watercraft exists, initial data suggest that the military only used vessels as target ships during the middle of World War I, the beginning of World War II, and during the Korean War and the Malayan Emergency.

Table 2. Vessels Scuttled as Target Ships in Australian Waters (by State)

Name	Built	Scuttled	State
George R. Crowe	1885	1887	QLD
Moltke	1870	1913	QLD
J.L. Hall	1859	1916	WA
Lalla	1874	1917	WA
Barcoo	1885	1924	NSW
HMAS *Australia*	1913	1924	NSW
Loch Ness	1869	1926	WA
J5 submarine	1916	1926	VIC
Torrens	1916	1930	NSW
Huon	1915	1931	NSW
HMAS *Encounter*	1905	1932	NSW
Hankow	1869	1932	NT
Pam	1864	1934	SA
HMAS *Anzac*	1917	1936	NSW
Psyche	1900	1940	NSW
HMAS *Success*	1918	1941	NSW
Bankfields	1876	1950	WA
Quorna	1912	1950	SA
Kyogle	1901	1951	QLD
Marjorie	1898	1952	NSW
Colonna	1878	1952	WA
HMAS *Kuramia*	1914	1953	NSW
Governor	1898	1955	WA
Kara Kara	1926	1973	NSW
Karoola	1947	1974	NSW
Trinity Bay	1912	1981	QLD
Colac	1941	1987	NSW
1208 oil fuel lighter	1945	1987	NSW
HMAS *Adroit*	1968	1994	WA

The remaining vessels either directly follow or immediately precede conflicts (this is especially true for the period between the two world wars). This may indicate two behaviors, the testing of weaponry as a show of power in the prelude or aftermath of war or the testing of weaponry in preparation for war. It is highly likely that both behaviors coexist. In some cases, target ships may not relate to actual conflicts. For instance, the commencement of target-ship testing in 1887 is more likely an indication of the "Russian scares" around the middle of the 1880s than the consequences of the aftermath of the Sudan War, which was not a major Australian conflict and never involved naval forces. Foster mentions proposals during the Russian scares of 1885 to scuttle hulks in the West Channel of Port Phillip, Victoria, to prevent its use by enemy vessels. The government eventually stopped the plan because of publicity concerning the prices paid for the unwanted ships.[93]

The practice of using target ships exists in three separate clusters of submerged vessels. It is noticeable in ten craft sunk as target vessels in the lead up to World War II and in the period after the Vietnam War (five sunk). Of more interest is the 1950s. If we take into account the positive economic effects of the Korean War, and the negligible economic impact of the Malayan Emergency, it could be that target-ship sinking activities in the 1950s were for the purposes of preemptive weapons testing in anticipation of future conflicts in Southeast Asia (such as in Vietnam).

The Aftermath of War

The aftermath of war, with the resulting transition into peacetime economy, is often associated with a brief depression. An example of this is the aftermath of the Crimean War, where freight rates reflected "the state of the depression that began after the war."[94] Likewise, changes in freight rates associated with a number of other conflicts, such as the Korean War (1950), Suez Crisis (1956), and Six-Day War (1967),[95] probably had substantial ramifications for Australian economic health by influencing the profitability of shipping, in turn influencing discard behavior. More often, the aftermath of war coexists with an "overtonnaging crisis" due to increased shipbuilding during wartime and a reduced demand after the conflict.[96] Davies notes that "wars created shipping shortages and conversely a glut when the wars ended,"[97] and James Culliton has mentioned that nations could build ships faster than they could sink them by World War II.[98] As Culliton also explains, the products of shipyards tend to accumulate in times of war. They also tend to be mass produced and lacking in the custom-built features that prospective shipowners desire. This is especially true in relation to combination cargo and passenger vessels.[99]

Furthermore, ships after the war were exceptionally cheap, and their purchase eventually led to the discard of older vessels:

> Although soon made obsolete by technical development, the war built ship could still earn money if purchased at the right price. The vessels were accordingly sold slowly by government at prices which started at $200 per deadweight ton, but rapidly declined to near scrap value in the early thirties.[100]

Crisis-level surplus tonnage does not always coincide with postwar situations and may simply be a product of uncontrolled shipbuilding. Nevertheless, it nearly always coincides with depressions in the shipping industry.[101] Overtonnaging crises are, however, made worse by the economic depressions following protracted conflicts and appear to be one of the major catalysts for increasing ship abandonment. Another contributing factor are the costs of laying up unused vessels for prolonged periods of time.[102]

It was the *aftermath* rather than the conflict of World War I that tended to predispose a shipowner to abandon a ship. This was partly due to the passenger-trade depression of the 1920s, but it was more attributable to the surplus of shipping on the commencement of peace and the fall in freight rates accompanying it.[103] Eventually, a large portion of the world's mercantile fleet could not obtain business and their owners had to either dismantle or discard them. This surplus was due to what Bach calls "the legacy of emergency wartime building,"[104] exacerbated by continued shipbuilding after the war, which was "in excess of the requirements of trade."[105] Consequently 2.5 to 3 million tons of shipping was laid up in British ports, and 20 percent (10 million tons) of the world's merchant ships were idle by 1922.[106] This is in direct contrast to behaviors in ship owning during the war. Vessels such as the American barque *St. James*, for instance, which was converted into a barge in 1909, underwent subsequent refitting as a barquentine due to the shortage of available tonnage emerging with the conflict.[107]

However, the aftermath of World War I also coincided with technological changes that would have dramatic consequences on a range of maritime industries. In particular, historians acknowledge this as the period after which the development of road infrastructure grew. Although this did not affect international vessels, it had a drastic negative effect on coastal watercraft.[108]

The innovation and increased use of the motor engine following the war had other results. Although the war had little effect on the fleet of small coastal trading craft in South Australia during its duration, the accelerated acceptance of the auxiliary engine and the increased competition following this had major repercussions for the future of coastal trade.[109] The increased conversion of vessels to engine assisted types reflects this trend.

The aftermath of World War II also had many effects on maritime trade. The peace that ensued was for most of Australia a time of marked general economic boom influencing both prewar trades and industries created out of wartime necessity. This was the case with many areas at the center of this research, such as at Strahan, Tasmania.[110] For many nations, but particularly for Australian coastal trades, the first postwar decade was one of steady decline. This was due to the cessation of certain trades, industrial unrest, and changes in cargo handling methods, a fall in the demand for passenger services, increased competition from land transport, and the astronomical costs associated with building new vessels.[111] The aftermath of World War II also saw a dramatic shift in the emphasis of vessel design. Shipbuilders in Tasmania, for instance, began building fishing and recreational vessels exclusively.[112] The changes in the design of vessels were a response to new technological and economic environments. Gustav Milne has cited a similar situation in a case study from the United Kingdom describing the conversion or motorization of war barges for other purposes.[113]

The aftermath of World War II is a major feature in the history of abandonment due to the scrapping of wartime merchant vessels en masse. Researchers have noted this in both American and Australian contexts.[114] As F. G. Fassett has stated,

> The mass production of ships of all types during World War II has resulted in a large surplus tonnage for peacetime commerce. The reduction in the number of shipyards today under way to contract operations to a peacetime basis is one of the most drastic industrial shrinkages and one of the gravest economic problems to be met in passing from war to peace.[115]

The effect of the aftermath of war on watercraft abandonment can be summed up in three areas: surplus tonnage, short-term postwar depression, and what Bach terms the "rude challenge" of technological innovation in relation to ship design, technology, and shipping techniques (such as cargo handling and berth design).[116]

Conclusion

The distinct economic processes of boom, depression, conflict and the repercussions of war are important factors behind the abandonment of watercraft in Australia. These processes provide important historical contexts against which we can assess watercraft discard trends, but the number, type, and configuration of the vessels discarded are also tools for the assessment of these events on maritime trades and general economic health.

It is no surprise that the tools of economic development (watercraft) are also the most sensitive to changes in the economic environment. The abandoned watercraft record illustrates these processes because the vessels that were engaged in trade did so until they were no longer required. Where catastrophic loss does not artificially shortens lifespans, vessel use-life becomes a representation of the life, success, and health of the trade and economy within which a ship operated.

There is a correlation between well-documented economic trends of national importance and trends in the discard of watercraft in Australia. These discard behaviors exist because of drawn-out decision-making processes that emerge throughout the life of a vessel but are redefined by the consequences of economic change. Moreover, we see this change in the analysis of the number of vessels abandoned throughout Australian history. This analysis shows that the discard of watercraft is an economic indicator and can be used in the assessment of the social consequences of economic events caused by cycles of boom and bust and interrupted by conflict.

5

Watercraft Abandonment in Australia

Environmental and Regional Perspectives

And in any port that had a 'rotten row' where vessels were laid up—
either temporarily or out of commission for good—they swarmed aboard
the steamers and barges. Each lad who could grab a wheel would stand
at it, pretending to steer, imagining himself already a skipper.

—Ian Mudie, *Riverboats*

The distribution of abandonment areas and the environmental, economic, and historical events that have contributed to the formation of vessel-discard sites in particular regions are also subjects ripe for investigation. On a regional level, some major historical events are the direct cause of changes in discard trends, whereas other historical processes amplify the tendency to discard ships. Discard trends on national and statewide levels are substantially different but nonetheless still relate to the fluctuating economic and technological conditions in nations and regions.

The Landscape of Abandonment

As Sarah Kenderdine notes, understanding landscape is pivotal in understanding discard behavior:

> Landscapes symbolically express the actions of groups and individuals conditioned by particular cultural values over a period of time. The landscape is a code that when deciphered reveals the meaning of the cultural and social significance of common but diagnostic features. . . . The natural landscape underwrites the subsequent interactions of humans and the environment, it precludes and dictates the activities that can be sustained within (and across) geographic regions.[1]

The abandonment of watercraft revolves around a singular and fundamentally important point: An abandoned vessel should never be a navigation hazard. The discard of watercraft in a location that will cause harm to other watercraft is usually unacceptable, except during war. When humans wreck ships in navigable sections of water, they usually attempt to destroy or substantially dismantle them.[2] To a large extent, ship-dumping areas form because of a socially organized use of space that is comparable to many other archaeological studies.[3] Findings in maritime archaeological research also support this premise of discard psychology. During an unsuccessful search for the abandoned ship *Ellen* (1857–90), for example, the Underwater Explorers Club of Western Australia discovered the shipwreck of the *James Matthews* (n.d.–1841). Although the *James Matthews* was not an abandoned ship, its discovery provides some insight into the rationale for the abandonment of unwanted watercraft in certain locations. As noted by Michael McCarthy, there are underlying human decision making processes relating to the risk of creating wrecks that guide the process of deciding the appropriate location for abandonment:

> It is thought unlikely . . . that the Harbor master would have allowed a vessel [*Ellen*] to be deliberately scuttled on the northern shore of Woodman Point as she would be a danger to vessels blown ashore from the Owen Anchorage area immediately to the north. . . . The wreck, therefore, is presumed to lie to the south of Woodman Point, in Jervoise Bay.[4]

Ships' graveyards are located where there is a concentration of commercial activities and a high volume of trade and traffic. In inner harbor environs, ships' graveyards generally occur in disused or "abandoned" stretches of waterway. In Tasmania, for instance, there is a correlation between areas used as gunpowder hulk–mooring areas (where a vessel is used for gunpowder storage) and eventual abandonment regions.[5] This may be due to the perception that such places are unimportant and underused. A place fit to moor a dangerous object, such as a gunpowder hulk, which may catastrophically detonate, is obviously a fitting resting place for marine detritus. When such places are in use, and humans target them for other functions, sites like ships' graveyards come under increased pressure, usually in the form of heightened salvage activities. This also supports an assertion that concentrations of refuse tend to occur where there have been previous discard activities.

Australian Abandonment: Site Location Factors

On the broadest level, the location of abandonment sites is associated with the establishment of the Australian states and the location of capital cities

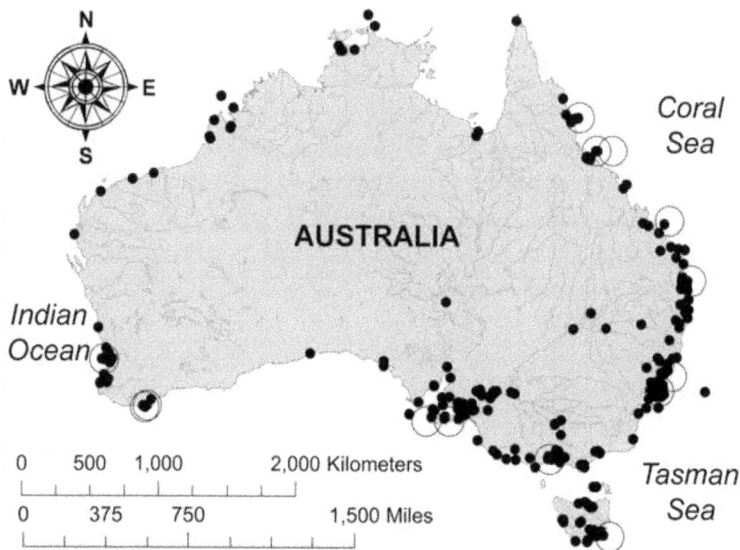

Figure 9. Map of Australia showing the distribution of abandoned watercraft and the location of designated Commonwealth dumping areas.

and port areas. The distribution of abandoned watercraft sites can be seen in figure 9. This does not simply illustrate the dispersal of these vessels; it also enables us to understand some of the site location factors that are evident when investigating the spatial aspects of ship-abandonment areas. Overwhelmingly, the distributions of abandoned vessels correspond with Australia's ports, and almost every major port has at least one watercraft disposal region. Further, the locations of major watercraft discard and demolition areas tend to be adjacent to the main ports of each state. These areas are usually in close proximity to ports because of the concentration of shipbuilding, repair, and salvage activities that take place there.

In 1969, the Australian Bureau of Statistics noted that Australia had sixty-one principal ports, twenty-five to thirty of which were of "statistical significance" due to their volume of trade. Of these, researchers only considered six as major ports.[6] It is within these premier ports that the vast majority of watercraft abandonment in Australia has occurred. Their location tells us much about the reasons for the placement of major, centralized ship-abandonment areas in close proximity to areas of port activity. Australian ports, due to their distance from each other, do not compete to the same degree as European ports, and therefore the most significant aspect of Australian port activity concerns the proximity to and size of their hinterland.[7] For this reason, the distribution of major watercraft discard areas tends to be equally far apart.

We also see this in the tendency of major ports to be close to, or have within them, at least one ships' graveyard, and for secondary ports to have isolated abandonment sites close by. Furthermore, it seems that where secondary ports undergo major development and become major centers of maritime activity, ships' graveyards of some type eventually follow.

Trade, Technology, and Distance

As Malcolm Tull has stated, "The basic function of a port is to provide a link between land and sea transport and to furnish means by which transfers of freight and passengers between the two systems can be made efficiently."[8] Ports in many respects, are microcosms of trade. Although they do not represent the journey of a vessel, they represent the causes, commencement, and conclusion of mercantile behavior. They are the locations of the successes and the failures of technology and economic enterprise. For this reason, it is not surprising that watercraft abandonment sites occur close to ports. These ports tend to be where trades evolve; people introduce, try, and test technologies; and unwanted, unused, or unsuitable vessels are laid up. Why they are laid up at these locations rather than other places is due to the concentration of obtainable trade at major ports and the fact such major ports are often more likely to have remnant trade opportunities in times of economic depression or recession.

In large ports, however, the location of abandonment takes on a level of technological dependence. Without a powered vessel to tow an unwanted ship to a deep-water scuttling location, it would have to travel under its own power. This is rarely practical due to adverse logistical circumstances such as ensuring crew safety. Additionally, if someone were to take the vessel out under its own power, he or she would have to scuttle it with many of its propulsion related components (masts, sails, rigging, and engines) unsalvaged, something not practicable at sea. Sailing ships likely could not tow unwanted vessels because of problems with maneuverability. In the age of steam, technology remedied many of these issues, but there were high costs associated with the use of steam tugs for moving vessels out to sea for scuttling. Moreover, the inefficient engines of early steam vessels made them slow and unreliable, limiting the distance they could travel.[9] Thus we can see that the dangers and costs associated with the abandonment of a vessel at sea increased with distance. Combined, these factors tell us how the locations of abandonment areas adjacent to major ports are technologically derived and due to perceptions of cost.

Inner Harbors and Abandonment

Abandonment areas correspond with certain inner harbor functions. Examples in Australian historical literature indicate that links between areas of ship breaking and shipbuilding exist. In most areas of Australia, shipbuilding places were initially determined due to their close proximity to suitable resources of shipbuilding timber, and in the early days of settlement, shipbuilding occurred all along the coastline. As the reserves for timber dried up, "batten built" vessels, ships with steam-bent knees, were increasingly built.[10] By this time, shipbuilding and the location of shipyards ceased to depend on close proximity to their own timber reserves, and carts, horses, or punts were able to supply a steady stream of timber. As a consequence, there was an increasing tendency toward the centralization of shipbuilding activities at ports, where shipbuilders could easily purchase materials.

The procurement of timber played a pivotal part in shipbuilding businesses located within inner harbor areas. Consequently, the salvage of timber from old, outmoded, or worn vessels was a major way of providing raw materials for new construction. Indeed, there seems to be a strong correlation between the intertidal ships' graveyards in many inner harbor locations and ship-breaking industries.

Another indication of the relationship between shipbuilding, abandonment, and salvage activities is that many shipbuilding places were also places where people carried out watercraft modification, conversion, and repair. In northern Tasmania, for example, some shipbuilding yards undertook repair and lengthening work on watercraft.[11] When ship repairers placed vessels undergoing repair, conversion, or modification back into the water and found new floatation problems, the shipyard soon became a demolition yard. Subsequently, it was often necessary to designate a place close by as a suitable ships' graveyard. Research has noted this in southern Tasmania, where many major shipbuilding locations along the Derwent River were also in close proximity to major ship-dumping areas.[12]

Australian Abandonment: Site Types

The Australian abandonment landscape has many layers. As noted elsewhere, abandoned vessels exist in Australia as isolated (solitary) sites or within large accumulations known as ships' graveyards. Forty-two known ships' graveyard sites contain at least 507 out of 1,542 vessels (approximately 33 percent) nationally. In addition, there may be another thirty-seven unconfirmed ships' graveyards constituting a further 154 vessels (10 percent), taking the accumulated 661 vessels to about 43 percent of the total.

The location of abandoned watercraft peripheral to shipping routes is indicative of strategies intended to avoid commerce-impeding navigation hazards. The graveyard sites comprise two main environment types: deep-sea scuttling areas and intertidal ships' graveyards found in inner harbor contexts. These sites are also peripheral to commercial activities, but in slightly different ways. Deep-sea scuttling areas tend to be substantial distances from major mercantile centers and trade routes. Ships' graveyards in harbor contexts are isolated from trade routes and channels, as well as areas of commercial activity, although their locations, being within a harbor, are still accessible. These two types of site also correspond with legal definitions and political jurisdiction. Ships' graveyards in Australia are either designated/official or nondesignated/unofficial. Designated graveyards are often enshrined within legislation and bureaucratic procedures. Nondesignated graveyards often predate the designated type or eventually become designated dumping areas. In Australia, deep-sea scuttling areas tend to be "Commonwealth designated areas" defined under the Beaches, Fishing and Sea Routes Protection Act of 1932.[13] Ships' graveyards within harbors are located inside state waters or state controlled areas, normally controlled by state harbors legislation and regulation.

Commonwealth Designated Areas

The regulations dictated by the Beaches, Fishing and Sea Routes Protection Act are also relevant to the landscape of abandonment because the accompanying Statutory Rules for Commonwealth Acts include maps of the areas where vessels can be dumped.[14] There are fourteen areas outlined in this legislation that correspond with certain Australian ships' graveyards. Their definitions include a number of details, among them, description of location, depth of water at disposal area, bearings to prominent shore based features, and distances from port.

Twelve of the areas are circular regions between three miles(in the case of Area 3—Melbourne and Geelong) and seven miles in diameter (in the case of Area 7—Fremantle), with the two designated areas off Albany being adjacent to land. The depths vary from twenty-five fathoms in the case of Area 3 to one hundred fathoms in the cases of Areas 1, 2, 4, 10, 11, and 14 (Sydney, Newcastle, Hobart, Brisbane, Rockhampton, and Cairns). The depth of Area 7 in undefined.

These areas, indicators of the concentration of trade in certain locations, correspond with the location of Australia's premier ports. These designated areas also show where there is major competition between ports. For instance, historical documentation contends that Fremantle had to compete for trade with other ports on the Western Australian coast (such as Albany).[15] Consequently, there is a small distance between Commonwealth Designated Area 7 in Fremantle and Areas 8 and 9 in Albany—a direct consequence of a period of major trade competition between them. Another spatial correlation exists between major ports, designated areas, and the length of the coastline of certain states. For instance, Queensland more than any other state has the largest number of separate abandonment locations as well as the most Commonwealth designated areas. This is due to an exceptionally long coastline, numerous profitable and concurrently working ports and settlements, and a dispersed population.

These locations give us some indication of the lengths to which regulatory bodies went to control watercraft abandonment. The analysis of the ANAVD, however, suggests that these designated areas were not a complete success—only about 15 percent of all recorded ships are located within these areas. Only five noted watercraft accumulations, or ships' graveyards, correspond with these areas. The Sydney Heads Graveyard (Area 1), Newcastle disposal area (Area 2) Barwon Heads Graveyard (Area 3), Rottnest Island Graveyard (Area 7), Albany Graveyards (Areas 8 and 9), and accumulations off Townsville and Cairns (Areas 13 and 14) correspond well with designated areas. Other areas, such as those designated for Adelaide and Gulf Ports and Brisbane (Areas 5 and 10, respectively) do not contain enough vessels to be considered major accumulations. Areas 4, 11, and 12 (Hobart, Rockhampton, and Bowen), it seems, were never used. In particular, there is a well-documented relationship between Area 4 (Hobart) and a site known as the Little Betsy Ships' Graveyard, which ship abandoners used instead of the designated site. The statutes make a special note for Tasmania: "The sinking area within the Hobart port limits is on the edge of the reef at the south end of Betsy Island situated to the eastward of the entrance to the Derwent River."[16]

In part, the lack of use of these designated areas relates to previously stated assumptions on the links between watercraft abandonment and distances from port. As Frank Broeze noted:

Distance, it should always be remembered, can be measured and perceived in many different ways: in length, time or cost, and according
to class, occupation or ideology. What is far to some can be close to
others.[17]

Although the distances of these Commonwealth areas from port are not
large by normal mercantile standards, they are exceedingly large when the
journey is to discard a ship, certain to cost much and have no financial reward. The expense of traversing large distances to faraway designated areas
to dump vessels would be a major disincentive. For this reason, one may also
speculate that some of the vessels intended to end up in these remote, deep-
water designated ships' graveyards did not end up in these areas; rather,
their owners secretly dumped them between the port of departure and the
designated area. This also explains why vessel owners used ships' graveyards
like the Little Betsy Island Ships' Graveyard (located about twenty-seven
kilometers by sea from Hobart) instead of the Commonwealth designated
area (located more than one hundred kilometers by sea from Hobart).

This is the case with other, underused Commonwealth designated areas.
Areas 5 and 6 for Adelaide are respectively located more than 160 and 250
kilometers from Port Adelaide, whereas the most densely packed discard
areas in Port Adelaide are between 100 meters and 6 kilometers from major commercial areas. It is also the case in Brisbane, where the major ships'
graveyard (Bishop Island) is in the mouth of the Brisbane River as opposed
to the designated area, some eighty kilometers away. Contrasting this are
the approximate distances of the successful (that is, used) designated areas
from major commercial areas:

Area 1	36 kms from Sydney
Area 2	64 kms from Newcastle
Area 3	77 kms from Melbourne; 75 kms from Geelong
Area 7	37 kms from Fremantle
Areas 8 and 9	22 and 27 kms from Albany (respectively)

The majority of these areas are closer to ports than the unsuccessful (unused) designated areas. Clearly, distance was a major part of the success of
Commonwealth areas, and the shorter distances represented by the existence of non-Commonwealth graveyards (some illegal) or under the jurisdiction of State regulatory bodies were a major attraction for those wishing
to dump unwanted vessels.

State Jurisdiction

In Australia, ships' graveyards within state jurisdiction tend to consist of beached (shallow or intertidal) rather than scuttled (deep-water) watercraft. This is due to Commonwealth jurisdiction over most Australian waters and state jurisdiction over inland waterways. Additionally, each state (and sometimes each port) may have a number of separate abandonment areas. If the Commonwealth areas are indications of the concentration of trade nationally, the predominance of abandoned watercraft adjacent to Australia's capital city ports represent the veritable monopoly on trade that each port has within particular states.[18]

Port Adelaide in South Australia, for instance, has a range of vessel abandonment areas (official and otherwise) scattered about the inner and outer harbor. Movement of the location of preferred vessel disposal areas appears to have occurred due to the changing use of the port and the changing nature of salvage throughout the nineteenth and twentieth centuries.

Ships' graveyards within state areas are of two types: those representing ship-discard activities and those representing ship-breaking activities. In relation to site formation theory, we can see ship-discard sites as *secondary refuse sites*, because some degree of salvage has already occurred at a ship-breaking yard located elsewhere. Where the breakers yard also culminates in the dumping of vessels on site, the term *primary refuse site* applies. Primary refuse sites are predominantly ship-breaking areas, where modern redevelopment or salvage activities have completely dismantled and recycled watercraft, cleaning up the area and filtering most archaeological material out of the record. Hence, such sites are not ships' graveyards in the way other sites are. Examples of these sites are found at American River and Kingscote (South Australia), Balmain and Pyrmont (New South Wales), and Battery Point and Prince of Wales Bay (Tasmania).

Intertidal ship-discard and ship-breaking sites are different from deep-sea scuttling areas because people abandon watercraft within them for salvage as much as disposal. These sites are, therefore, more likely to accumulate the signatures of placement assurance and hull-reduction strategies that may coincide with economic or technological trends.

Surviving sites in Australia that represent ship breaking and ship discard together can be found at the Jervois Basin (Port Adelaide), Homebush Bay (Sydney), and Point Lillias (Corio Bay, Geelong). Ships' graveyards at ship-breaking yards are also notable because although they often contain some abandoned watercraft remains, these are only a small proportion of the vessels ever abandoned and dismantled there. These sites, despite their relatively scarce material remains, are also important because they represent many more reuse, discard, abandonment, and reclamation processes.

Special Cases: Territories and Rivers

In most Australian states, the locations of official ship-abandonment areas relate to the division between state and Commonwealth rights and responsibilities. In the case of the Northern Territory, however, the situation is different. Because the Northern Territory, at the time of the writing of the 1933 legislation, did not need to control vessel disposal, the discard pattern there is considerably scattered. Historical records only note three distinct regions as dumping areas. The first, loosely termed a ships' graveyard, is found in Darwin Harbor. The other two regions are considerable distances from Darwin; one is around Ashmore Reef and the border of Australia's Exclusive Economic Zone (about 470 nautical miles west of Darwin) and the other is located at New Year's Island (approximately 150 nautical miles northeast of Darwin). The majority of the abandoned vessels in the Northern Territory (about 98 percent) lie inside or within close proximity to Darwin Harbor. Inside this area, there are a number of locations that have served as focal points for vessel disposal.

Kenderdine has also noticed spatial patterning in relation to the location of watercraft on the Murray River in South Australia, Victoria, and New South Wales.[19] Of relevance to deliberate discard, she noted that, first, sites are more common in the lower reaches of the river, indicating that vessels moved down river as trade declined; second, discard locations were predominantly in tributaries removed from the main river to ensure safe navigation; third, sites cluster around sawmill operations in New South Wales and Victoria, the barges often built for these particular enterprises; fourth, tributaries of the river often serve as ships' graveyards; fifth, the growth of railway networks and the construction of bridges had ramifications on trade and discard behavior; sixth, more sites exist in the lower reaches of the South Australian section of the river than any other region (which indicate that the normal response to trade decline was to deliver last services to downstream ports); and seventh, sites cluster around major ports—each usually with a rotten row. Discard analyses in this research mirrored all of the above, with the major towns and settlements along the river found to be focal points for abandonment activities.

The spatial constraints of operating a vessel on a river (only being able to travel up river and down river) also affect options as to where you may discard a vessel. Nevertheless, there are still links between riverine and marine

Table 3. Number of Watercraft (with Known Date of Build and Abandonment) Organized by State of Abandonment (n = 1,267, "Unknown State" Excluded)

State	Number	% Known
New South Wales	319	26
Unknown	275	—
South Australia	256	20
Queensland	185	15
Victoria	181	14
Western Australia	164	13
Tasmania	120	9
Northern Territory	42	3

Table 4. GRT of Watercraft (with Known Date of Build and Abandonment) Organized by State of Abandonment (459,390.7 Total GRT, "Unknown State" Excluded)

State Total	GRT	% Known
New South Wales	138,175.970	33
Victoria	72,097.588	17
Western Australia	69,414.375	17
Queensland	58,569.930	14
South Australia	52,203.300	13
Unknown	43,981.908	—
Tasmania	24,497.780	6
Northern Territory	449.850	<1

abandonment in the location of discard areas. For instance, trade will define working locations, and perceived threats to navigation will define the site of abandonment. Babits and Corbin-Kjorness found this to be true in a similar study on the Pungo River system in North Carolina, where the most likely places for watercraft disposal were secondary and tertiary streams.[20]

As indicated, there are 1,542 separate abandoned watercraft sites in the data set of this study. Of these sites, 275 (approximately 17 percent) were abandoned or dismantled in a state that is currently unknown and have, therefore, been excluded from regional analysis. The remaining 1,267 vessels are dispersed as depicted in tables 3 and 4, according to number and tonnage.

As with national analyses, these values may change as researchers identify additional undocumented abandoned vessels.[21] Similarly, there are some vessels in the database without currently known tonnage values.

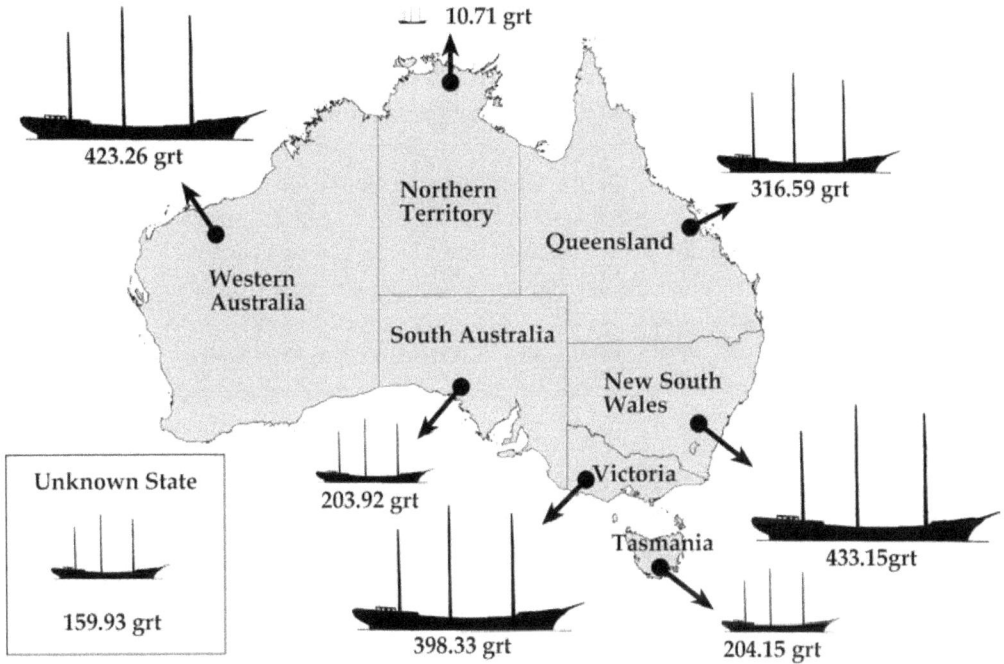

Figure 10. Average gross tonnage of watercraft abandoned in each state and territory (equals total gross tonnage abandoned divided by total number abandoned). Figures are rounded to two decimal places.

These figures illustrate the importance of gross tonnage as a value for the analysis of abandonment trends. A comparison of the number of watercraft and the total gross tonnage of watercraft abandoned in each state and territory show that there are small ranking differences in the distribution of each data set. This also illustrates that although some states have had many vessels abandoned, their size on average was much smaller than other states (see figure 10).

As the breaking up of smaller watercraft tends to be invisible in historical records, and as the "unknown location" vessels tends to be smaller ships, this also explains why there are so many watercraft of unknown location of disposal. Additionally, these values may also reflect the size of vessels working in the major ports of these regions and, over time, may illustrate the effect of developing port infrastructure and the consequences of dredging operations.

There is a large variation in the number of vessels abandoned in each state and territory of Australia. For instance, the watercraft abandoned in the Northern Territory account for only 3 percent of all abandoned vessels throughout time. Additionally, the entire ship-abandonment resource of the Northern Territory equates to only forty-two vessels, roughly the equivalent to a single ships' graveyard in most other states. If we assume that the number of abandoned vessels in a place is proportional to the volume of trade in that place across time, such a correlation is not surprising. Nevertheless, this also means that some analyses will be less reliable due to considerably smaller sample sizes. Due to the large differences in the number and total gross tonnage of watercraft discarded in each state, no combined abandonment trend on a single graph can be adequately displayed, hence figures 11 to 24 show the number and gross tonnage of watercraft abandoned in each region (arranged according to number of watercraft) between 1800 and 2000. Periods of major economic change (national and regional) and drought years (compiled from historical sources) have been superimposed on the graphs to illustrate the degree of correlation between natural and economic and watercraft discard trends.

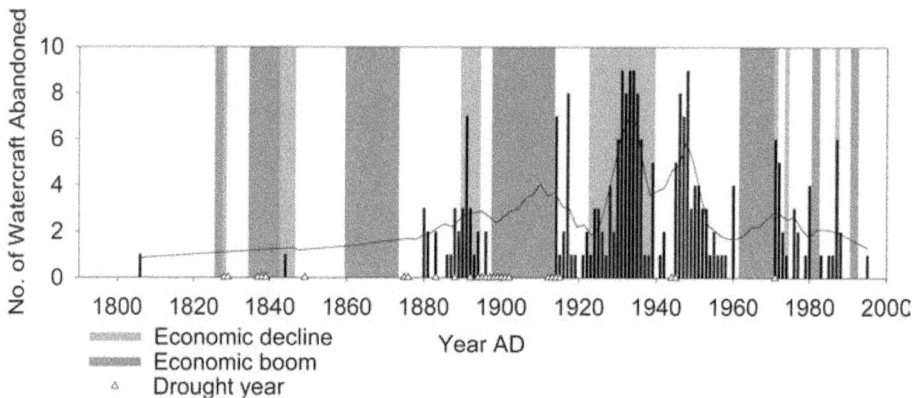

Figure 11. Watercraft abandoned in New South Wales (1800–2000) by number of watercraft (n = 319 watercraft).

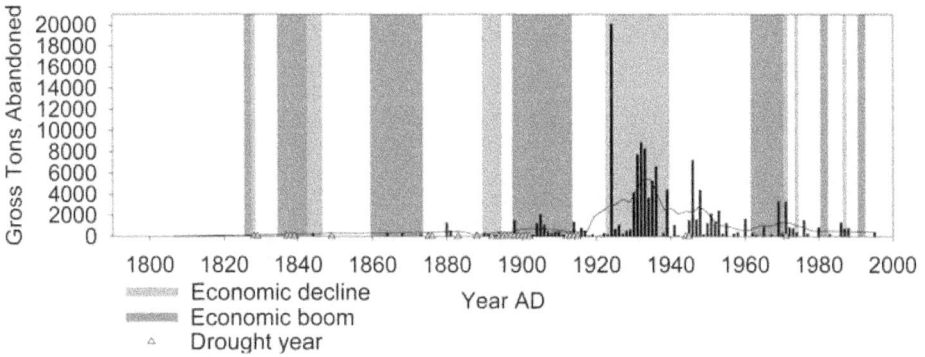

Figure 12. Watercraft abandoned in New South Wales (1800–2000) by gross tonnage (n = 319 watercraft, 138,175.97 GRT).

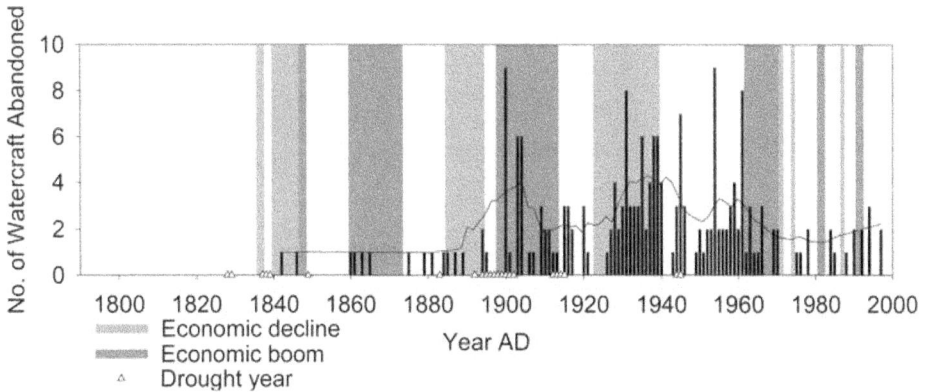

Figure 13. Watercraft abandoned in South Australia (1800–2000) by number of watercraft (n = 256 watercraft).

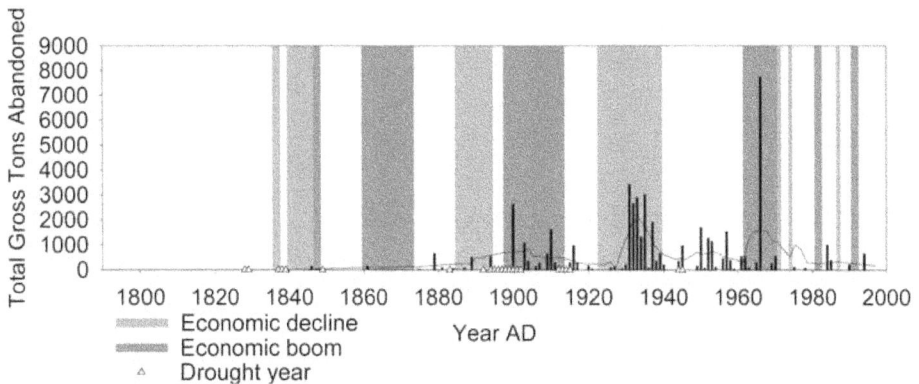

Figure 14. Watercraft abandoned in South Australia (1800–2000) by gross tonnage (n = 256 watercraft, 52,203.3 GRT).

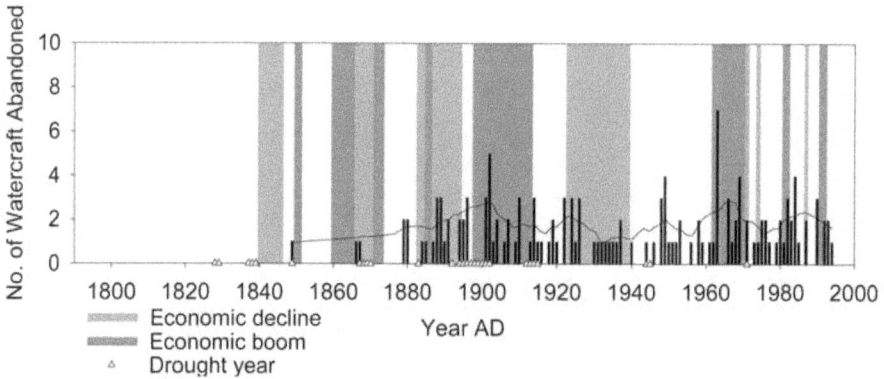

Figure 15. Watercraft abandoned in Queensland (1800–2000) by number of watercraft (n = 185 watercraft).

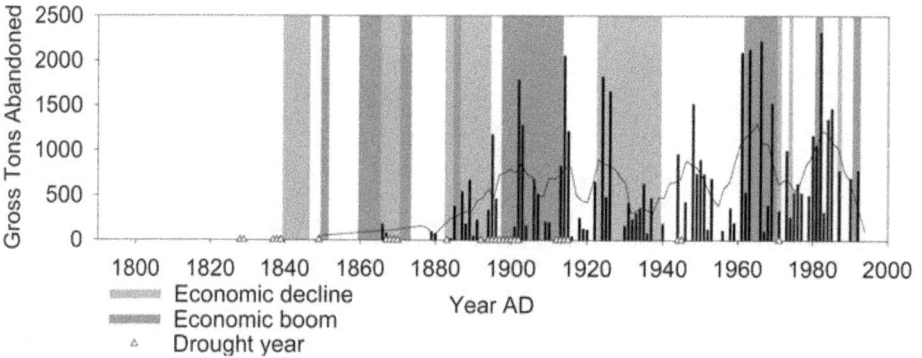

Figure 16. Watercraft abandoned in Queensland (1800–2000) by gross tonnage (n = 185 watercraft, 58,569.93 GRT).

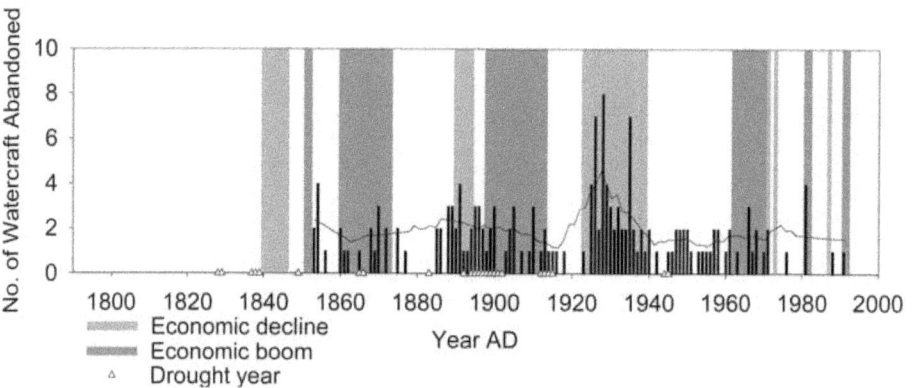

Figure 17. Watercraft abandoned in Victoria (1800–2000) by number of watercraft (n = 181 watercraft).

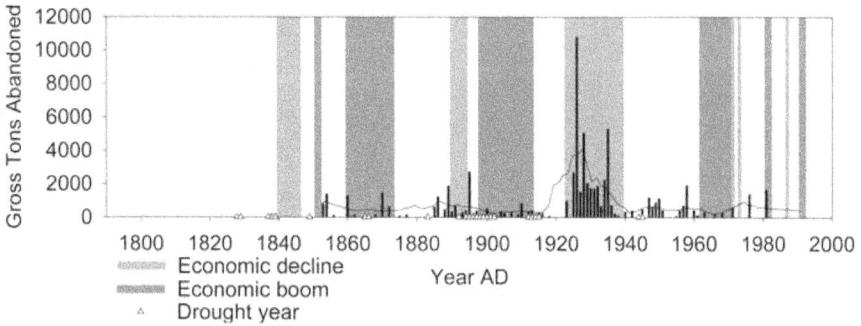

Figure 18. Watercraft abandoned in Victoria (1800–2000) by gross tonnage (n = 181 watercraft, 72,097.588 GRT).

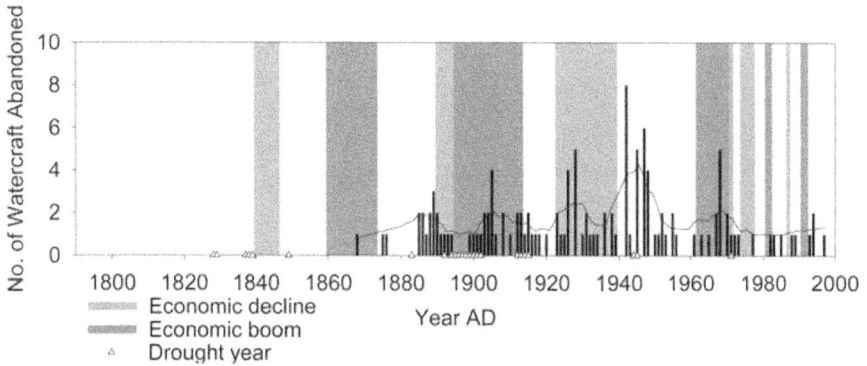

Figure 19. Watercraft abandoned in Western Australia (1800–2000) by number of watercraft (n = 164 watercraft).

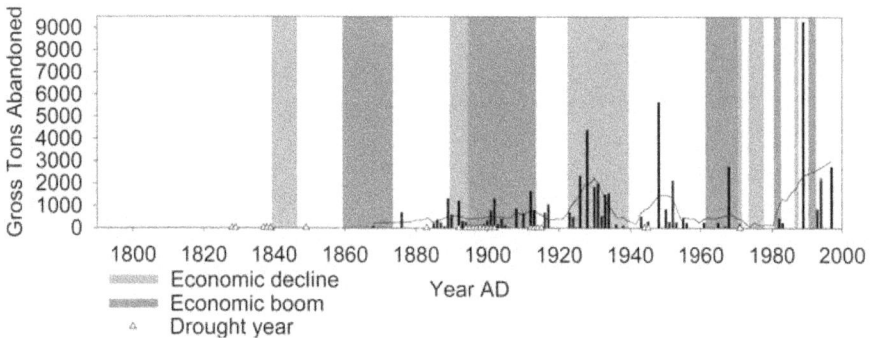

Figure 20. Watercraft abandoned in Western Australia (1800–2000) by gross tonnage (n = 164 watercraft, 69,414.375 GRT).

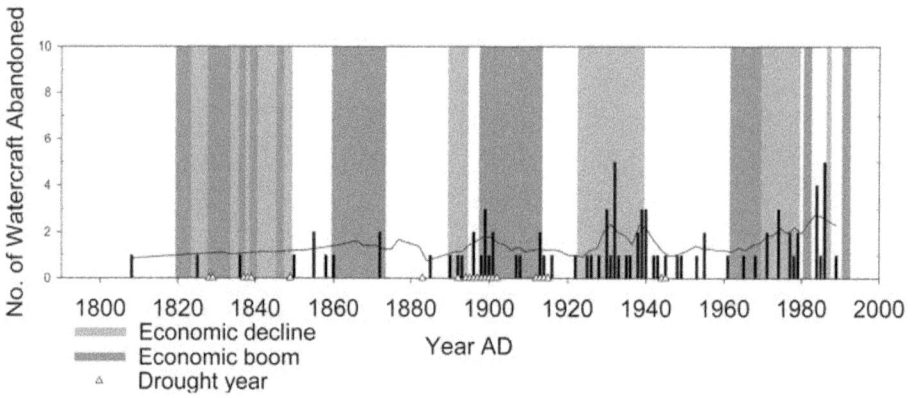

Figure 21. Watercraft abandoned in Tasmania (1800–2000) by number of watercraft (n = 120 watercraft).

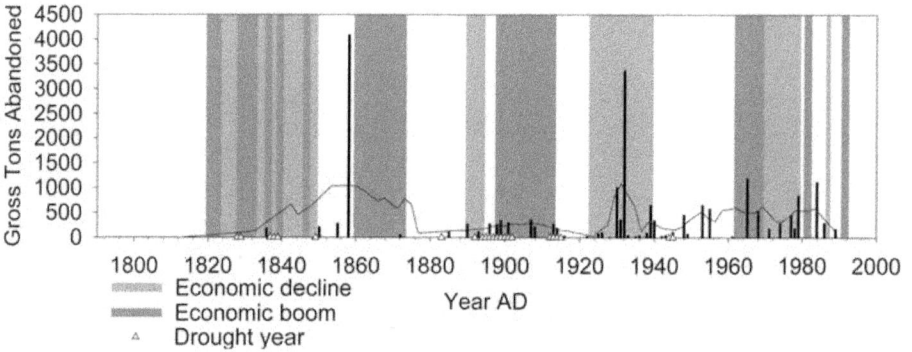

Figure 22. Watercraft abandoned in Tasmania (1800–2000) by gross tonnage (n = 120 watercraft, 24,497.78 GRT).

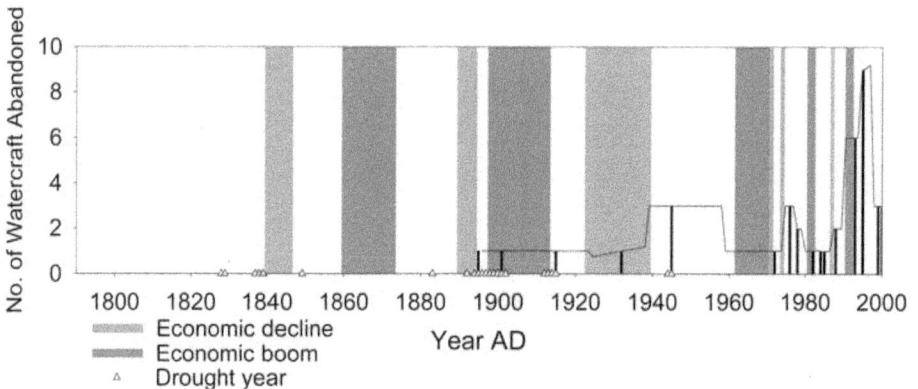

Figure 23. Watercraft abandoned in the Northern Territory (1800–2000) by number of watercraft (n = 42 watercraft).

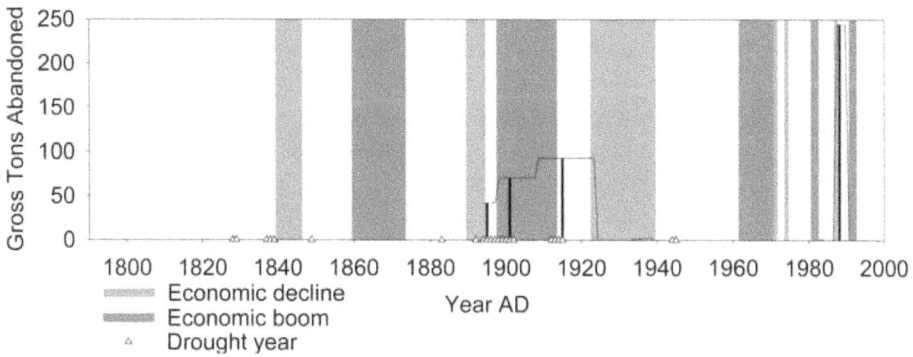

Figure 24. Watercraft abandoned in the Northern Territory (1800–2000) by gross tonnage (n = 42 watercraft, 449.85 GRT).

Environmental Aspects of Ship Abandonment

Although this research is concerned with the cultural site formation processes that create ship-discard sites, the environment and environmental change may also play an important role. We can best analyze the environmental aspects of ship discard on a state level because such events are generally regional. In this way, individual state discard trends may reflect the environmental events that affect regions along state boundaries.

Environmental damage has played a role in the creation of ship-discard areas. Such occurrences, however, are not evident in the maritime site literature, and environmental damage appears to play no part in the process of abandoning vessels in Australia. This is probably because key developments causing environmental damage along the inland waterways of Australia have only recently become major problems. Moreover, in most cases the ships that were discarded in Australia were constructed *after* the conclusion of the use of inland waterways as major transportation routes.

Broadly, environmental damage only appears to influence trades centered on riverine and lacustrine environments, not marine ones. There are, however, some links between environmental catastrophe and the tendency to abandon vessels. For instance, although droughts may result in the drying up of waterways and increase the possibility of stranding vessels, this does not seem to have been a major problem in Australia. Yet droughts have undeniably devastating influences on economic conditions in Australia, particularly through the effect of hot, dry climates on crops and vegetation. This in turn changes trade along rivers, and ultimately alters the economic health of regions and states. As with any other historical events influencing national economic health, this translates to an increase in the abandonment of vessels used in drought-affected regions.

There have been countless droughts reported throughout nineteenth-century Australian history, and the ebb and flow of environmental extremes is a topic central to that history.[22] The earliest mention of a devastating drought was in 1828–29; it caused a dramatic fall in the prices of the major staples of the Australian economy. Later, equally ruinous droughts (1837–39) coincided with other detrimental economic events, such as the cessation of the use of convict labor in most states (commencing in New South Wales in 1840).[23] The droughts of 1849, 1883, and 1892 produced similar results.[24] Some researchers have cited droughts in the early part of the twentieth century as the cause of the abandonment of vessels. One such example is the paddle steamer *Melbourne*, which for the period 1902–5 was laid up and eventually abandoned at Mildura, Victoria. The vessel's owners deposited the vessel on the remains of the paddle steamer *Jane Eliza*, abandoned some twenty years previously after concluding duties as a pumping plant.[25] Although it is important to acknowledge that there are cases where abandonment directly relates to environmental catastrophes, the discussion below indicates that they are statistically irrelevant.

Despite the fact that these environmental catastrophes are said to have had national economic consequences, a perusal of figures 2 and 3 depicting the number of vessels and the gross tonnage of vessels abandoned in those years does not reflect the increase in abandonment that would be expected (although there is a slight increase around 1850). It may be that environmental events, such as droughts, have their greatest influence on regions within, and across state boundaries.

Many historically documented droughts have affected particular regions, and a reading of general Australian histories indicates that different areas of different states felt these effects at different times. On a state level, for instance, drought had a major effect on all of Victoria in the summer of 1865–66, and drought coupled with depressed cattle prices ravaged Queensland between 1868 and 1870.[26] Similarly, New South Wales suffered shortages of water throughout 1888.[27] On a regional level, drought affected Wilcannia (New South Wales) between 1875 and 1876, and Maitland (South Australia) was in the depths of a drought in January 1901.[28]

The "dry nineties" was a period of Australian history that refers to a veritable national drought. This period saw most states suffering from 1894 until the "Sahara year" of 1902, and before this time there had been five years of abundant rainfall for many states.[29] Later periods of drought also occurred between 1912 and 1915, 1944 and 1945, and, in Queensland, Western Australia, and New South Wales in 1971.[30]

Although historical records note vessel abandonment occurring in these years, as well as the years directly following, none of these times correspond with major periods of increased abandonment. Furthermore, where a drought coincides with a marked increase in ship abandonment, the reasons are attributable to other economic developments. From this reading, such events are relatively minor in comparison to other events in Australian history, and at best worsen preexisting economic problems. History notes other environmental catastrophes for their dramatic effects on certain sectors; a hurricane in 1870, for example, ended the cotton and sugar industries in Townsville.[31]

Fundamentally, these environmental events are only catalysts contributing to, and multiplying economic change. It is my view that although there is some degree of environmental determinism in the abandonment resource of Australia, it cannot be considered a primary factor in watercraft disposal psychology. In an Australian context, the influence of the environment on abandonment trends relates almost entirely to the threat, perceived threat, or occurrence of widespread natural disaster and the subsequent economic problems caused by such events. From this perspective, we can see that the catalysts for changes in abandonment trends have an economic origin.

Economic Aspects of Regional Abandonment

The economic aspects of regional watercraft abandonment relate to the themes of economic boom, bust, war, and the transition to peacetime economy as outlined in the previous chapter. Additionally, the abandonment trend of a region may reflect the influence of developing port infrastructure and alternative transportation methods.

Tull has stated that shipping and trade is a barometer of a state's prosperity.[32] If this is the case, then trade is also a major factor in the abandonment of vessels, and with peaks in economic prosperity, abandonment should theoretically decrease. On an intrastate level, however, competing ports within a state tend to influence the predisposition to abandon watercraft at one location over another. On Australia's southwestern coast, the development of Cockburn Sound, and Albany, in particular, drew trade away from Fremantle in the 1950s, culminating in extensive abandonment regions at both locations.[33] Research cites Albany as having competed with Fremantle as Western Australia's premier port from the 1830s, which is reflected in the spatial arrangement of official and unofficial ship-discard areas in both locations. Economic expansion and growth of port infrastructure at both of these places were central causes of this competition.[34] In this way, the intrastate dynamics of trade may influence changes in the use of ship-disposal areas in individual ports.

Of course, if abandonment is trade-dependent and regional trade is reliant on commodities that may be unique to certain ports, the tendency to abandon certain kinds of vessels in some ports is dependent on the health of particular industries. For this reason, ship-disposal areas have a local or regional context, which researchers may draw out of vessel histories. These issues will not be discussed here, but they illustrate how the analysis of abandonment trends on statewide, or even more local, scales have much to contribute to understanding economic change across regions.

Economic Feast and Famine

One problem when trying to understand regional economic boom and bust cycles is that regional histories do not often communicate whether the economic depressions they discuss were local, regional, or national. This is especially the case when they discuss the prefederation period (before 1901), when the current states were separate colonies. Charting economic developments in every trade of every colony and state over time is impossible within the scope of this research. Every change in policy, increase in freight rates, new trade monopoly, conference on passenger shipping, or enlargement in wharfage dues directly influences and controls economic conditions.

Analysis shows that an increase in abandonment correlates with documented economic decline in a number of regions, including South Australia in the early 1840s (1841–46) and two decades of depression commencing in the 1880s (around 1885) that joined with the national depression of the 1890s.[35] Queensland experienced economic decline in the 1860s (1866–70) due to the collapse of the banks that funded initial colonization, and in the 1880s due to competition from German sugar (1883–89) and a slump in gold mining (1888–89) (see figures 15 and 16).[36] Western Australia was economically depressed from 1974 until 1977 due to downturns in the container trade (see figures 19 and 20),[37] as was Tasmania in the 1970s due to the decimation of the fruit industry (see figures 21 and 22).[38]

Although early regional depressions appear in the abandonment trend, they are not as distinct as in national analyses. Increases in abandonment do not appear to correspond with the earliest economic depressions that gripped the colonies after their establishment. This may be due to a number of factors that define the early economic development of Australia, including the rate of immigration, the system of land grants and land rents, and government expenditure, but it more likely was attributable to the relatively small size (and often experimental nature) of trade in new colonies, as well as the options for vessels to trade in nearby colonies. There are many examples of this. First, New South Wales from the 1790s due to labor shortages, and in the late 1820s (1827–29) due to English financial crises and a fall in wool prices (see figures 11 and 12).[39] Second, South Australia in the 1830s despite economic hardships that date from the establishment of the colony in 1836 (see figures 13 and 14). Third, Tasmania from the 1840s due to the cessation of convict transportation (and hence cheap labor) and the mass exodus of people from this colony because of the California Gold rush (1849), the establishment of the new colonies of South Australia (1836), Victoria (1850), and Queensland (1859), and the New Zealand gold rushes (see figures 21 and 22).[40] This trend is also obvious on a national level in the 1840s (1842–44) (see figures 11–24).[41]

In some cases, this corresponds to economic growth in other sectors. For example, in Tasmania, the economic expansions brought about by the development of timber and produce export industries (because of the rushes in California, New Zealand, Victoria, and New South Wales from the 1850s) may have canceled out much of the hardship. Indeed, the abandonment trend poorly represents the economic depressions of Tasmania, which historians cite lasted from the 1840s until the 1870s, probably due to the drastic fall in shipping arrivals to Tasmania over this period. Certainly, Hudspeth and Scripps cite that between 1857 and 1872 the tonnage of shipping plummeted from 105,000 to 50,000 tons, representing a drop in yearly ship arrivals from 547 to 195.[42]

The analysis of regional booms and busts in Australian colonies and states has tended to concentrate on trade cycles defined in relation to English trade cycles.[43] For example, R. W. Hartwell cites that because Tasmania was a dependent colony, it went through trade cycles that reflecting the English economy over the same period.[44] Van Diemen's Land was very depressed during the periods 1826–27, 1834–35, and 1841–45; had moderate depressions in 1824–25, 1838, and 1848–49; and experienced a boom in 1839–40. It had periods of mixed prosperity 1820–23, 1828–33, 1836–37, and 1846–47. However, many of these cycles are too short to expect a corresponding change in the abandonment trend, which we can expect to occur only during protracted advantageous or adverse economic change. This can be noticed in any number of the cycles communicated by Hartwell in relation to Tasmania, and in the short lived economic depressions of particular ports (such as Townsville in 1876), as well as more modern recessions, such as in Western Australia in 1952–53.[45]

Not all states appear to have had the same response to the national economic depressions mentioned in the previous chapter. Although the depression of the 1890s is clearly evident in the examination of trends in South Australia and Queensland, it is not nearly as marked in the Tasmanian trend, despite its documented adverse effects.[46] Likewise, the unfavorable influence of the Depression of the 1930s on all states of Australia is not as marked in the Tasmanian abandonment trend.[47] This may be due to record produce crops and port arrivals in the early 1930s, the lifting of coastal clauses in the navigation act in 1932, the reduction of wharfage rates in the mid-1930s (both stimulated trade), and documented problems in gaining business after the depression (due to increased competition in a number of trades). Combined, these factors may have "smoothed out" this trend. Additionally, Tasmania is credited with being in the midst of depression by the 1920s, which deepened in the 1930s.[48] Likewise, other data suggest that South Australia was in the midst of economic depression by the 1920s, and the state's economy was in very bad shape by the early 1930s.[49] All of these events appear in regional abandonment trends. Similarly, the effect of the Middle East oil crisis of 1974 and the stock market crash of 1987 varies markedly from state to state.

A decrease in abandonment corresponds with documented economic expansion in New South Wales in the 1820s and between 1835 and 1840 (see figures 11 and 12).[50] In South Australia, a similar correlation exists in the late 1840s (after 1846) and the 1870s (see figures 13 and 14).[51] The trend is also seen in Queensland throughout the 1850s, due to the expanding pastoral industry and mineral booms; the 1860s, due to the American Civil War (which maimed the American cotton industry), subsequent mineral rushes, and the growth of wool exports; and the mid-1880s, due to the "sugar boom" and expansion of beche-de-mer fishing (see figures 15 and 16).[52] In Western Australia, the expansion of gold mining and a growing population caused booms in the 1890s (see figures 19 and 20).[53]

Early, short-lived economic growth periods are often difficult to determine due to the low amount of trade at some ports. The economic boom periods that lasted from 1829 to 1832 and 1839 to 1840 in Tasmania, for instance, are too short to expect a corresponding change in abandonment behavior.[54] This is also the case with booms in New South Wales in 1826–27, 1838–40, and 1841–42.[55]

Warfare

The economic effects of war vary markedly between state trends. The Boer War (1899–1902) and the Boxer Rebellion (1900) helped Queensland, for instance, because of the demand for horses that they created, but they were of little benefit to other states.[56] Similarly, the commencement of the two world wars had special effects on different Australian settlements that are discernible in abandonment trends.

For example, despite the fact that historians credit World War I with speeding up economic development in Australia, the abandonment trend does not reflect this in all states. In Tasmania, its influence is reputed to have been negligible until 1917, when the effects of the decline in shipping due to wartime adoption of merchant tonnage began to have ramifications. Much later, when it was a source of major disruption to trade throughout Australia, it still did not deter many states from expanding their port infrastructure. This would subsequently change due to the prolonged nature and intensification of the conflict. June 1918 saw the prices of quayage and port dues rise substantially, despite general hardship in the state brought about by the shipping decline following the outbreak of World War I. The changes in how these dues were determined (a change from net tonnage calculations to gross tonnage calculations) constituted a major financial drain on struggling merchants and shipowners. The cessation of hostilities in late 1918 did not see a major change, with high fees now coupled with a seaman's strike causing a postwar continuation of hardship. When the big ships did return, it was soon found that they had indeed become bigger, mainly due to the establishment of new, more direct routes in international trade (London to Hobart), a problem for the port due to the depth of water.[57] Similarly, in North Queensland, the outbreak of World War I caused havoc in the mining industry due to fears of unpredictable foreign markets among buyers, in the process shutting down smelters. In South Australia, historians credit the war for bringing about a depression.[58]

Additionally, World War II brought about a slow turnaround of shipping in Tasmania and became a reason for vessels not to visit the port. This in turn meant that Hobart suffered from a lack of trade at this time, made worse by the requisitioning of vessels for use in the conflict. The level of shipping, which was at its highest in 1938, would not reach the same level until 1958.[59]

The Growth of Alternative Modes of Transportation and Communication

Alternative modes of transport and communication have been credited with creating competition that adversely affected many forms of maritime transportation in Australia and overseas.[60] Despite the fact that most road networks were still unsealed in the 1950s and air services did not really exist until the 1940s, the growth of alternative forms of transportation were pivotal in the replacement of maritime trades.[61] This occurred where alternative methods replaced the transportation of people, merchandise, or information. Although it was mainly the physical barriers broken by the growth of rail, road, and air networks that facilitated this, it was also the product of the expansion of telegraph, radio, and pipeline technologies.[62] The expansion of these developments, however, spread at different rates in different places and had a direct impact on the abandonment trend through the influence that it had on maritime trades. In some cases, the growth of these networks facilitated more commerce to ports, and in others, it replaced marine trade. Researchers have noted this in relation to North Queensland ports, especially following World War I, where by the 1950s these modes had eroded many of the traditional markets of maritime trades.[63] As one author has noted, "Competition from railroads and road transport, and in more recent years, from airlines provoked the prophecies of doom that are inseparable from the shipping industry the world over."[64]

Transportation methods vary according to a range of attributes in relation to both passengers and cargo, such as comfort, safety, and efficiency. The major difference between water and land transport relates to infrastructure. Part of the success of sea transport depends on the concentration of infrastructure at the site of port development. Infrastructure in relation to both road and rail transportation, although still requiring centralized facilities such as warehouses, terminals, and repair establishments, is much more dispersed, requiring much more time, expense, and effort to become established. Once established, the costs of maintenance and use are much less in relation to sea transportation, providing major competition and, therefore, drastic change.

In particular, land alternatives influenced intrastate shipping because

intrastate shipping is short-haul work, unable to maximize its time at sea with respect to time in port. The limited cargoes, the short runs, the physical problems of most of the ports, the time lost, owing to weather conditions at the bar entrances, would have been by themselves severe obstacles to the expansion and modernization of services. When an alternative means of transport was freely available, the outcome was inevitable.[65]

As Kerr notes, steep, hilly, and densely forested land by nature is poorly suited to land transportation.[66] Hence, topographic features influence the growth of land infrastructure, which in turn play an important part in the growth, development, and eventual decline of maritime trades and seaborne transportation. From the examination of the establishment of land-based infrastructure (road and rail), it is clear that their spatial orientations are important to consider when examining the growth or decline of maritime transportation and trade. The overriding formulas for this seems to suggest that land transport infrastructure running parallel to the coast will cause a decline in maritime trades, except under exceptional circumstances related to economic conditions in adjoining regions that see en masse migration from the region in question.

There is also a relationship between economic conditions and the expansion of alternative modes of transportation. To some degree, economic decline may have been beneficial for maritime trades. For instance, Geoffrey Bolton credits the depression of 1892 and drought conditions that concluded in 1902 with stopping road development in Queensland.[67] Another ramification of the expansion of alternative transportation was technological changes within marine transport. Matthews, for instance, has commented that the conversion of ketches in South Australia to motor vessels was undertaken because it allowed for greater competition between these watercraft and emerging road and rail systems.[68]

Railway Transportation

As with other nations, in Australia the decline in maritime trades and the growth of rail networks are related. Some colonies such as Victoria began building railways from the 1850s, and some authors credit the linking of Adelaide to Brisbane by rail in 1888 as "stealing" traffic from shipping.[69] Other colonies, such as Western Australia, had natural obstacles that inhibited the construction of railways and therefore did not feel the effects of competition until much later.[70] Indeed, on the upper north coast of New South Wales, the railroad only began to have an adverse influence on maritime trade around 1924, when it played a large role in the destruction of trades along the Hawkesbury River.[71] Nevertheless, the expansion of railway mileage in Australia from 800 miles in 1870 to 13,500 miles in 1900 and the opening of the Trans-Pacific Railway in 1917 would not have been advantageous to Australian coastal trades.[72] Likewise, the development of railways to Perth, between Sydney and Brisbane, and between the towns of Queensland caused a major drop in passenger transport, triggering the disposal of interstate passenger vessels.[73] These events were a contributing factor to the increased abandonment of watercraft in mainland states in the late 1910s and 1920s. This has also been the case in Australia more recently. The modernization of newsprint production facilities, namely, the introduction of rail facilities at Boyer, Tasmania, was the one of the reasons for the abandonment of the barges used in newsprint transportation (the barges *ANM 3*, *ANM 4*, and *ANM 6* in 1984 and *ANM 5* in 1986).[74] However, as with other instances from around the world, some ports, such as Fremantle, benefited from radial rail networks.[75] Indeed, rail had the added affect of changing the role of regional ports and thereby influenced the balance of trade.[76]

The growth of alternative methods of transportation was particularly important in the case of riverine trades. Ian Mudie notes that government attitudes toward riverine transport on the River Murray influenced policy and railway planning.[77] In this case, the Australian colonial and, later, federal governments perceived the trades in the river as out of their control and planned railways to travel to the rivers in order to facilitate its decline. This, coupled with the development and use of motor lorries, was to have great ramifications on trade, finally culminating in the total drying up of major commercial activity on the river. Indeed, in the economic warfare between the colonies along the river, alternative transportation seems to have been the most effective and decisive weapon, with the South Australian control of the river (and hence trade) evaporating as the Victorian and New South Wales governments extended their railways.[78]

Others have noted these changes. When Kenderdine says that "wreck-site distribution tends to reflect the dynamics of the decline in the river economy and trade, the advent of the railways and the building of bridges, and the adaptation of alternative forms of technology that helped supersede the River Murray steamer as a form of transport,"[79] she is actually referring to abandoned vessel distribution.

Road Transportation

Alan Moore has commented that the economics of land transportation and the influence of the petrol engine were major sources in the early decline of waterborne transportation.[80] Similarly, Louis Hunter has stated that the quality of the road or waterway is a variable that is crucial to the viability of any mode of transport.[81] These assertion illustrate the reasons for the initial unimportance of early road transport and the growing importance of road transport once costs associated with road construction and upkeep dropped in relation to the costs associated with dredging. Competition from road transportation was also a cause of the death of many maritime industries around the world. This is especially the case in Australia. By 1932, there was one car for every twelve Australians, making the country the fourth largest car-owning nation and the fifth largest importer of petroleum.[82] In 1932, the South Australian Parliament reported that

> the use of motor transport has had an effect on reducing business at many of the ports on Yorke Peninsular [*sic*]. The commissioners recognize that whilst the public naturally seeks what it deems to be the cheapest means of transport, nevertheless where such an operation displaces forms of transport that efficiently and economically serve the public, and have been established at great cost, it inflicts a loss on the community as a whole. Should the territory hitherto using water carriage be served by other means of transport, it must be recognized that many ports will not pay, and it will be difficult to justify the maintenance of the shipping facilities now provided.[83]

However, the changes to maritime trades through the expansion of road networks came earlier in coastal commerce, such as the South Australian "ketch trade," as noted by Ronald Parsons:

> Changes of ketches to auxiliary power was forced upon owners after World War One through economic necessity. Road transport was cutting into their remaining trade and road delivery, although often more expensive was usually faster.[84]

After World War II, the development of road infrastructure was to be a major force in changing the barge trade in Tasmania, as well as causing a decline in the timber trade.[85] Roads also played a large role in the destruction of maritime trade along the Hawkesbury River north of Sydney and the decline of the passenger trade along the Richmond River between 1920 and 1950.[86]

Road transport often followed railway expansion and compounded the detrimental effects of railways on river transportation corridors. Workman, for instance, has linked the decline in the use of ketches from the 1920s in Port Adelaide directly to the emergence of the motor truck and semitrailer.[87] John Tregenza, also writing about South Australia, cites the direct influence of the "unreliability of the maritime work force and the competition of air and road transport"[88] as the main reason for the end of the interstate passenger and freight line trade. The growth and steady improvement of road infrastructure also changed the transport spending priorities of businesses such as Port Adelaide timber merchants Le Messurier, who had traditionally upgraded their ships but by 1968 had in their possession six diesel-fueled semitrailers operating between Adelaide and Melbourne.[89]

Citing evidence from Tasmania, Kerr has noted that the direct impact of road transport from the 1920s (coupled with the effects of the Great Depression) was a drastic drop in available freights.[90] This meant that vessel operators had few choices: convert vessels to fishing trades, sell them interstate, or lay their ships up. Road transportation also contributed to the abandonment of vessels in Tasmania. When the Australian Newsprint Mills Company changed to road transportation, they scuttled their fleet of barges in 1986.[91] Graeme-Evans and Wilson also cite the use of semitrailers for the transportation of grain in 1956 as the main reason for the sale (due to fears of the vessel's redundancy) and modification of the vessel *Leillateah*.[92]

Air Transportation

With the exception of Bach, who has noted that expanded aviation services replaced passenger trades, researchers have commented very little on the competition between aviation and maritime transport.[93] This is probably because the development of airborne trades generally occurred after land transportation had made substantial inroads into many marine trades. Indeed, Scott Baty notes that, at least in the passenger trades, air transportation only began to have an influence on seaborne passenger trade in the 1950s.[94]

As one government committee commented:

> Because of the different operating conditions, pattern of usage, technical requirements, state of development and other factors peculiar to each of the transport modes, the adoption of new technology within these modes has progressed at different rates and in different directions. A little cross-fertilization of technology between modes has occurred, but each mode has remained essentially different and independent.[95]

In the modern world, this situation is gradually changing with the creation of "transport systems" that facilitate intermodal (sea-road-rail-air) freight transfer through the efficient transshipment of goods between different modes of transport.[96] Such systems (like containerization) also decrease the likelihood of abandonment by reducing competition between modes of transport.

Changes to Port Infrastructure

The development of appropriate port infrastructure is central to port use, productivity, efficiency, and success. Hence, the development of port infrastructure has an affect on the types of vessels operating at a port, and therefore it affects what vessel types are available for abandonment at a particular port.

Infrastructure, such as the provision of marinas, boat sheds, and moorings, will affect the use-life of vessels by saving them from strain and wear. During a regional depression in 1850s, Tasmania redundant water taxis were granted boat ways and a boat harbor so that the vessels did not have to be beached for prolonged periods while there was no work.[97] From this perspective, deliberately beached and abandoned vessels represent not only the abandonment of the actual vessel but also the abandonment of a mooring and, consequently, a total cessation of useful function.

These developments influence abandonment trends in a number of ways. On one hand, the improvements to the usability and safety of ports can stimulate trade and create economic expansion. This growth should decrease watercraft abandonment. Such is the case with the port of Fremantle, an unsafe harbor until authorities removed the bar across the mouth of the Swan River and constructed the inner harbor in the 1890s.[98] These poor port facilities ensured that Albany remained Western Australia's principal port throughout most of the nineteenth century. The importance of the major port at Fremantle increased in the 1870s, reflecting a growing population and economy.

The other side of this economic expansion is that subsequent economic downturns will bring about a substantial increase in watercraft discard activity, due to the larger number of unused vessels in port. Likewise, the conclusion of port development and expansion phases will often see the abandonment of the vessels (many of which are often custom made for work on port expansion projects) that construction crews used in the project. These activities may be seen as "multiplying factors" in the abandonment trend, something demonstrated by the fact that construction work had concluded at Fremantle by 1903 and breakwater schemes were completed in Port Kembla in 1901 and at Adelaide and Newcastle in 1909, all of which coincide with levels of high vessel abandonment.[99]

Commercial vessels and ports operate in a delicate symbiotic relationship.[100] A change in one often requires changes to the other. As one source notes, "Many technological changes in transport cannot be introduced, or all of the benefits may not be derived from their introduction, because of the inability of the physical infrastructure to support them properly."[101] Similarly, Daniel Lenihan has referred to the relationship between changes in watercraft design and support infrastructure: "During the Industrial Age, what was an innovative design in one decade could be made obsolete in the next, as mass-produced support facilities became incompatible with vessel design."[102]

Ports can also reflect world shipping. For instance, Bach notes that the projected depth of the Suez Canal meant that ports such as Fremantle and Melbourne had to increase their harbor depth if they wanted to have equivalent vessels in their port.[103] It is also clear from some port histories that the forces that direct port growth and decline (such as war, economic depression, and labor stoppages) are the same pressures shipowners contemplate when considering watercraft abandonment.[104] The specifications and circumstances of the vessels found within the disposal areas of ports the world over are signifiers of the development and decline of these pivotal commercial centers. Thus ports are mirrors of shipping, and vice versa. In early periods of port development, the changes to ships that most impinged upon the workable nature of a port were the size and number of ships. The technical difficulties this caused for ports were few and predictable. Where the numbers of ships grew, more space was required, and the impetus to accelerate wharfage and harbor development grew. Likewise, the nature and size of the port, and the harbor and dock facilities that serviced these vessels, limited the size of the vessels and cargo handling methods.[105] Where vessel size grew greater, the time and energy harbor authorities needed to invest in dredging and channel improvement activities also grew.

Arguably, the latest revolution in shipping is the advent of containerization. Besides the revolution in ship design, a concurrent revolution in waterfront work practices, centralization policies and the transformation of ports themselves became manifest. As Bach has noted, "Unlike traditional technologies, containerization could not be introduced gradually; the enormous implications and ramifications of the concept had to be considered in detail before the service was started."[106] This was not the first step in the revolution, with technology such as larger containers, stern-loading roll-on/roll-off (ro-ro) vessels, and lighter aboard ship (LASH) technology introduced from the 1970s. Although some changes to ship design are not symbiotic to the same degree as others (for instance, LASH ships operate at many types of ports due to their ability to unload barges of goods), all of these technological changes illustrate the transition to highly specialized technologies in the design of ships.[107]

The year 1965 saw shipping companies turn seriously to the container system. LASH ships and container ships are a part of a process that "extends ideally from factory floor to distributor's store, involving a complex of land and sea movements and documentation that calls for all available experience and skill."[108] Some Tasmanian ports, however, did not begin to undergo the process of containerization in earnest until the 1980s.[109]

Indeed, there is also a link between deepening activities, public works, and abandonment because of the types of vessels discarded in an area. For instance, Hobart had very little dredging carried out, due to its suitability as a natural harbor, and hence there were very few dredges abandoned. This is in direct contrast with ports such as Adelaide, Brisbane, and Launceston, which required extensive harbor modification and had to employ dredges extensively. Dredging also has an effect on the design of watercraft, specifically in relation to the dimensions of a vessel. This is a global phenomenon, with the depth and width of the Suez and Panama Canals, the locks at Sault Ste. Marie, and the St. Lawrence Seaway playing a large role in limiting the dimensions of watercraft the world over.[110] Similarly, the lack of port infrastructure in the Australian colonies in the early days had a major influence on watercraft design.[111]

A successful port was one that kept abreast of these changes and moved with the times.[112] This is another reason for the drastic effects of economic depression, which tend to stop or inhibit wharf expansion. The Great Depression of the 1930s, for instance, laid up the development of wharfage in Melbourne.[113]

Generally it could be said that the only aspect of ship design that was important to the design of early ports were the dimensions of a vessel, due the considerations of channel depth and width, and wharf length. A new hull design or marine technology would have had minimal consequences in port design, expansion, and use. This could even be said during the transition of sail to steam, with the only changes being the need for bunkering facilities. This was the case until comparatively recent times. Bach notes that there were three developments in modern maritime technology that required changes to the matching facilities ashore: bulk carriers, cellular container ships, and ro-ro vessels.[114]

The relationship between ports and ships on a technological level is complex. For a change in the design of a ship to work, it must be compatible with the ports with which it wishes to engage in trade. Likewise, a major change to port infrastructure is useless unless there are ships that can use it. In essence, both ships and ports have had to adapt to new technologies in trade, shipping, and cargo.[115] In many cases, we can see the remnants of a certain portion of the abandoned watercraft resource as representative of this inability to adapt and the unveiling of shortcomings in design illuminated by such changes. A shipowner would have to replace a vessel that could not adapt to an innovation in cargo handling or other port-related activity.

Other Factors

Other factors that have influenced regional abandonment trends are the increased tendency to sink unwanted vessels as artificial reefs and the destruction of "illegal" vessels (refugee and seized fishing boats). Although both of these activities may skew the abandonment trend, on a regional level they have very little effect. This is because the tendency to sink vessels for postabandonment uses such as fish aggregation devices and artificial reefs (pursued in earnest since the 1970s) are as much about the economic health of a region as normal discard activities. Additionally, the destruction of "illegal" vessels is a phenomenon more or less confined to the Northern Territory, where it comprises the vast majority of abandoned watercraft for that region.[116]

Conclusion

The distribution of discard locations in Australia suggests a number of things. From one perspective, it reflects cultural constraints, such as the legislation that defined Commonwealth designated areas in the 1930s designed to control the abandonment of watercraft. From another angle, it illustrates the failure of these Commonwealth initiatives due to logistical and jurisdictional issues.

Indeed, part of the lackluster use of these Commonwealth areas is attributable to their focus on harm minimization issues at the expense of the economic issues associated with distance. For this reason, discard sites tend to be associated with ports and are normally in close proximity to ship-breaking areas. The distance between primary and secondary refuse sites is the major factor in the creation of ship disposal areas. Additionally, these Commonwealth areas appear to have been used only where there were issues associated with space availability in a port (linked to port traffic, which is itself an economic issue) or where the close proximity of scuttling locations made the activity cheap to undertake.

The discard trend is an economic index on a regional level in the same way it can be on a national level. Although economic events precipitating changes to discard behaviors resemble those already mentioned in the national analyses undertaken in this research of boom, bust, war, and the aftermath of war, an analysis of a smaller geographical area needs to take in a number of other processes that serve to multiply the advantageous or detrimental economic effects of these events.

These so-called multipliers exist in the form of changes in the development of port infrastructure, the cessation of dredging and deepening, environment change, and the growth of alternative methods of transportation. Although these events have influences on discard behavior, their effects are varied, are largely indiscernible in the abandonment trend, and are not as marked as better defined economic developments.

6

Archaeological Signatures of Use

Hulks, no matter how bedraggled, barnacle-encrusted or time-worn, provided they have some mark of connexion with an earlier glory, carry with them a proud and romantic dignity which their up-to-date sisters cannot claim.

—R. W. Glassford, "A Fleet of Hulks"

A watercraft's former function may often be discerned from its remnant hull in the form of an "archaeological signature." These signatures, evidence of site formation processes and behavioral change, relate to the use, modification, and discard of watercraft. Use and modification processes are important because they have direct influences on discard processes and influence the time and nature of the transformation of a vessel from a systemic to an archaeological context.

In cases of deliberate abandonment, the term *use* has many meanings. For instance, the design and construction of a vessel is a signature of intended function as well as evidence of consumer choice in ship purchasing. It is therefore a representation of the adherence or resistance to technological norms. Also, indications of the modification or conversion of a watercraft's design or construction as seen in the archaeological remains of watercraft is an indication of changing technological and economic situations and the reuse processes that accompany them. In other cases, the clues of functional postabandonment use are evident. All of these stages in the evolution of a vessel's life are significant because they can shed light on economic change in the ship's lifetime as well as the reasons behind its abandonment. This chapter will concentrate on these processes (represented in figure 25) because of the consequences they have on watercraft use-life and thus on deliberate abandonment. They are also important because the technology represented at the time of a vessel's construction has a direct influence on the inclination of shipowners to discard vessels or use them in postabandonment functions.

In this research, the primary phase of a vessel's use-life refers to the original intended function of a vessel. There are two variations of this phase. The *primary mercantile* phase refers to the construction of vessels to fulfill

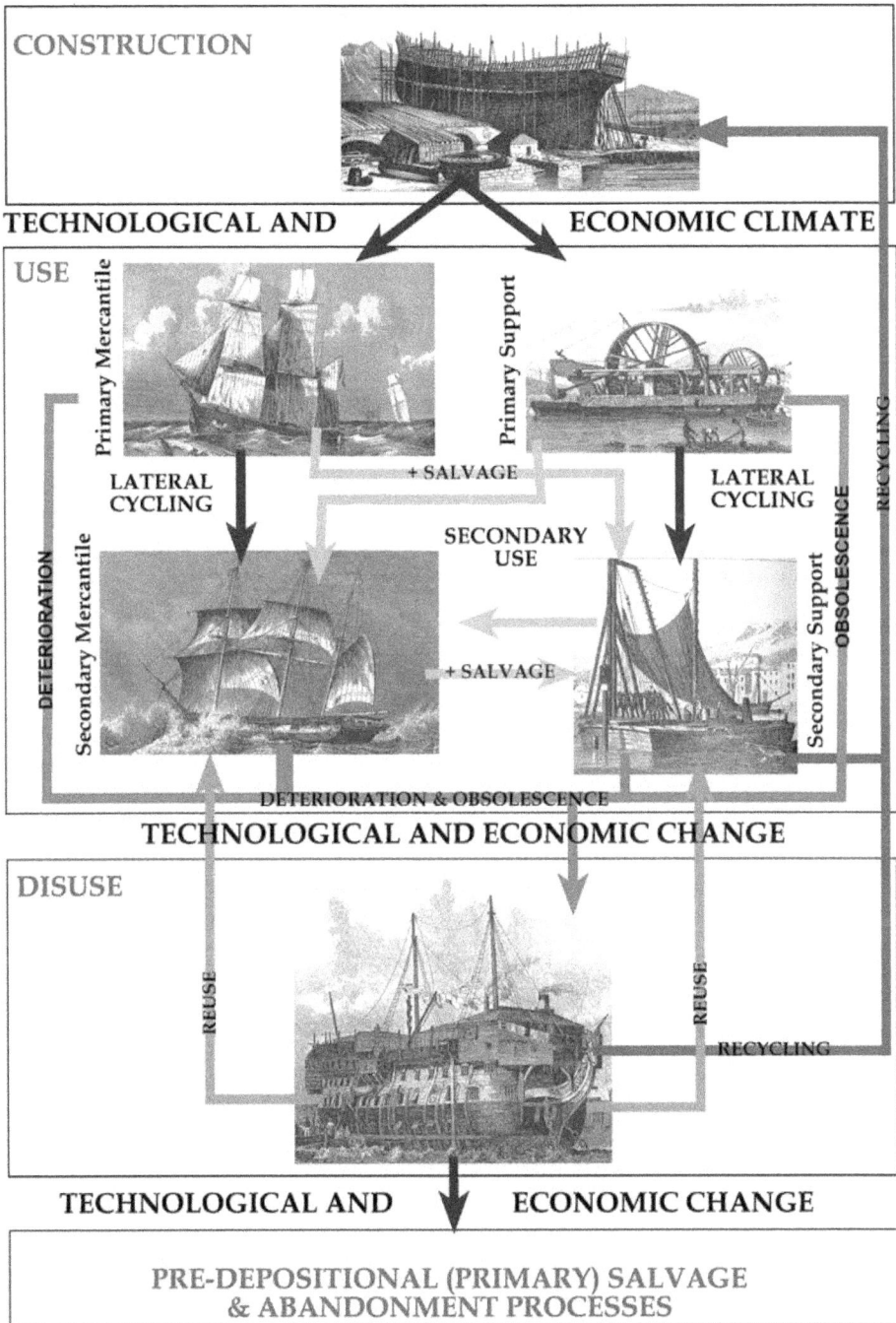

CONSTRUCTION

TECHNOLOGICAL AND   **ECONOMIC CLIMATE**

USE

Primary Mercantile

Primary Support

LATERAL CYCLING

+ SALVAGE

LATERAL CYCLING

RECYCLING

SECONDARY USE

DETERIORATION

Secondary Mercantile

OBSOLESCENCE

Secondary Support

+ SALVAGE

DETERIORATION & OBSOLESCENCE

TECHNOLOGICAL AND ECONOMIC CHANGE

DISUSE

REUSE

REUSE

RECYCLING

TECHNOLOGICAL AND   **ECONOMIC CHANGE**

PRE-DEPOSITIONAL (PRIMARY) SALVAGE & ABANDONMENT PROCESSES

Figure 25. Site formation processes acting on watercraft in their systemic context.

an intended mercantile or commerce related function (such as a collier or tramp steamer). The *primary support* phase refers to watercraft constructed by people for the fulfillment of a noncommerce function as custom-made support vessels (such as towed barges or dredging vessels).

The secondary phase refers to the transformation of a vessel from its originally intended mercantile or support function to another function. Here, there are also two variations. The *secondary mercantile* phase occurs when a shipowner modifies their ship to fulfill a new mercantile role in a different trade (such as the conversion of a cargo steamer into a passenger steamer). *Secondary support*, on the other hand, refers to a shipowner's modification of a vessel to serve nonmercantile, support functions (such as a hulk, barge, or lighter).

There are two important dichotomies in this terminology: primary/secondary where there is a transformation in the *form* of a vessel (intention of build versus intention of modification) and mercantile/support where there is a change in the *function* of a vessel. These terms link with language in site formation theory. Transformations from primary mercantile/support to secondary mercantile/support, for instance, correspond well with Schiffer's definition of secondary use. Changes in the ownership of a vessel with no corresponding change in function or form, whether in a use or support capacity, equate with Schiffer's notion of lateral cycling. As these processes are not readily evident in the archaeological record (due to the lack of alteration to watercraft structure), they do not warrant much discussion here. In some cases, vessels also undergo conversion from a primary support function to a secondary support function. Sarah Kenderdine has illustrated this process in her description of River Murray barges (primary support vessels) converted to pump supports for use in irrigation schemes.[1]

Conversion and Modification

Conversion and modification are processes that occur in watercraft in their systemic context in both primary and secondary (preabandonment) phases. In site formation terms, we can understand this as relating to reuse processes connected with secondary use. Conversion is a process that has been going on for hundreds of years. The conversion of merchant vessels to naval vessels (and vice versa) in particular has occurred for a long time, such as the conversion of the merchant vessel *Baltic* into a confederate ironclad gunboat.[2] Kenderdine has touched on how economic change guides watercraft conversion:

The abandonment of a vessel before the decline of the trade was un-usual unless the hull was difficult to employ in the trade. The conver-sion of . . . [a] vessel from paddle steamer to barge and the fact that it was built by a marine shipwright may indicate that . . . [it] was not particularly capable to carry out the function required of it in the riverine environment.[3]

We can see that there are links between the modification of a ship and the processes that define obsolescence. James Culliton outlines this:

Apart from the physical life of a ship, there is also the possibility that obsolescence will end the economic useful life of a ship. It is not easy to prove that any given ship is obsolete in the sense that the operator would be better off financially to scrap it and replace it with a new one. Frequently, too, a ship which is obsolete for one service can be transferred for to another where competition is not so keen, much in the same fashion as automobiles with useful life were typically traded in by some people who replaced them with new ones, while the old automobiles continued to be used by someone else.[4]

Modifications from Primary to Secondary Mercantile Contexts

Shipowners make many kinds of modification to vessels. The main types of modification are those made to propulsion (as represented by propulsion source and rig) and to the hull (either in dimension or materials). These alterations will normally bring about a change from a primary to secondary mercantile context. Because the owner makes these modifications to their watercraft when they desire it to continue to operate within a trade more efficiently, or to enable its transfer to a new trade, it is implicit that there are correlations between modification activities and times of abandonment. This is because the process of modifying a vessel in order to make it more suitable or commercially competitive is a mechanism designed to save a ship from being discarded (it is in effect a curate behavior). There is often also a correlation between the modification of the hull of a vessel and the addition and modification to its propulsion.

Modifications to Propulsion

Modifications to propulsion normally serve the purposes of technological augmentation or the "upgrade" of a propulsion system to a new, more ef-

Table 5. Percentages of Vessels Undergoing Propulsion Methods Modification

Type	%
Sail (unassisted)	36
Paddle (side wheel)	26
Steam (single screw)	15
Paddle (stern wheel)	11
Steam (twin screw)	4
Sail (auxiliary motor)	5
Motor (single screw)	4

ficient type that will not require the replacement of the entire vessel. Where there is a conversion from one use or from one source of propulsion to another, we may use the term *retrofit*. This term distinguishes types of conversion and more adequately resembles the process of conversion in which owners change vessels to suit the economic climate or new technological standards.[5]

Propulsion modification processes are largely a natural reaction to the introduction of new technologies, especially ones that threatened to overtake and replace old vessel types. Many sail vessels in Tasmania after the 1870s, for instance, had internal combustion engines fitted as a reaction against the economic influence of steamships. As one source has suggested, this modification "fostered a greater challenge in the design of ketches and schooners; they had to be fast to compete!"[6]

A comparison of the earliest configuration of ANAVD vessels and their latest configuration (using Customs House registration documentation) indicates that only fifty-three vessels (about 3.4 percent) underwent changes to their propulsion system. Of these, most changes occurred to unassisted sailing vessels, followed by side-wheel paddle steamers and single-screw steamships (see table 5). This is not surprising considering that shipowners replaced all of these propulsion systems at some time with newer technologies and that these three categories are the three most statistically dominant propulsion types in the database of sites (and about 65 percent of the entire database).

However, if we examine each transition in propulsion system (see table 6), we notice that changes occurred to certain systems, which, if compared to the accepted histories of technological change, appear to be retrograde technological steps. When we consider the types of activities that these changes represent, we can hypothesize the possible economic causes and repercussions that they may exemplify. These changes can all be grouped within the following system. *Technological reduction* refers to the removal of a particular system of propulsion, such as the conversion of powered

Table 6. Types of Modification to Original Propulsion of Abandoned Vessels

Original Propulsion	Final Propulsion	Number	%
Sail (unassisted)	Sail (auxiliary motor)	11	58
	Steam (single screw)	4	21
	Sail (auxiliary steam)	2	11
	Motor (single screw)	1	5
	Motor (twin screw)	1	5
Paddle (side wheel)	Steam (single screw)	5	36
	Paddle (stern wheel)	3	22
	Steam (twin screw)	2	14
	Sail (unassisted)	2	14
	Sail (auxiliary motor)	2	14
Steam (single screw)	Motor (single screw)	4	50
	Sail (unassisted)	2	25
	Sail (auxiliary steam)	1	12.5
	Paddle (stern wheel)	1	12.5
Paddle (stern wheel)	Paddle (side wheel)	5	83
	Steam (single screw)	1	17
Steam (twin screw)	Paddle (side wheel)	1	50
	Motor (single screw)	1	50
Sail (auxiliary motor)	Sail (unassisted)	1	50
	Motor (twin screw)	1	50
Motor (single screw)	Steam (single screw)	2	100

watercraft into sail vessels. This process would be relatively inexpensive and simple and would not generally require substantial rebuilding of the vessel. *Technological augmentation* constitutes a process of addition in which an owner adds new or different technologies to the existing structure, normally as an "upgrade." These processes include the conversion of unassisted sail vessels to auxiliary sail, steam, and motor or paddle vessels. Augmentation activities are comparatively difficult and expensive to carry out. Finally, there is *technological substitution*, by far the most complex process of change, as it involves the removal of one form of motive power and the addition of another. Such a change may constitute substantial structural changes and rebuilding of a vessel at high cost.

In light of these processes, it may be possible to equate events of technological reduction and augmentation with economic issues related to fuel costs, or savings in fuel, and technological substitution with issues relating to fuel efficiency, or changes in trade requirements. For instance, early motor vessels operating on a benzene fuel often converted to steam power because of the prohibitive costs associated with the procurement of that fuel.

Modification to Hull Dimensions and Materials

Modifications to the hull are usually changes in the dimensions and hull material of a vessel. An analysis of the ANAVD shows that historical references to vessels changing the material of their hull is very rare (under 0.5 percent) and is only reflected in seven individual cases (see table 7).

Additionally, these changes seem to be limited to transitions in the use of iron, with five out of the seven vessels changing from iron-hulled to composite-hulled watercraft (in all cases, these vessels remained iron framed), and two changing from timber-hulled to iron-hulled watercraft. This is likely attributable to the fact that (with the exception of the vessel *Manawatu*) all of the vessels were river craft (paddle steamers or barges).

Changes to the hull of a vessel normally constitute an extension or contraction of dimensions and tonnage. The main, and apparently easiest, modification that is made to vessels, especially wooden ones, involved the

Table 7. ANAVD Watercraft that Have Undergone Changes in Their Hull Material Type

Vessel Name	Original Material	Year of Change	Final Material	Propulsion
Rapid	Wood	Unknown	Iron	Paddle steamer
Kelpie	Iron	1875	Composite (iron frames)	Paddle steamer
Pride of the Murray	Wood	1891	Iron	Paddle steamer
Ariel	Iron	1876	Composite (iron frames)	Paddle steamer
Corowa	Iron	1921	Composite (iron frames)	Paddle steamer
Manawatu	Iron	1882	Composite (iron frames)	Screw steamer
Albemarle	Iron	1914	Composite (iron frames)	River barge

Table 8. Dimension Modification in Modified Abandoned Watercraft, the Number of Vessels Represented, and the Percentage (Rounded to Nearest .1%) of Changes to Dimensions (n = 153 Watercraft)

Dimension	Change	Number	%
Length	Increased	80	52.3
	Decreased	22	14.4
	Unchanged	51	33.3
Breadth	Increased	54	35.3
	Decreased	25	16.3
	Unchanged	74	48.4
Depth	Increased	30	19.6
	Decreased	44	28.8
	Unchanged	79	51.6

twofold increase to length and tonnage through the cutting of a vessel in half and the building of a new amidships section. ANAVD data shows that at least 153 (about 10 percent) abandoned vessels underwent modifications to increase size. These values are presented in table 8.

Although a simple analysis (as seen in table 8) suggests that dimension changes tended to constitute an increase to length with no changes to breadth or depth, a more detailed investigation shows that changes to length generally had little effect on corresponding changes to breadth or depth. However, changes to the breadth of a vessel often brought about substantial changes to its depth dimension. This is illustrated in figures 26, 27, and 28, which present this data according to changes in the length, breadth, and depth measurements in relation to one another.

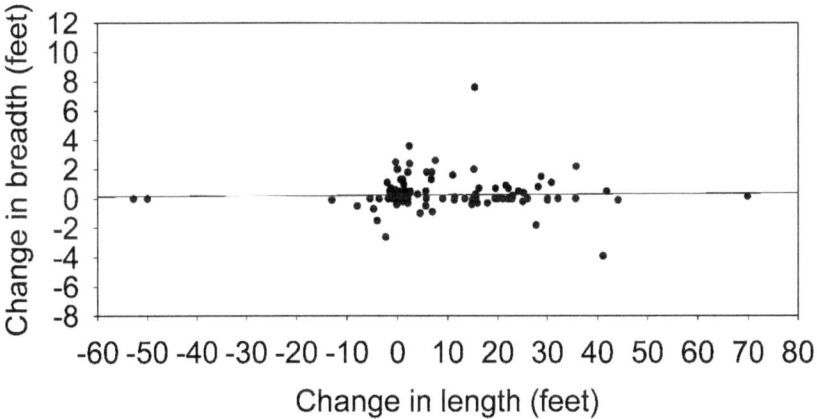

Figure 26. Changes in length dimension with corresponding changes in breadth dimensions.

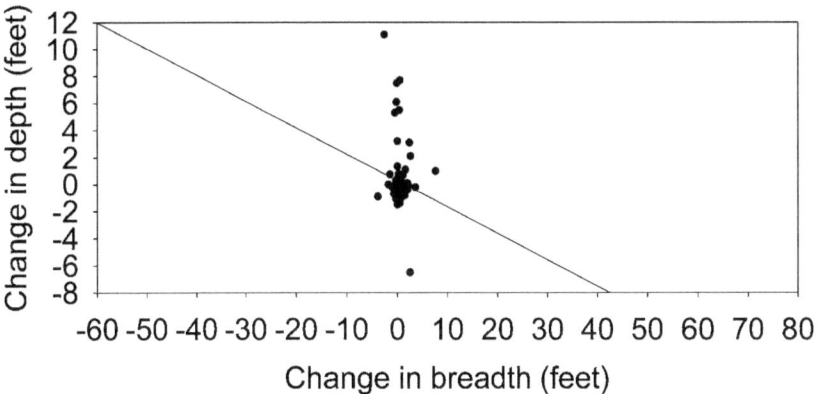

Figure 27. Changes in breadth dimension with corresponding changes in depth dimensions.

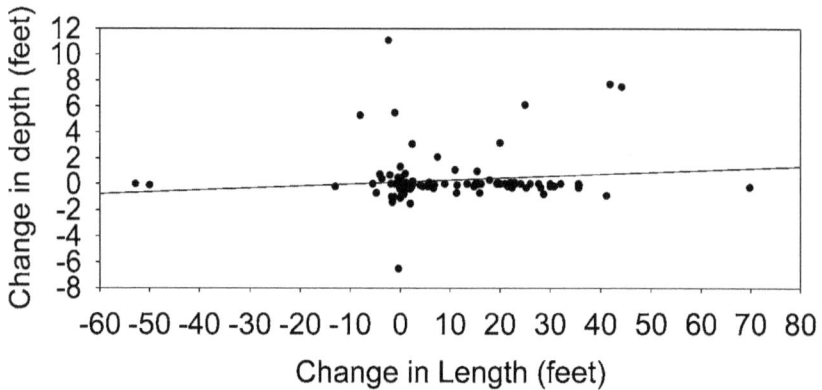

Figure 28. Changes in length dimension with corresponding changes in depth dimensions.

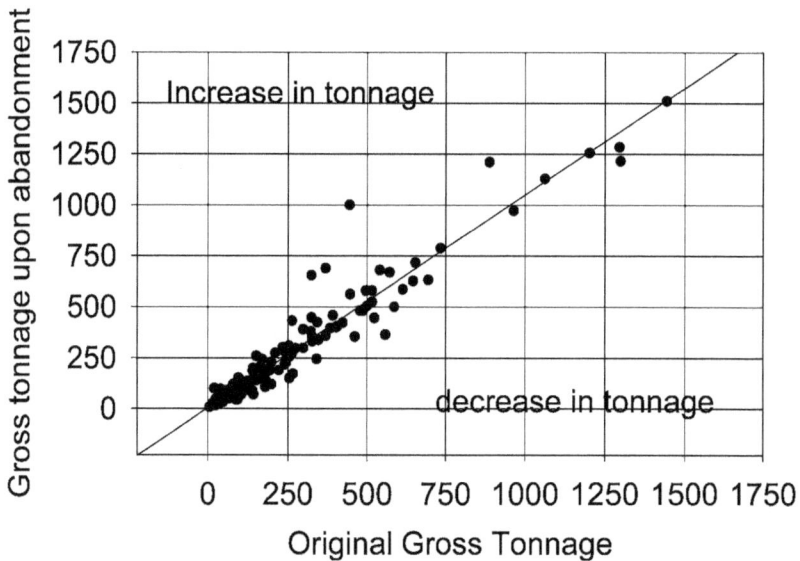

Figure 29. Changes in tonnage due to modification (n = 153 watercraft).

The database also lists 153 vessels as having undergone modifications that changed their gross tonnage. The simple analysis of changes in tonnage (table 9) shows that the majority of conversions actually reduced the tonnage values of most of the vessels. If we examine this in relation to the actual size of the changes that occurred (fig. 29), we can see that in most cases the change in size of a vessel was normally not substantial.

Table 9. Change in GRT Following Vessel Modification (n = 153 Watercraft; Percentage Rounded to Nearest 0.1%)

Change	Number	%
Increased	67	36.6
Decreased	107	56.5
Unchanged	9	4.9

Arguably, these figures suggest that the vessels are not going through modification for the purposes of simply increasing their capacity to carry more goods or transport more passengers but are undergoing modification for other purposes. This may be because of a change in trade that requires operation in new locations with certain environmental constraints, or it may indicate that modifications are occurring to increase the efficiency of watercraft. These modifications, however, also have consequences on the duration of use of a vessel. In relation to the use-life of abandoned watercraft, the analysis of the ANAVD suggests that the investment in modification added an average of nine years to vessel use-life. In relation to watercraft dimensions, the ANAVD has data on 1,388 ships for which there is no mention of major modification to a length, breadth, or depth and 159 ships that underwent such modifications.

Of the 1,059 vessels in the database with known dates of build and abandonment, 928 had no changes made to their dimensions, and 131 went through modification. Likewise, with regard to changes in the gross tonnage of vessels, there are 1,359 vessels cited as not having undergone modifications to their gross tonnage and 154 that had. Of the 1,059 vessels in the database with known dates of build and abandonment, 905 were unmodified and 154 were. According to this analysis, modified vessels lasted on average a decade longer (expanded below).

Support Functions and Modification

Of special interest is the conversion of vessels from their primary and secondary mercantile uses to other functions. In particular, their conversion for secondary support functions, such as conversion to lighters and hulks, is of interest because in some cases this reuse mechanism can represent both secondary use and recycling processes.

There are many types of hulk, the most common of which was the cargo hulk.[7] Cargo hulks, or vessels used for the storage of materials, were mainly coal and gunpowder hulks (see fig. 30).[8] Each descriptive category of vessel

Figure 30. The *Aladdin* as a Tasmanian government powder hulk. W. L. Crowther Library. By permission of the State Library of Tasmania.

has further variations according to what kind of barge, hulk, or lighter it was. This tells us something about the demand for watercraft fulfilling support roles, the types of stresses subjected to these ships, and the duration of hulk use-life. The choice of a wooden vessel as a gunpowder or explosives hulk, for instance, would not have made much sense in the late nineteenth or early twentieth centuries when ferrous-hulled vessels were available because wood absorbs nitroglycerin from sweating TNT and becomes explosive.

The categorization of secondary support vessels is problematic because of the nature of the work these watercraft engaged in. Although some may have fulfilled a singular secondary support role, others carried out many functions at once, or throughout their secondary support lifespan. Of the 532 vessels, the ANAVD lists at least 95 as fulfilling two secondary support roles and at least five as performing three secondary support roles. In some cases, this is also because of gray areas in how researchers describe support vessels. For example, a "coal hulk" is different from a "coal lighter" according to definitions that indicate that "hulk" refers to stationary vessels and "lighter" refers to a towed vessel.

Conversion of a vessel to a secondary support role happened for a range of economic reasons. Normally a vessel became unwanted because of its condition and age (and hence an inability to gain marine insurance) or its representation of an old technology seen as uneconomic. In other cases, it was because a particular trade disappeared or ceased to be viable, or instances where a vessel had been damaged. However, for a ship to be turned into a hulk there needed to be a demand for the fulfillment of such a secondary role, and the vessel had to be of an appropriate type for its new function. In addition, Lincoln Paine notes that many-masted schooner rigged vessels required a large crew, and that this was the main reason the rig became obsolete in Maine.[9]

Large crew requirements were also responsible for the conversion of schooners into barges and other secondary support vessels more than any other type. Additionally, Stanley Gerr has suggested that schooner rigged vessels underwent increased wear and tear because their swinging booms and gaffs act as energy sponges that contribute to higher rates of loss and shorter lifespans.[10] Understanding this, we may be able to determine a correlation between rig and rig transition through a vessel's working life and a correlation between a ship's final rig configuration and the tendency to convert to secondary use. Of the 532 vessels listed in the ANAVD as hulked, 307 were rigged, and historical documentation lists their rig configuration. Of these, the two most common rig types were the barque rig (36 percent) and schooner rig (35 percent).

There is currently no published analysis of the rig configuration of watercraft operating in Australia over the period covered by this study (1806 to 2001) that is comparable to the ANAVD. The data pertaining to "vessel type" in the AHSD (accessed 24 June 2002) was the closest comparable data set found. There are 5,972 shipwrecks and forty-two "vessel type" designations. Of these, there are eighteen separate designations of rig ("schooner rig" is made up of five separate designations), which cover 3,499 shipwrecks (or 58.59 percent of the database). A breakdown of prevalent rig configurations shows that the abandonment data is significantly different from shipwreck data, with the five most common rigs being the schooner rig (33.58 percent), ketch rig (16.09 percent), cutter rig (14.4 percent), barque rig (11.49 percent), and brig rig (6.49 percent). It should be noted that this field is an amalgam of "rig," "type," and "function" attributes and not set up for this kind of analysis because type and function descriptions tend to obscure rig configurations (i.e., a vessel designated as "fishing boat" may or may not be rigged).

Although we can often find support vessels described in the historical literature, researchers have not explored support roles in depth. What is obvious is that the demands for these functions varied over time depending on economic issues (local as well as international), port infrastructure, port

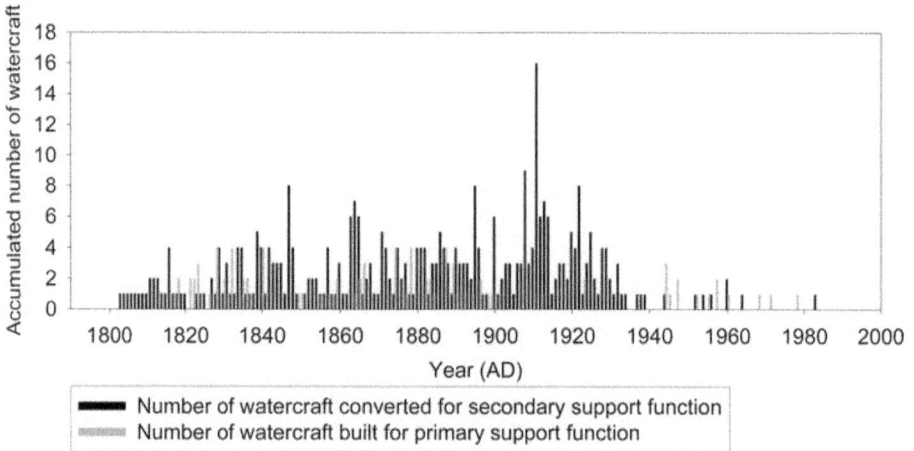

Figure 31. Comparison of the years of build of primary support vessels and the years of modification of vessels to secondary support functions (n = 296).

development, and a range of other influences. It appears that custom-made (primary) support vessels have tended to be barges, punts, pontoons, and sometimes lighters, whereas vessels fulfilling secondary support roles have almost exclusively tended to be described as hulks or lighters. The distinction between categories of support is important. If shipbuilders constructed vessels with the intention of fulfilling support functions, there is likely to be less of a chance that there will be a high demand for the conversion of other watercraft into hulks. The consequences of this are that shipowners are more likely to repair vessels for the continuation of their primary role or will abandon them earlier due to the lack of demand for any alternative function. Figure 31 shows that shipbuilders tend to construct primary support vessels in years when there is low demand for the conversion of commercially active watercraft for secondary support. We can expect these correlations to be more marked in riverine trades because of the reliance on the use of barges in many river trades in Australia (such as wool transportation).

Many vessels seem to have undergone conversions from functional merchant vessels to barges and lighters.[11] This process often occurs to vessels with a history of costly repairs. Such substantial investments tended to make owners choose a particular vessel for the fulfillment of a subsequent support role rather than a continued mercantile function. Another trend evident in the historical literature is that before the rise of steam propulsion, it was more likely that an owner would not condemn a vessel before converting it into a barge.[12]

On the Australian rivers, the trend is the same, with functional paddle steamers such as the *Lady Augusta* and *Lady Daly*, which often towed barges, becoming barges for a period before finally being abandoned.[13]

As R. W. Glassford points out, vessels have been hulked in Australia from at least the 1830s, but most of the details regarding these vessels have been lost. In particular, he points to some of the earliest examples being lighters employed as prison and powder hulks and wool lighters. He also mentions grain hulks and grain-mill ships but admits that the coal hulk was the most common form of hulk.[14] The overwhelming need for the conversion of vessels in Australian ports into hulks was due to demand for coal-bunkering facilities. With the growth and popularity of the oil-fired and diesel-powered vessel, the need for such bunkering facilities ceased, causing a new wave of abandonment.[15] From the 1930s, changes in technology began to have an influence on the usefulness of hulks:

> The oil-fired boiler, the diesel engine, and now the gas turbine have between them rendered the coal hulk obsolete, while the ports of the wheatfields have built silos to take the place of grain hulks. As a result, the number of surviving hulks in Australia is dwindling rapidly, and very soon now there will be none left at all.[16]

In other words, these technological transitions ushered in a period when the obsolete mercantile vessels converted by their owners into coal hulks became obsolete a second time. One newspaper noted this in relation to the breaking up of the vessel *Graham* in 1933: "With the passing of sail the *Elizabeth Graham* became the hulk *Graham*, but oil burning vessels have now made even a coal hulk an anachronism."[17]

Glassford, however, had noted that "the States which produce no steaming coal of their own suitable for firing marine boilers were those that had the greatest number of coal hulks, namely, Victoria, South Australia and Western Australia."[18] Analysis of the abandonment data suggests a different conclusion: The three states with the largest number of coal support vessels (that is, any hulk, lighter, or barge used for coal bunkering) were abandoned in Western Australia, Queensland, and Tasmania (see table 10).

Indeed, a more in-depth investigation of coal bunkering in Tasmania illustrates that the ANAVD is a better reflection of reality than Glassford's information. Tasmania's ports used hulks extensively, as indicated by the Marine Board's boast that they had more coal bunkered at Hobart than any

Table 10. Breakdown of States with Abandoned Watercraft that Had Been Coal-Trade Support Vessels

State	%
Western Australia	26
Queensland	21
Tasmania	17
South Australia	11
Victoria	10
Unknown	8
New South Wales	6
Northern Territory	1

other port outside of Newcastle (New South Wales). Coal hulks were to be an integral part of trade in Hobart well into the 1930s, and some vessels, such as the *Jessie Craig* and *Aldebaran*, were still in operation (mainly due to their exemption from marine survey) into the 1940s.[19] Likewise, hulks were used extensively in Queensland, mainly because of the joint influence of Burns, Philp and Company and the Australasian United Steamship Navigation Company, which from 1888 co-owned the Carpentaria Lighterage Company, which operated along most of the Queensland coastline.[20]

If we look at the time of abandonment of coal hulks/lighters/barges between 1850 and 1970, we can see that the early 1900s, mid-1920s, and especially the early 1930s and late 1940s were the main periods of the abandonment of coal hulks (fig. 32). In other ports, barges, hulks, and lighters were in use until replaced by new port infrastructure. This was the case at Port Adelaide, where ship operators used secondary support vessels until the construction of the outer harbor.[21] This was due to a combination of factors, with some vessels built for the construction of the harbor no longer required and others no longer needed due to new fuel storage facilities.

Special Support Roles

Not all modification of vessels to secondary support functions relates to the internal workings of harbors. In many cases, owners converted their ships to exceptionally specialized uses. Likewise, not all hulks were dead ships into which no investment went. The vessel *Fortuna* (former *Macquarie*), for instance, was converted into a coal hulk in 1909 and then augmented with mechanical elevators in 1920 to become a floating plant and mechanical coal hulk.[22]

One common procedure for reuse was for vessels to become lodgings after hulking (and some after abandonment). The vessel *Snimos King*, for in-

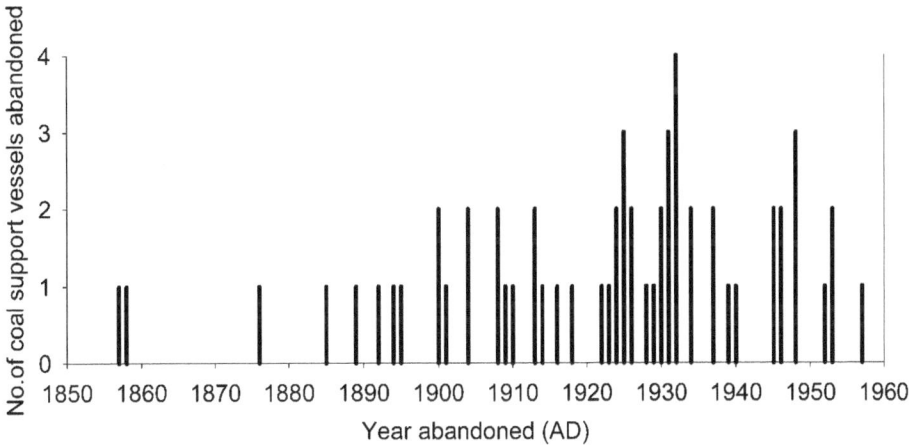

Figure 32. The abandonment of support vessels associated with coal bunkering, 1850–1970 (n = 75).

stance, was rumored at one stage to be about to be converted into a floating circus big top by a Japanese consortium, and the *Prince George* was sold to become an Alaskan hotel.[23] In many cases, these conversions occur because of the same economic circumstances that precipitate the modification of vessels. Sometimes they proceed due to the whims of corporations and the gimmick value of juxtaposing new, nontraditional functions on watercraft.

A number of vessels are noted as having served "specialized" roles (see table 11). These watercraft served functions such as accommodation vessels/residences, bathhouses, bridges, fish depots, chapels, restaurants, sugar mills, crushing plants, workshops, and wreck-raising hulks. Additionally, at least three vessels served more than one specialized role. Historical sources show that the *Fitzjames* served as a reformatory hulk and quarantine hulk. The former HMVS *Cerberus* served as both a floating magazine and floating workshop, and the *Garthneill* was a floating grain mill/grain grading plant and residence (fig. 33).

The Consequences of Support-related Modification

Scholars have written very little on the actual process of converting a vessel for a secondary support role. Ian Warne has briefly described the process of the conversion of the vessel *Lalla* to a lighter around 1906.[24] It entailed the slight shortening of the vessel, the removal of masts, and the addition of a towline. In most cases, the transformation of a vessel into a secondary sup-

Table 11. Vessels Known to Have Fulfilled Special Support Roles upon Conversion

Name of Vessel	Function
Anson (1812–1850)	Accommodation/residence
Ben Bolt (1852–1864)	Bathhouse
City of Adelaide (1864–1915)	Bathhouse
City of Grafton (1876–1930)	Accommodation/residence
Clyde (1884–?)	Fish depot
Excelsior (1882–1948)	Floating workshop
Gem (1868–1927)	Bridge
Jupiter (1866–1940)	Fish depot
Pride of the Murray (1865–1910)	Floating workshop
Sesa (1869–1928)	Accommodation/residence
Sir William Molesworth (1848–1876)	Accommodation/residence
Sir William Wallace (1824–1850)	Floating chapel
Sophia (1800–?)	Floating chapel
Sunbeam (1857–1909)	Wreck raising hulk
Swan (1916–1934)	Accommodation/residence
Trinity Bay (1912–1981)	Floating restaurant
Walrus (1864–1879)	Floating sugar mill/crushing plant

Figure 33. The *Garthneill* as grain silo, 1930. Ron Blum Collection. By permission of Ron Blum.

port vessel was the last stage in its working life. For this reason, the hulking of a vessel is a functional preabandonment use (adaptive reuse). This was not always the case. Sometimes, such as during World War I, the shortage of coastal shipping in Australia meant that authorities refitted or converted coal hulks for primary trade functions.[25] Hulks and lighters would have had their function as support vessels continually assessed much in the same manner as if they were fulfilling primary functions. When the vessel started to leak, and it became uneconomical to repair, someone would salvage and discard it.[26]

The hulking of a vessel had substantial economic ramifications for a shipowner. Although a shipowner may have liked his vessel to be in use forever, of course, such a situation was never a reality. For this reason, the next preference was to use a vessel for some purpose other than its "as built" function. Here, the most obvious opportunity was the hulking of a vessel. Of ships in the entire ANAVD, 532 (34.5 percent) were used for support roles. Out of this number, 90 (16.9 percent) fulfilled this role upon construction (primary support) and 442 (83.1 percent) fulfilled this function after hulking (secondary support), a reflection of the options undertaken by shipowners to gain money from unusable vessels or make money from hulk trades. There are 1,059 vessels with known date of build and known date of abandonment in the ANAVD. Of these, 346 were built for one purpose and hulked (secondary support), 45 were built as hulks (primary support), and 668 were never hulked (used in primary use roles only).

Culliton has commented, "It is sometimes accepted, especially by legislation, that the life of a ship is twenty years. Experience seems to indicate that physically at least ships last much longer than 20 years."[27] The results displayed in table 12 indicate that the life of a ship was more than twenty years, confirming Culliton's assertion about extended existence. The averages of the lifespan for each category illustrates the advantages of hulking, with a difference of twelve years between the vessels that were never hulked and the vessels that served as hulks (see table 13). The vessels that were built as hulks (primary support vessels) only lasted on average about three years longer than vessels that had never been hulked, illustrating that they were probably more cheaply built and subjected to more wear, tear, and rough handling while also being used in more protected working environments. These figures confirm those presented by Nathan Richards regarding the average age of abandoned vessels in the Garden Island Ships' Graveyard.[28]

A more complex examination that incorporates a comparison of modified vessels from the perspective of changes in dimension and gross tonnage supports this assertion and backs up earlier conclusions concerning the

Table 12. Average Lifespan of Unhulked and Hulked Watercraft (Rounded to Nearest Number) (n = 1,059 Watercraft)

Category	Years
Primary and secondary use only	39
Primary support	42
Secondary support	51

Table 13. Average Lifespan of Modified and Unmodified (Based on Changes in Dimension), Unhulked and Hulked Watercraft (Rounded to Nearest Whole Year) (n = 1,059 Watercraft)

Category	Modification	Years
Overall	Modified	51
Overall	Unmodified	42
Primary and secondary use only	Modified	48
Primary and secondary use only	Unmodified	38
Overall support	Modified	55
Overall support	Unmodified	49
Primary support	Modified	43
Primary support	Unmodified	42
Secondary support	Modified	56
Secondary support	Unmodified	48

advantages of modification (see tables 13 and 14). These figures clearly support the theory that support vessels survive longer than other vessels and that modified vessels in all categories outlast unmodified vessels. However, this analysis also illustrates that modification was a substantial benefit to vessels fulfilling primary and secondary uses, and that modification was only of slight benefit to vessels built in primary support roles. This may be because people made high-quality repairs to primary use vessels and shoddy repairs to low-quality primary support vessels.

Additionally, a diachronic analysis shows that across time, and despite technological innovation, watercraft use-life decreased drastically between 1790 and 1990 (fig. 34). Although this trend is undoubtedly influenced by the smaller number of vessels built at the beginning and end of this period (as seen in figure 1), it may indicate the influence of the steam engine in replacing sail vessels in the early nineteenth century. Another factor was the replacement of steam technologies in the 1920s and 1930s. This brought about the replacement of support vessels, particularly for coal bunkering purposes, and played a major role in the reduction in the duration of watercraft use-life. We may also attribute this to the transition toward the

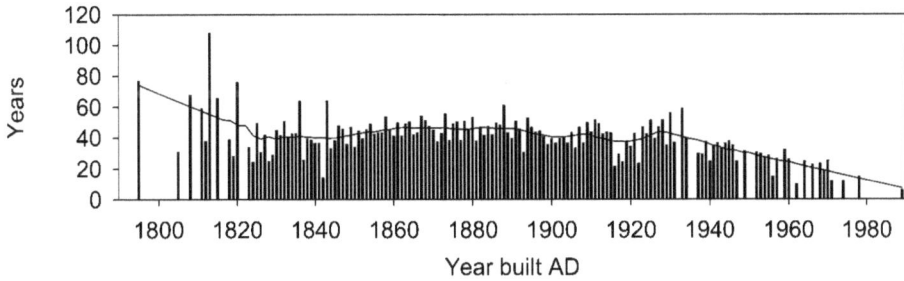

Figure 34. The average lifespan of abandoned watercraft (1790–1990) (n = 1,059 watercraft).

Table 14. Average Lifespan of Modified and Unmodified (Based on Changes in Gross Tonnage), Unhulked and Hulked Watercraft (Rounded to Nearest Whole Year) (n = 1,059 Watercraft)

Category	Modification	Years
Overall	Modified	52
Overall	Unmodified	42
Primary and secondary use only	Modified	49
Primary and secondary use only	Unmodified	38
Overall support	Modified	55
Overall support	Unmodified	49
Primary support	Modified	42
Primary support	Unmodified	42
Secondary support	Modified	56
Secondary support	Unmodified	50

mass production of watercraft and the increasing perception of ships as throwaway items with limited "use-by dates."

Functional Postabandonment Use

The term *postabandonment use* implies that a vessel has been discarded, but with a continued functional role in mind. In these cases, a vessel, while undergoing a range of placement assurance, salvage, and hull reduction processes (see the following chapter), will remain largely within a systemic context. Postabandonment use is multifaceted. The most common functional postabandonment use for unwanted vessels was as breakwaters. Of this there are many examples, such as the vessel *William Pitt*, sunk at Fortescue Bay, Tasmania, in the 1960s as a breakwater for small vessels (fig. 35).[29]

Figure 35. The *William Pitt* at Fortescue Bay, Tasman Peninsula, Tasmania. Photo by Nathan Richards.

Indeed, Jack Loney suggests that people used many old iron-hulled vessels specifically for breakwaters around small islands or in harbor contexts. The choice of iron-hulled vessels, especially as breakwaters, is attributed to the hardy nature and slower rate of corrosion and deterioration of iron when compared to both wood and steel.[30] This, however, was not just restricted to metal-hulled vessels, and there are cases where people used wooden-hulled ships for similar functions. Once again, the use of unwanted vessels as breakwaters illustrates the economic issues that surround their abandonment. In 1912, the *South Australian Register* newspaper quoted the president of the Marine Board of Port Adelaide as being a "firm believer in the efficacy of using hulks on the formation of breakwaters."[31] The government offered two hulks to the engineer in chief at Hog Bay, Kangaroo Island, for the purposes of breakwater construction. On the decline of the offer, the government proposed a similar scheme for the outer harbor at Port Adelaide. On this matter, the Marine Board sought correspondence with the Public Works Department of the New South Wales Government. Despite information that the use of hulks at Newcastle (apparently for the construction of the Northern breakwater) had saved the New South Wales government more than four thousand pounds in stone costs, the South Australian plans were again declined, and the strategy was never enacted.

Other postabandonment functions include the use of the barque *Othello* as a landing stage and wharf at the Kaipipi Shipyard, Paterson Inlet (New Zealand), in 1927, a common function for unwanted watercraft.[32] In 1949, the newspaper the *News* similarly reported the use of a sunken ship as a wharf:

Port Moresby—A Japanese ship of about 10,000 tons, which was bombed and sunk in Rabaul Harbor during the war is now being used as a wharf for a small ship. The vessel is upright in shallow water near the shore. A wooden approach has been built to the ship from the shore and much of the superstructure has been removed. The new wharf is speeding up the turn-around of coastal ships.[33]

The database lists only about 7 percent (115 vessels) of abandoned vessels as fulfilling postabandonment uses. Of these, 112 (about 97 percent) served as structures. Some of these vessels have served a range of functions related to their use as items of port or out-port infrastructure. Watercraft such as the *Python*, *S.F. Hersey*, *Margaret Poynter*, and *St. George* served as piers, the *Induna* as a wharf, and an unidentified lighter at Port Welshpool was reputed to have served as an immovable coffer. Additionally, the Penrice/No. 1 hulk is known to have served as an immovable explosives storage depot (and later was used to reinforce an embankment), and the vessel *Rhea* was scuttled off Sydney Heads with a load of waste.

More common postabandonment uses come in the form of artificial reef formations (45 vessels), breakwaters (30 vessels), reclamation devices (20 vessels), and protective structures (eight vessels). For some sites, such as the Tangalooma artificial reef (fig. 36), categorization is more problematic because it can be regarded as an artificial reef, boat harbor, and breakwater. The three other nonstructurally used watercraft include the vessels *Psyche*

Figure 36. The Tangalooma Ships' Graveyard, Moreton Island, Queensland. Photo by Nathan Richards.

and *W. H. Gemini*, which were explicitly sunk to provide a dive training site, and the vessel *Inca*, which was deliberately burnt for the movie *For the Term of His Natural Life* (1926).

Artificial Reefs and FAD

Artificial reefs pose a small problem in the analysis of ship disposal because of their relationship to other aspects of sea dumping. These artificial reef systems are not exclusively composed of vessel material, having a broad range of other materials used in their construction. For this reason, vessels abandoned as artificial reefs are often also found with other materials. Darwin Harbor, for instance, has numerous artificial reefs made up of vessels and other materials such as freight containers and even a large bottle-washing machine.[34] Queensland artificial reefs, on the other had, contain a diverse array of materials, from old Brisbane trams and dry dock gates to old concrete pipes. An additional problem in researching artificial reefs is that people often dump many small pontoons on site. These vessels are often unnamed and accompanied with very little documentation, making them part of the "invisible" abandonment resource that may change the analyses undertaken in this research.

The domination of artificial reefs in postabandonment contexts is a worldwide phenomenon, and many artificial reef organizations exist in many nations that vie for unwanted vessels for the creation of such sites. One of the best examples of this are the Liberty ships of the Texas Artificial Reef Program.[35] This program commenced in the mid-1970s with the scuttling of twelve World War II Liberty ships in the Gulf of Mexico. This allowed for some degree of preservation (as dive sites) and enabled the vessels to serve the community as fish aggregation devices (FADs).[36] The federal Congress had originally offered the surplus vessels to the coastal states of the United States in 1972. The enacting of the federal Abandoned Shipwreck Act of 1987 has meant that Texas has had to provide private-sector access and develop cultural education on the heavily salvaged vessels.[37]

The Canadians also have had a long and successful history in the use of vessels as artificial reefs, mainly through the Artificial Reef Society of British Columbia. The Canadian navy antisubmarine warship HMCS *Chaudiere* (1959–93), sunk off Nanaimo, British Columbia, in April 1994, is reputed to be the largest artificial reef in North America (and the third largest in the world). Creation of this artificial reef, however, stirred up much debate about the issues of environmental management.[38] Other examples, such as the sinking of the *G. B. Church* near Sidney, British Columbia, in August 1991, has parallels with Australia regarding the financial benefits that were projected to result from the sinking (five million Canadian dollars). Similarly, the *West Australian* newspaper projected that the sinking of the HMAS *Swan* in Western Australia would produce about one and a half million Australian dollars.[39]

Indeed, artificial reef schemes have been operating for some time in Australia, and the use of obsolete vessels for the purposes of creating artificial reefs and fish aggregation devices have occurred in every state. Organizations have established a number of artificial reefs in Victoria, including the vessels *George Kermode* and *Uralba*.[40] The Department of Primary Industries and Fisheries began the first official artificial reef, known as Fenton Patches, in Darwin Harbor in 1988.[41] The Darwin Port Authority is also responsible for "strategically" locating several "steel derelict vessels to further enhance fishing opportunities,"[42] illustrating that the continued creation of FADs is an ongoing part of fisheries management.

The decision to use an obsolete vessel for either an artificial reef or FAD is not straightforward. Today organizations create these sites with safe, clean vessels, and there must be inspection of the seabed prior to scuttling to ensure that the vessel will not damage sea grass. Additionally, the vessels should come to lie on a flat seabed, containing little marine life.[43] An application for a permit under the Environmental Protection (Sea Dumping) Act of 1981 for the creation of an artificial reef must also be made. This application covers many issues, such as community consultation, financial and business matters, safety (navigational and diver), environmental factors, purpose, location, site selection, vessel preparation, sinking management, logistics, and postscuttling management.

Studies in Darwin Harbor on two abandoned vessels, the *Marchart 3* and the so-called dumb barge, have suggested that in order to make a vessel an appropriate and effective artificial reef, modifications should be made to the structure to be sunk. This includes the addition of protruding objects and the removal of solid or continuous horizontal surfaces.[44] Often structural modifications are also made for dive tourism purposes in order to allow for greater diver safety.[45] Coupled with the lack of substantial salvage, this shows that the behavioral aspects of the abandonment are enshrined in the material remains of the vessel on sinking. The use and modification of vessels as artificial reefs, FADs, and dive tourism sites will have consequences on the perception of historical significance under law. Current studies indicate that vessels with a high surface area, many holes, and few continuous horizontal surfaces such as decks are best suited in this capacity because they encourage three-dimensional growth, small coral reef fish, and predatory fish habitation. In order to ensure high surface area modifications to the hull of the would-be scuttled vessel, researchers recommended cutting into it and adding additional protruding features.[46] If organizations sink these vessels in Commonwealth waters, after seventy-five years federal legislation will reclassify them as historic wrecks.

Fish attraction and fish productivity are the two major reasons for the creation of artificial reefs. Due to this, scientists base the effectiveness of an artificial reef on the accumulation of nutrients, adequate water flow, and levels of light. Different species and fish of different ages require different amounts of these variables. Although initially thought to be the perfect way to create enriched marine environments, recent discussion has shown that there is a range of positive and negative aspects to the formation of artificial reefs. The perception of these negative environmental factors can stall attempts at the creation of artificial reefs, irrespective of their intended purpose.[47] The environmental concerns often tabled are multifaceted and range from fear of environmental pollution due to materials (such as asbestos) or fuels (causing chemical slicks) left onboard the vessel on their sinking to their impact on fish stocks. There are also concerns among some experts that vessels do not generally make good fish habitats.[48]

Nevertheless, the sinking of vessels is now commonplace due to the direct and indirect benefits to communities through dive recreation and tourism rather than environmental benefits.[49] This is evident from the way the abandonment of vessels for postabandonment uses has become a major social issue. The sinking of artificial reefs in Australia has become important to tourism strategy, as it is in Canada, but on a more localized scale. In Australia, regional artificial reef societies are powerful lobbying groups. Indeed, the Western Australian artificial reef program has been substantially influenced by Canadian circumstances, with advice from the Artificial Reef Society of British Columbia being sought.[50] This is particularly the case in the decommissioning of former Australian navy vessels, which have become the focus of the most recent phase of vessel abandonment. The deliberate scuttling of these vessels is not a continuation of the use of the sea as dumping ground but has serious ramifications for local communities.

In many instances, communities have forcefully petitioned for the right to have vessels scuttled near their shorelines in order to attract dive tourism and for fish aggregation. The debate over the sinking of the HMAS *Derwent*, according to government sources, became so heated that the vessel was mentioned in Commonwealth Parliament, as was the case of the HMAS *Swan* before it.[51] This phenomenon has seen local communities in Western Australia becoming increasingly competitive in gaining control of the scuttling location of these vessels. Arguably, this began with the scuttling of the HMAS *Derwent* to attract visitors and allow the Australian navy to conduct experiments on the ship. These experiments were designed to help "the Navy build more durable and safer ships for the future."[52] This continued with the abandonment of the *Swan* in 1997 and the scuttling of the Australian Destroyer HMAS *Perth* on 30 August 1999.[53] Sources cite the costs for the initial sinking of the *Derwent* as about fifty thousand dollars, but it was said to have blown out "exponentially."[54]

A dispute over the *Swan* erupted in 1994, with battle lines drawn between the Western Australian towns of Rockingham and Busselton. During this fight, the vessel seemed to become a political bargaining tool, often involving state and federal tourism and environment agencies and even prominent politicians.[55] The eventual disposal of the vessel off Dunsborough, Geographe Bay, on 14 December 1997 made front-page news.[56] Likewise, the sinking of the HMAS *Hobart* off the South Australian coast (scheduled for December 2002) has proved problematic for a range of reasons.

This transition toward an abandonment strategy for vessels that revolves around tourism and fish aggregation is significant because it changes the traditional spatial dynamic of abandonment. It has precipitated a transition from inner harbor abandonment at major ports to isolated, regional abandonment.

Conclusion

This chapter has outlined a number of issues. On one hand, it gives credence to the need to reassess the role of support vessels in maritime economies and in port development. This is especially clear in relation to the long lives of modified watercraft and support vessels, the connections between the manufacture of support vessels and hulking activities, and their prolonged use as tools of trade. Vessels fulfilling support functions are also important reminders of economic trends through the financial opportunities that they represented to shipowners when their vessels became useless. They are also indicators of the costs of technological innovation when changes to fuel and propulsion technologies brought about their displacement.

However, this research is of archaeological interest because it illustrates the connection between conversion and reuse processes and other associated behaviors that are evident in other countries. Even today, most discard and postabandonment use occurs because of perceived economic benefits, irrespective of any legislative or regulatory changes. And the signatures of these processes are evidence of behavioral change.

The modification and conversion of the function, form, and material of watercraft are important to consider in archaeological site formation for a number of reasons. Transformation processes in systemic contexts have direct and quantifiable effects on the archaeological record, especially in relation to lateral cycling and secondary use processes. In this way, we can see that preabandonment circumstances have a large effect on abandonment processes and potential postabandonment use. Use and modification processes are important because they have direct influences on discard practices and change the time and nature of the transformation of a vessel from a systemic to an archaeological context. We can see this particularly in use-life analysis of abandoned watercraft. Moreover, the analysis of use-life is also an analysis of technological change—an analysis that challenges notions of unilinear technological change. Conversion processes are themselves linked with economic and technological changes. Conversion and hulking is dependent on economic demand for support roles, and this demand is itself dependent on the demand created by new technologies. This demonstrates the interconnectedness of technological, economic, and archaeological processes.

7

The Signatures of Discard

A reverberating explosion, followed soon by another, then another, as gelignite explosions opened the ship to the ocean. The vessel shuddered, then listed to port, sending loose gear tumbling in chaos down the rapidly sloping deck as the green seas poured greedily into open holds, forcing her down by the head. The stern reared high into the air and within a few minutes the ship had gone, leaving great eddies and whirlpools tossing flotsam in ever widening circles.

—Jack Loney, *Jack Loney's Maritime Australia*

As with the use of vessels, the discard of watercraft leaves behind unique archaeological signatures. In many ships' graveyards and, indeed, for more isolated deliberately abandoned vessels, the telltale signs of abandonment are highly articulated structural remains, the absence of rigging and other evidence of propulsion, and a scarcity of portable material culture (if not artifact sterility).

Generally, humans do not design watercraft with their deconstruction in mind. Their very nature reflects the human desire to create improved tools of commerce. Although no shipbuilders or shipowners believes that their vessel is an indestructible object at the all-time pinnacle of technological achievement, they certainly wish that it were. A ship's hull is a hardy and expensive item; its maker imbues it with certain abilities that make it a difficult object to disassemble or destroy. Although its functional role is finite, its component parts and materials may survive for many generations. Couple this with the understanding that unlike domestic waste, vessels are generally too large and heavy to conceal easily, and we can understand the problems associated with vessel disposal.

The destruction of a ship needs to be systematic in every way. A large part of the destruction involves dismantling, whether the vessel is to be scuttled, beached, or demolished. When a shipowner makes the decision to scrap and totally dismantle a vessel (whereby there will be no extant archaeological remains able to be located), this procedure is nevertheless similar to abandonment. The belief that the salvage and dismantling of vessels at the end of their functional life constitutes their total destruction is just one common misconception in maritime archaeology and history. If

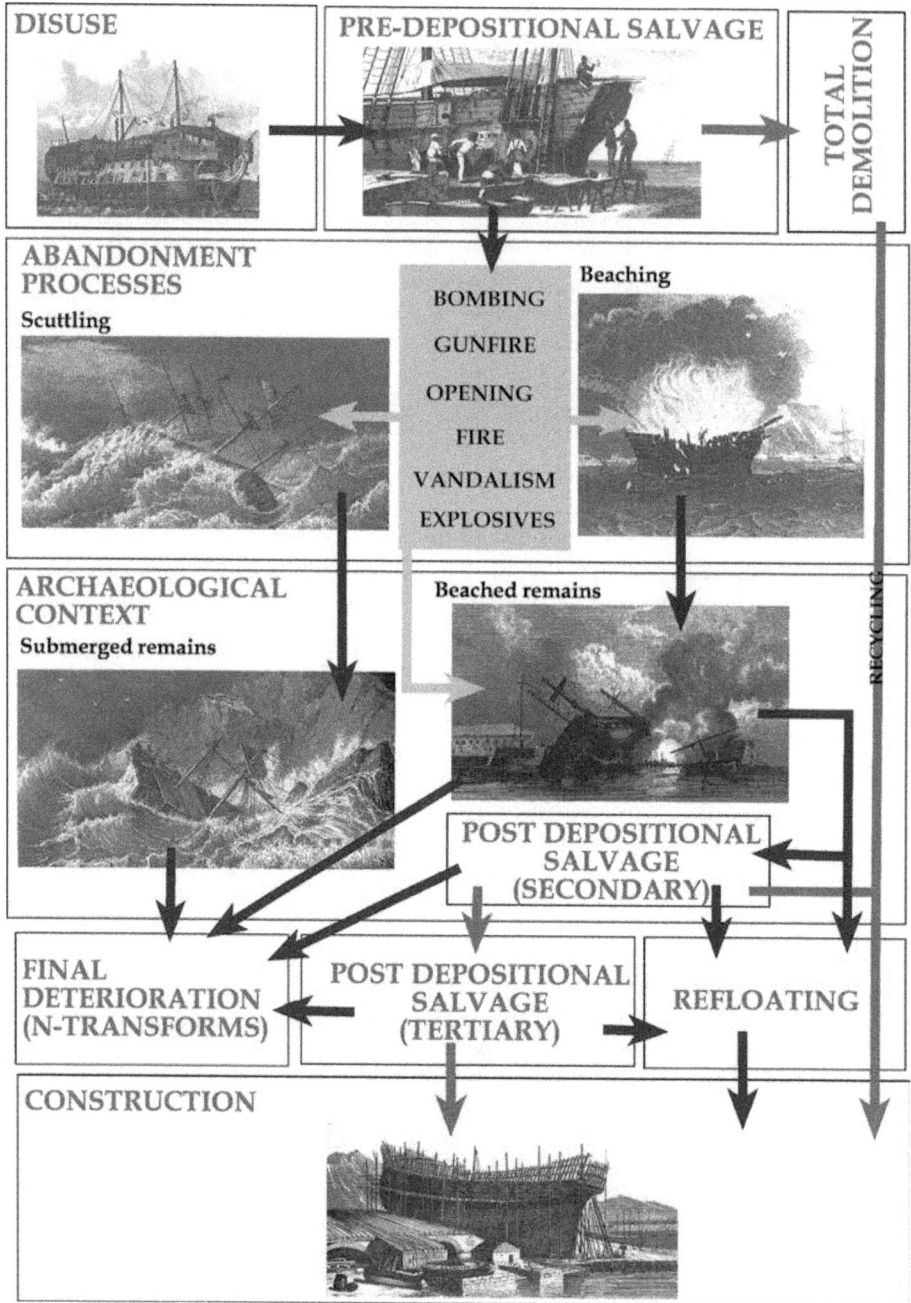

Figure 37. Site formation processes following the disuse of watercraft, illustrating the processes contributing to the transformation of vessels between systemic and archaeological contexts.

this were the case with all dismantled vessels, we would have no evidence of vessels used in a reuse context, or indeed of abandoned watercraft.

Salvage can take the form of pre- and postdepositional salvage. This distinction is an important one, as both types are detectable in different forms in the archaeological record. Additionally, they are indicative of behavioral differences. Vessel salvage is not simple, and the dismantling of watercraft is as dependent on technology as vessel construction. For example, Smith, Arnold, and Oertling describe a case in which a group of men salvaged an antitorpedo raft from the American Civil War, beached at Dolly's Bay, Bermuda, in 1868 for its timber.[1] The attempts were unsuccessful, because of the massive timbers and the extensive use of fastenings on the vessel. Its discoverers eventually left it to rot.

The ability to reduce the hull of a ship to its smallest dimensions also influences another aspect of ship abandonment: the location of abandonment. Here, too, a range of influences and conditions play a role in the logistics of the abandonment act in order to ensure that the shipowner can assure the permanent placement of a vessel on a beach or seabed after abandonment.

It is clear from historical sources in Australia and abroad that there are certain processes in the deliberate abandonment of watercraft that illuminate the psychology of disposal. Although such processes can tell us much about the perception of a vessel's hull as a structure, they can also outline some of the archaeological signatures that the archaeologist may find on sites. These relate to the location of disposal of vessels and the processing of the unwanted hull in the lead up to and aftermath of a dumping event. This chapter discusses these processes and the behaviors they represent, as well as the reasons for such treatment. They have been depicted graphically in figure 37, a synopsis of the site formation processes outlined in this chapter. These processes relate to the most practical way to dispose of unwanted vessel remains, and they shed light on the technology and economics of disposal and the socioeconomic status of the people carrying out such activities. Moreover, changing methods of vessel disposal can tell us about the economic health of regions and nations. It also can inform us as to what degree the technology used in dismantling a vessel follows the technology used in its initial manufacture.

Structure Minimization and Hull Reduction

An important aspect of the logistics associated with the abandonment of unwanted vessels comes in the form of *harm minimization*. In an abandonment context, harm minimization takes the form of the systematic destruction of a vessel via processes that allow for the reduction of the hull to its smallest size as dictated by technological, temporal, economic, and environmental constraints. We can define these processes as *structure minimization* or *hull reduction*, terms defining strategies of systematic reduction when vessels become threats to navigation. The greater the minimization of a hull's structure, the less the potential harm that can occur to other vessels operating near the area of abandonment.

This aspect of vessel abandonment also serves to highlight a range of problems for shipowners. On one level, harm minimization is required to enable the safe abandonment of a vessel and ensure that there are no ongoing costs in the control of vessel remains. On another level, the costs associated with harm minimization strategies can be expensive. Every aspect of abandonment is economically driven and has economic consequences. The historical and archaeological literatures contain a number of well-documented hull-reduction techniques.

Salvage and Scrapping Behavior

As already acknowledged, abandonment and salvage go hand in hand, and "scrapping" behavior is one major aspect of abandonment. Indeed, "abandonment" implies that people have engaged in some sort of salvage activity. As Sarah Kenderdine has noted, "Abandonment and eventual sinking implies that a vessel would have been stripped of all moveable items, and even the not so moveable but valuable boiler and engines. Cargoes and material remains of the crew would be unlikely to remain in the archaeological record."[2]

These are important considerations, because they illustrate what archaeological signatures to expect on a discard site. Kenderdine also noted that "the extant remains of vessels potentially leads to an accurate chronology of design and a typology of machinery, boilers and engines which reflects the environment, economy and function of these vessels."[3]

We can link salvage activity with the economics of the procurement of raw materials for shipbuilding, construction, and the costs of maintenance. In this way, although the abandonment of a vessel is an economic burden to a shipowner, it can also be an economic benefit. In particular, the salvage of recycled materials from ships was a common practice. As Ronald Parsons has noted, "It was, particularly in the early days, quite unusual to find any . . . vessels completely new throughout—great use was made of salvaged materials from larger craft that had been wrecked, dismantled, altered or for some reason or other were no longer serviceable."[4]

The economic factors in decision-making processes concerning salvage have always been the same. Lionel Casson has discussed ancient Athenian methods of dealing with the cost of maintaining fleets of triremes in relation to the ongoing costs of maintenance and the stimuli for the dismantling of vessels. Triremes were vessels of light construction with an expected use-life of between twenty and twenty-five years. Indeed, considering this, the Athenian navy classified their trireme fleet by their age and condition. The tiers of this system were, in an initial distinction, "old" and "new" vessels, then, following a more specific system of classification, they were divided into "selects," "first-class," "second-class," and "third-class." Any vessels beyond these categories the navy would convert into transports, sell out of service, or break up for use in other vessels or for other purposes.[5]

There is a convenience in selling off your vessel before it is useless, and always much organizing required in being the owner of a condemned ship. However, if the price is right, and the economic climate and scrap metal market are good, the salvage, dismantling, and abandonment of a vessel becomes lucrative. Indeed, there are many references to the breaking up of vessels simply for the value of their component materials. This economic aspect to the salvage of unwanted vessels is an integral part of what makes an abandoned watercraft an archaeological site. Evidence from Australia and overseas often suggests that certain elements of a vessel's build are regularly missing. In the case of intact, beached vessels, this tends to be the ship's rudder, which Mensun Bound notes in the case of the *Jhelum* in the Falkland Islands.[6] Furthermore, it is common to find abandoned vessels that have no masts, or evidence of rigging, and it is even more common to find these vessels without in situ boilers, engines, prop shafts, or propellers (see figure 38).[7] The fact that the characteristic elements missing from abandonment sites center on the propulsion of a particular vessel illustrates their perception as composite objects. It also shows the easy reuse of major aspects of a vessel guides their salvage and hence facilitates their integration into the archaeological record. Often these reuse behaviors will see disarticulated vessel materials used in other structures. Harry O'May, for instance, notes that builders reused the timbers from the vessel *Frederica* in a slipway in Tasmania.[8]

We can, however, also define scrapping processes according to cultural conditions. In particular, economic conditions and the prices of scrap material drive where and when salvagers carry out scrapping activities. Michael McCarthy has previously noted this in relation to the salvage of copper and copper alloy fastenings from ships.[9] Even where owners abandoned their vessels and allowed them to deteriorate for many years, they may have

Figure 38. Stern of the *Moe* at the Garden Island Ships' Graveyard (South Australia) showing missing rudder. Photo by Nathan Richards.

subsequently scrapped them because of an increase in scrap prices. One example of this was the barque *Otago*, which was broken up at East Risdon in Tasmania when scrap prices were high.[10] Another example was the vessel *Iluka*, which was accidentally beached after slipping its moorings at Hawks Nest, New South Wales, in the 1920s and then cut up almost fifty years later when steel prices escalated.[11] At other times, the abandonment of vessels occurs without substantial salvage. One such case was the scuttling of the barge *Premier* in the Rottnest Island Ships' Graveyard. In this case it was stated, "In view of her age, it was considered that, despite the high price obtainable for the metal, the amount of steel that would be gained by breaking up the hull would not return the amount of money spent on the work."[12] Despite the assertion that there was a "high price" for steel at the time, if the price had been even higher, the issue of adequate return would not have been important and the vessel would have been dismantled instead of scuttled. This has continued in more recent times with the International Maritime Industries Forum advising shipowners during a tonnage imbalance in 1982 to "scrap now before prices collapse even further."[13]

From at least the late 1930s, the normal method of undertaking salvage work on submerged, ferrous-hulled vessel remains was through the use of the "submarine blowpipe."[14] The technology involved was simply an adaptation of the technology used in cutting steel above water. This process reduced the cost of cutting steel underwater, previously done with manual tools, saving both time and money. Salvagers used these tools primarily in cases of collision where vessels could be refloated (opening bulkheads, cutting away damaged side plating and removing rivets), and for a range of harbor related functions, such as dock and harbor maintenance.[15] Such methods were expensive in relation to both money and time and would not have been used extensively in abandoned watercraft, where by and large salvage would occur before final discard or after discard at locations where materials were above water and still relatively accessible.

Scrap metal was particularly important because of its role in determining the price of pig iron.[16] Although we may assume the price of scrap was always below the price of newly manufactured iron and steel, the elevated price of new raw materials have, at times, been so much higher than scrap that salvaged metal became an attractive alternative. Although the costs of fuel in smelting, delivery, and manufacture in the steel and iron industries may fluctuate at any time, scrap, as a resource that can be stockpiled, would be less likely to fluctuate as drastically and would arguably only change in accordance to the scrap dealer's awareness of prices of new materials. In Australia, the scrapping of ships for iron in particular was a major industry.

Specifically, the dependence of the Scottish iron and steel industry on scrap metal was a force that drove fluctuating scrap prices, as stated by Neil Buxton:

> The Scottish iron and steel industry, indeed, did come to rely on scrap more than elsewhere. Imports of scrap through Scottish ports rose from 32,500 tons in 1929, 35 per cent of total scrap imports into the U.K., to reach a peak of 507,000 tons in 1936, 47 per cent of the U.K. figure. Even more revealing is the fact that by 1936/8, the volume of scrap imports into Scotland amounted to no less than 90 per cent of the volume of the country's production of pig-iron.[17]

The stories behind the salvage of many vessels demonstrate the close links between the scrap metal industry in Australia and the Japanese demand for metal, especially in the years before and following World War II. Here, there is an obvious link between the high prices offered by the Japanese for scrap iron and steel around the world and an increase in salvage activity in Australia. The Japanese were the major consortium engaged in the salvage of the vessels that they destroyed in air attacks upon Darwin during World War II and removed much of the structural remains of many vessels from the harbor.

In certain cases during World War II, salvagers rejected some vessels for scrapping, not because they were still usable but because there was an oversupply of certain qualities of scrap material. This was the case with the vessel *Hinemoa*, rejected in January 1944 for this very reason.[18]

In modern times, ports such as Fremantle have seen seven or eight ships each carrying twenty semitrailer loads of scrap metal bound for destinations in South and Southeastern Asia per year.[19] At these places, this scrap is prepared to meet the standards of steel mills and foundries so that it can be effectively recycled. Loney has also described how for months before abandonment, ship breakers would undertake the process of stripping a vessel of all valuable materials before handing it over to the tug operator, who would transport it to its final resting place.[20] However, often the actual scrapping of ferrous-hulled vessels would not occur in Australia. Indeed, works such as Scott Baty's *Ships that Passed* (1984) illustrate that no large passenger liners were dismantled in Australia and that Italian, Greek, Taiwanese, English, Belgian, Chinese, German, Scottish, Mexican, American, and, especially, Japanese ship breakers dominated the industry.[21] Although this is no surprise, considering that the larger-order liners were not built in Australia and only visited for short periods, smaller passenger vessels were often broken up in Australia (as evidenced by the breaking up of vessels such as the *Karatta* and *Flinders* in South Australia). At other times, the scrapping of vessels was an important subsistence industry.

The real establishment of scrap salvage as a subsistence industry occurred from the time of the Great Depression of the 1930s. Survival in these times was difficult for many, but especially for the unemployed. In Adelaide, where the unemployed ration was the lowest, most of the day was spent in trying to obtain foodstuffs by any means possible, whether it was by raiding vegetable gardens, or begging for thrown away lamb's tongues. This desperation for food was also a central feature of the poor and unemployed in other states.[22] Finding fuel for cooking and heating was just as difficult, with hordes of individuals searching railways lines for lumps of coal to heat their houses at night or wandering the beaches in search of driftwood.[23] Under these conditions, it is not surprising that a subsistence salvage industry developed focused on the salvage of material from discarded materials and abandoned watercraft. This is true of Port Adelaide, although the controls on the legality of the salvage appear to have been particularly stringent. Indeed, port authorities went to great lengths to make contracts for the salvage of material from watercraft. Removal of material without permission was considered illegal and only occurred clandestinely. Also in Port Adelaide there are case studies that illustrate the impact of the Great Depression on the local population while providing valuable insight into the growth of the salvage industry in that state.

The *Fides* was a four-masted Norwegian barque of 430 gross tons burden built in 1918 at a cost of thirty-five thousand pounds. In 1926, it took fifteen months to sail from Gothenburg, Germany, to Australia with a cargo of Baltic timber, during which time storms, calms, mast damage, rigging damage, engine troubles, and crew sickness forced the vessel to put into port on two occasions (in the Amazon at Rio Para and in Queensland). The vessel was destined for Adelaide, where its owners intended it for the trade between South Australia and New Zealand. When the *Fides* arrived at Port Adelaide in early 1928, the timber trade had collapsed, and the vessel could not find work. In late 1928, its owners berthed the vessel, and for four years, it laid idle. The laying up of vessels due to a lack of trade was to become a common occurrence during the downturn. For example, the *Leeta May* was laid up at Melbourne in 1931 due to a lack of cargo and, hence, a lack of trade.[24]

By 1931, the situation in Port Adelaide was desperate. The Reverend T. P. Williason of the Port Adelaide central Methodist Mission and captain of the *Fides*, J. A. Olsen, embarked upon a plan to recondition the vessel and crew it with the unemployed of Port Adelaide to conduct fishing operations off the west coast of South Australia and in the Great Australian Bight. Two prominent Adelaide men, Sir Langdon Bonython and a Mr. Barr-Smith, promised five hundred pounds toward the project. However, the initiative did not get off the ground because of the unsuitability of the vessel for fishing and the unsound nature of its hull. Finally, the owners of *Fides* sold some of its spars for the manufacture of other ships and then gave the ship to the Methodist mission, which donated the vessel to the unemployed and destitute, who used the barque for firewood. The mission charged these people with the responsibility of stripping the vessel in the Jervois Basin (South Australia) but requested that it remain in a floating condition so that someone could transport it to the Garden Island Ships' Graveyard (South Australia) for disposal. Instead, the vessel was broken down too extensively and was left were it lay, abandoned in the Jervois Basin in 1933, only thirteen years after its construction.

Another example was *Dorothy H. Sterling*, a 2,526-ton, six-masted wooden schooner built in 1920 by the Peninsula Shipbuilding Company of Portland, Oregon, for a cost of fifty thousand pounds. When the vessel arrived in Port Adelaide in 1929, the American crew found themselves abandoned in port without wages and provisions. After many attempts to provide for themselves, the crew took to stealing stores and destroying sails, selling the fabric for tablecloths. Eventually the Harbors Board seized the vessel for unpaid harbor dues and sold it at auction for an undisclosed amount (believed to be fifty pounds). Although the vessel was only nine years old, a salvage crew broke it up over a period of three years. Its salvage featured prominently (almost monthly) in local newspapers over that time.[25]

The salvage of the vessel appears throughout primary source documentation and illustrates the degree to which humans reuse the elements of vessels. The ship breakers transformed much of the vessel into other usable items. Some sections, such as the masts, became masts for other ships or harbor fenders, the wheel became a pergola, the cabin became a holiday shack, and the rest of the ship became firewood. Although the vessel was broken up in the customary way, with wedges and hammers splitting and rending frames and planks apart, oxyacetylene was also used (probably for the first time in Port Adelaide), allowing for more sections to be dismantled at a faster rate, hence saving time and money. The Garden Island Ships' Graveyard became its final resting place in March 1932.

Salvage Processes

Evidence from many sources, and concerning sites spread out over a long period, has shown that there are certain behaviors pertaining to the salvage of deliberately abandoned vessels that have persisted to the present day. There is evidence from the HMS *Vixen* site in Bermuda, for instance, that both official (predepositional and postdepositional) and unofficial salvage activities can, to some degree, be inferred from archaeological remains.[26]

Scholars have attempted the separation of salvage into phases for the purposes of appropriate interpretation in the past. McCarthy suggests that *primary salvage* is a term that aptly describes the salvage of materials of shipwreck remains after their wrecking by the "owners, insurers or their agents," and that *secondary salvage* describes work activities by "professional salvers or sports divers."[27] This study of abandoned vessels suggests that there are three main phases in the salvage of vessel remains. This scheme differs with McCarthy's because it concerns a deliberately disposed of resource that is defined by its use as a material source. For this reason, the system commences before any section of the vessel has become part of the archaeological record. First, primary salvage refers to predepositional salvage carried out before final deposition or abandonment. Second, secondary salvage comprises the phase of salvage that occurs in a postdepositional (postabandonment) context in the short term normally by the owner/abandoner of the vessel. These salvage attempts relate to the appropriate abandonment of the vessel, or are a part of the cost recovery efforts associated with the decision to abandon. *Tertiary salvage* encompasses attempts at salvage that occur through time following abandonment. These activities are intermittent and opportunistic and will usually occur after a change in ownership to an individual or group of individuals not related to the primary and secondary phases of salvage (as this is a site formation quite removed from initial postabandonment salvage activities it is not discussed in this research).

Not all three phases occur on all vessels. In cases where the appropriate infrastructure for ship breaking does not exist, often very little or no primary salvage activity occurs, and the vessel's owner simply discards it. Likewise, primary salvage is often substantial enough not to warrant further demolition of the hull and it may simply be left.

Primary Salvage

Primary salvage involves the reduction of the hull in such a way that the most expensive or accessible items are removed before the vessel is deposited at its final resting place. The most important aspect of this is that the hull remains in a floating condition, so that it is moveable to a final dumping place before further salvage or breaking up. There are demonstrated cases where overzealous activities of predepositional salvage have in fact destroyed the floating capacity of the hull, effectively stranding it (as with the *Fides*). There are also places where pre- and postdepositional acts of salvage have occurred at the same location. In discussing the Port Stanley hulk *Jhelum*, Stammers and Kearon have noted:

> It would be interesting to know if she was stripped of her gear before or after she was beached. Is it likely that much of the re-usable, easily removable equipment such as sails, boats, steering gear, winch, upper masts and spars was removed close to the FIC's stores and workshops for they probably had the most use for such materials.[28]

Although it is obvious on many discarded vessels that salvaging of hull material has occurred, often evidence of predepositional salvage does not translate well into the archaeological record due to the further removal of hull material (which is, after all, the purpose of such activity). More specifically, any evidence of predepositional salvage may not be evident due to confusion with the results of postdepositional salvage. Hence, we can see the dangers in describing all activities in relation to salvage as postdepositional.

During this study, I researched or inspected a number of sites that represent areas where primary-stage salvage activities occurred: the Jervois Basin (Port Adelaide, South Australia), Corio Bay (Geelong, Victoria), and Homebush Bay (Sydney, New South Wales) (fig. 39). Where there are structural remains of watercraft left at these sites, it is almost impossible to determine pre- and postdepositional salvage activities from the archaeological signatures left behind.

Secondary Salvage

Due to the reasons outlined above, the line between pre- and postdepositional salvage, from an archaeological perspective, is blurred. Owing to the need to keep a vessel in a floating condition, and in order to get it to a final resting place, the only real evidence of postdepositional salvage likely to exist on extant ship remains is the absence of material from areas crucial in maintaining flotation. In this way, a vessel salvaged of structural material toward its keel and garboard strake, below the turn of its bilge, has invariably been subjected to postdepositional salvage activities. We can see the

Figure 39. Homebush Bay Ships' Graveyard (Sydney, New South Wales) showing remains of the *Mortlake Bank* and *Ayrfield*. Photo by Nathan Richards.

importance of making the distinction between pre- and postdepositional salvage in comments made by McCarthy concerning the vessel *Amur* (the former *Agnes Holt*):

> She was fastened entirely with yellow metal, and her abandonment would have likely been followed by subsequent heavy salvage for her valuable fastenings. If she was afloat, her owners would have required for moving her to an area away from shipping, and the nearby grave-yard including Jervoise Bay appeared a likely possibility.[29]

From these statements, we can see that if an owner does not coordinate appropriate planning processes in the breaking of a ship, and subsequently a vessel is broken down too much, unwanted consequences may arise. One possible scenario is that the vessel, no longer in floating condition, is not moveable and has to stay where dismantling occurred, thus polluting an area not intended for discarded vessels. Where such events happen continuously, the only outcome is the creation of an area for ship breaking and abandonment—a type of ships' graveyard that is analogous to Schiffer's definition of a *primary refuse site*. As ship breaking often occurs where appropriate facilities are present, and because facilities are most often located

Figure 40. The *Grace Darling* after disposal in the Garden Island Ships' Graveyard. By permission of the South Australian Maritime Museum.

in inner port or harbor locations, the demolition or salvage of vessels can have serious repercussions for port use. Where the location of salvage is the same as the eventual disposal location, no predepositional salvage will generally take place. On the other hand, a lack of facilities imposes limitations by not enabling the appropriate minimization of the hull. In other words, salvage activities can determine whether its owner will totally dismantle a vessel or dump it in an isolated or ships' graveyard context—effectively guiding its final location of discard.

The degree to which postdepositional salvage occurs is evident in a photograph of the vessel *Grace Darling* in the Garden Island Ships' Graveyard (fig. 40). The image depicts the vessel in a postabandonment context, showing it relatively intact (and probably watertight). Although it is not clear whether salvagers removed the noticeably absent hull material before or after discard (potentially, the vessel was towed to the ships' graveyard in this condition), comparison with recent photographs shows the degree to which secondary salvage has occurred (fig. 41).

The reason why archaeologists can still detect abandoned ships, and why their owners did not totally dismantle them, is both a technological and an economic issue. To get access to the submerged portions of a hull takes time and specialized infrastructure. Without the aid of a cradle (or some other type of support), vessels tend to sit off center. Additionally, large vessels are not often flat bottomed. In other words, it takes more money to abandon

Figure 41. The *Grace Darling* (view to stern) after disposal in the Garden Island Ships' Graveyard. Photo by Nathan Richards.

Figure 42. The *Margaret* burning. Richard McKenna Collection. By permission of the Western Australian Maritime Museum.

them, with less opportunity for economic reward. Furthermore, these sections of the hull are very hardy and much less easily demolished.

The use of fire is a major aspect of postdepositional secondary salvage, as well as a hull treatment used in association with placement assurance strategies (discussed later). In the case of wooden vessels, or hulls with substantial wooden structural components, fire is the easiest way to destroy hull material not wanted for salvage or not cost-effective to recover (see figure 42). Marshall and Miners have noted the probable use of fire on the vessel dubbed "the wreck of stones" (believed to be the *Redemptora*), which they surveyed and undertook test excavation on in Western Australia in 1979.[30] The vessel was most likely set alight after all of the accessible materials were recovered during salvage (it is not known whether the vessel is indeed an abandonment or a wreck site). Another case study of an Australian vessel showing evidence of burning is the vessel *Day Dawn*, abandoned in Careening Bay, Western Australia, about 1890 and said to have been "stripped and burnt, perhaps deliberately for recovery of fittings."[31] Indeed, fire is evident as a common strategy for salvage and structure minimization (to be discussed) in the ANAVD, with forty-three instances of vessels being burned. Of these vessels, the majority were wooden (thirty-seven), followed by unknown material (two), composite hulled (two), and iron hulled (two). The iron vessels mentioned as being destroyed by fire, the *Gannet* (1884–1946) and *Moolgewanke* (1856–1940), were both paddle steamers that had been used in riverine trades and therefore would have had substantial wooden components.

In many cases, the burning of wooden hulls also relates to salvage strategy. There are many cases of people burning American merchant ships in order to gain the metal (usually copper and iron fastenings) used in the hull.[32] The vivid description of the burning of one of these vessels, *Glory of the Seas* (dated 23 May 1923), provides us with some insight into the effect of burning upon ships, and the attitudes associated with the destruction of these vessels:

> Nearing the beach, instead of her topmasts through the trees, I saw a thin cloud of smoke and felt that she might have been smoldering for a week and I would see nothing but her keel.
>
> Down to the beach and found that she had been burning only a few hours but at that nothing was left of her but a fire-punctured shell, a section of which would occasionally fall into the waters of Puget Sound with a dull explosion. Her badly charred fore and main masts were alongside, the mizen [sic] hanging over the port quarter, the whole mixed up with bolts, wire and remnants of another burned hull. The picture made one think of the effect of a tidal wave followed by fire.
>
> The only spectacular bit I saw was when, from the weight of the bowsprit, the entire bow from catheads to stempost at the bobstays fell overboard in one huge chunk. I felt glad that the goddess who formerly capped the stem, was saved the humiliation of being smashed to splinters by gravel and shallow water in a junk yard.
>
> That the old ship was to be burned that day was not made public so only a few residents, mostly children, saw the end of what was to them merely a lot of wood bolted together and called a "boat."[33]

Abandoners also used fire in the salvage and destruction of vessels; from those discarded during the California Gold Rush in the 1840s and 1850s, to the remnants of the "Emergency Fleet" in Maryland from the 1920s, as well as in Australian cases, with vessels, such as the barque *Maida*, listed as having been "burnt for her copper rods and bolts."[34] McCarthy also refers to the coal-burning steamer *Zephyr* "being progressively burnt and hauled up the beach till her hull was completely destroyed and all the copper fastenings recovered" around 1966.[35]

Although fire is the most obvious way of reducing a hull, and is an apparently efficient means of destroying a wooden vessel, how this translates into the archaeological record is problematic. Fire is associated with the salvage of valuable fittings from vessels, but it may be hard to distinguish this method from subsequent vandalism not associated with the salvage of such materials. Concerning the ships' graveyard in the inner harbor of Kingston, Ontario, Jonathon Moore has suggested that there is "some historical evidence that vessels entering the graveyard were bonfired" (Moore found no archaeological evidence of this).[36] One other example of this is the vessel *Myall River* (1912–?), abandoned at Witts Island, Port Stephens (New South Wales), and subsequently burnt by children at a much more recent time.[37] Evidence of this event were still evident when I inspected the site in 2001.

In these cases, the reasons for a lack of an archaeological signature can be due to cultural and/or natural site formation processes. For instance, where postdepositional salvage has occurred, the salvager may remove evidence pertaining to salvage. If water conditions expose burnt timbers in an intertidal or submerged environment, the subsequent action of natural forces such as wear or consumption by shipworm will reduce the evidence. It can be hypothesized that such activity will only be detectable where the remains of the vessels were covered by an anaerobic layer of sediment soon after the vessel has burnt, stopping subsequent natural or cultural impact.

Placement Assurance

Salvagers often use fire as a way of sinking a vessel and assuring that it remains submerged. The burning of vessels in order to make them sink sometimes met with disastrous results. Deirdre Jordan describes one such scenario in relation to the vessels *Palace* and *Birchgrove* in Port Phillip, Victoria:

> The tug crew set the two vessels on fire and cast them adrift, however, the fires went out, before burning the vessels to the waterline. The

vessels drifted ashore . . . where they were broken up, by the action of the sea.[38]

The scuttling or sinking of vessels at sea has often been the preferred option for the disposal of watercraft. This has traditionally been because of a desire not to "slew the coastline with old wrecks."[39] Jack Loney describes this traditional way to dispose of a vessel at sea:

> With a tug boat ahead the hulk was taken seaward on a lengthened tow line and once the distance was run the position was checked to ensure that there was no risk of the vessel sinking in shallow water where it might foul fishermens' nets. Then the explosive charges were fired.[40]

Sometimes, however, scuttling simply does not work:

> The old paddle steamer *Hygeia* made a bold attempt to escape her destroyers while being towed by the tug *Eagle* to be sunk outside Port Phillip Heads in 1931. In rough seas and a strong westerly she broke away from the tug late in the afternoon of 27 August, bumped across Mud Island and disappeared in the darkness with two men still aboard. Next morning she was found aground near [the town of] Rosebud with about 400 tons of water in her but was eventually refloated and taken out to her grave.[41]

The issue of placement assurance is an important one, especially in an examination of the cultural aspects of site formation. The methods used in ensuring the appropriate abandonment of a vessel, whether it relates to the burning, salvage of materials, or hull perforation activities will leave certain archaeological signatures behind that enable interpretations to be made on other sites less adequately described in historical sources. This has been a neglected area within maritime archaeology, although most archaeologists would take it for granted that such a process occurs. McCarthy, in his report on the "Black Cat" Catalina aircraft scuttled off Rottnest Island, Western Australia, in 1945 and 1946, reinforced the relationship between abandonment method and the subsequent in situ remains: "The mode of disposal of scuttling of these aircraft will have an effect on the nature of the remains and the method used in the abandonment process will have ramifications for the recovery, conservation and exhibition of the remains."[42]

Historically, placement assurance has always been an issue when abandoning a vessel because the ownership of abandoned vessels is much the same as that of shipwrecks: Someone is always the owner. However, whereas an insurance payout may compensate the owner of a shipwreck (transferring ownership to the underwriter), there is usually no agency that would seek to own an obsolete and unwanted vessel. The only exception to this occurs where the agency or individual was confident that they could make money from salvaged material. From this perspective, once someone salvages or abandons a vessel, the owners, although still responsible for the remains of the vessel, would like to have nothing more to do with it unless there are postabandonment uses in mind. In order to dispose of a vessel, the owner needs to ensure that it will not cost them money by floating off or moving and causing damage to other ships or port structures. There have been cases of vessels not being properly abandoned and causing subsequent problems for their owners. The case of the American clipper ship *Twilight*, for example, illustrates this point:

> It was found inexpedient to make repairs and in May she was sold at auction for $4575, to be stripped and broken up. As though objecting to this ignominious end, she floated off the beach one night at high tide, drifted through Raccoon Straits into the upper bay and stranded near California City. From there she was towed back to Sausalito, securely beached and then broken up and burned.[43]

Fred Hopkins notes similar problems in association with the Mallows' Bay Graveyard: "The WWI hulls in Mallow's Bay would not sink quietly into mud. In the years prior to WWII there was constant concern that the hulls would break loose and drift into the Potomac shipping channel."[44]

One Australian case study in particular illustrates the need for placement assurance. The owners of the iron barque *Moe* abandoned their vessel at the Garden Island Ships' Graveyard sometime after August 1926. Years later, the vessel was taken up by a high tide on two separate occasions (25 July 1929 and 1 February 1930), damaging a wharf in the latter incident. Subsequently, on 25 September 1931, the vessel required reabandonment in the same area. Part of this last abandonment procedure included the dumping of an unwanted pontoon on its stern (see figure 43).[45]

Placement assurance takes many forms but can generally be separated into two categories, the appropriate treatment of the hull and the choice of an appropriate environment. Although placement assurance techniques are the mechanisms designed to facilitate the transferal of a vessel from a systemic context to an archaeological one, this process may reverse. There have been isolated documented cases of individuals refloating vessels for their reintegration into mercantile or support functions. One such example

Figure 43. Iron pontoon deposited on the remains of the *Moe*. Photo by Mark Staniforth.

was the vessel *Seminole*, abandoned initially at the Garden Island Ships' Graveyard in 1906, subsequently refloated, reused (and probably partially rebuilt), and reabandoned around 1908 within the same disposal area.[46] The systemic reintegration of such vessels, however, is rare.

Appropriate Hull Treatment

Besides guaranteeing that adequate salvage has occurred to ensure the loss of the vessel's flotation, salvagers used many other processes to affect the buoyancy of a waterborne hull, and ensure that it remained discarded. These processes are generally the same in the case of both beached and scuttled watercraft. The difference between them relates to the lack of extensive pre- and postdepositional salvage in the beached ships and to the greater level of buoyancy required if transporting vessels to sea. Mention of these hull treatment procedures is not common in the historical record, and there are problems with the detection of many of them from the archaeological record because of postdepositional processes that mask or destroy them. At least ninety vessels in the ANAVD are listed as having had hull treatment procedures (including the use of fire, as already discussed) undertaken on them before abandonment (table 15). Of these, historical sources suggest that only five underwent multiple procedures.

Explosives and Other Hull-Breaching Procedures

Obviously, the easiest method of breaching a vessel in order to inundate a hull is to open it to the sea. Although the most common way of facilitating this would be by opening a vessel's sea cocks, historical records do not often elaborate on the process. The use of explosives is the most common method (reported in thirty-nine cases). Although someone may use explosives in conjunction with postdepositional salvage for the purposes of loosening plates of hull, it is also one of the most popular ways of ensuring that a hull does not maintain its water-tightness. The use of explosives on the hull of a ship is one procedure well attested to in the historical literature. For instance, descriptions from primary and secondary sources indicate that the method is the same whether ensuring rapid sinking at sea or striving for steadfast placement on a beach; explosives need to be set off within the bilges of the vessel.[47]

Indeed, very few historical sources outline the procedures used on vessels in the prelude to their abandonment. There is some literature on the deliberate scuttling of vessels when they are in danger of total wrecking without hope of refloating or salvaging them. These references exist in many

Table 15. Breakdown of Hull Treatment Procedures in the ANAVD (n = 90)

Procedure	Number	%
Exploded only	35	39
Burnt only	41	46
Filled only	6	7
Opened only	3	3
Exploded and filled	2	2
Opened and Burnt	1	1
Opened and Exploded	1	1
Exploded and Burnt	1	1

of the second volumes of the *Manual of Seamanship*, books issued by the lords commissioners of the Admiralty to British seamen.[48] The procedure outlined involves the deliberate breaching of a hull in order to allow water to flow in and sink the vessel. Specifically mentioned are choices concerning methods and positions for hull breaching. The methods suggested include the chiseling, hammering, drilling, or perforation by oxyacetylene equipment to allow for the creation of a clean hole. In urgent circumstances, the source endorses the use of small charges of explosives. It is stressed that the holes should be accessible at low tide (that is, above water), and that these should be small holes with minimal distortion or rough edges so that the patches used in refloating attempts can be made watertight easily. Although this gives some insight into the methods where refloating is the primary aim of such activity, it may also give us some insight into the behaviors associated with discard related deliberate scuttling.

It appears as if the precepts outlined above could be reversed in relation to deliberate scuttling, where the archaeological evidence suggests that large amounts of explosives set off as low as possible was the preferred method. This makes sense for two reasons. In the first instance, large holes low in the water will allow for fast and efficient foundering irrespective of water depth. This also maximizes the potential for total inundation, which assures the vessel's placement on the seabed or beach. The use of large amounts of explosives, which has been seen to greatly distort and bend the intact plates while causing large "peeling back" of other sections of plate (as with the *Garthneill* in figure 44), will, in the case of beached vessels, serve as a deterrent to people wishing to refloat the vessel illegally.

One problem when sinking a vessel is that it may not sink quickly enough. The *Musgrave*, for instance, was due for scuttling in the Little Betsy Island Ships' Graveyard (Storm Bay, Tasmania) in 1930 but drifted for around four hours before settling in a different location off the island.[49] Additionally, the

Figure 44. Exploded metal plates in the bow of the *Garthneill*. Photo by Mark Staniforth.

West Australian newspaper cited the sinking of the *Norwhale* off Rottnest Island as taking three attempts with explosives to sink it.[50]

The use of explosives, as with any other method designed to ensure the sinking of a vessel, is an economic issue. Generally, the principle is the more explosives used, the more likely the vessel is to sink properly. In cases where the military have scuttled large, former RAN vessels, up to twenty detonator charges are used.[51] This is in direct contrast to the scuttling of other watercraft, where two or three charges may be used. Although the increased use of explosives is an indication of the size of the unwanted ship, it is also a suggestion of the costs required and the money people are willing to spend to create artificial reefs and recreational dive sites. In certain cases, there are complications. Vessels such as the HMAS *Derwent* were "used to test the effects of various types of explosives"[52] and could therefore not be taken as an indication of the number of explosives normally needed to sink a vessel of this size.

Many of the vessels examined during fieldwork for this research had obvious signs of explosives evident in their remains. Of particular interest were the vessels at Tangalooma, which had "dynamite charges . . . exploded in the bottoms of the ships to sink them."[53] The use of explosives in the abandonment of vessels for functional postabandonment uses in intertidal contexts, such as those vessels at Tangalooma, is not a simple matter. Watt describes this in the following excerpt that documents the scuttling of the *Tarawera* as a breakwater, wharf, and store ship in New Zealand in December 1927:

> A coil of gelignite was . . . laid by a diver . . . unfortunately, on detonation, the hulk tipped the wrong way. The result was that her deck, rather than her bottom, lay outward and exposed to the sea, and as a result she subsequently broke up faster than expected; the old iron bones never did satisfactorily serve their purpose.[54]

Filling

Likewise, historical and archaeological literature attests to the filling of salvaged hulls (with eight vessels listed as "filled" in the ANAVD). If an owner had to beach their vessel in order to save them from wrecking, some advised, "Ballast should be taken in during the beaching operation to cause the ship to settle securely on the bottom."[55] This was also the sensible thing to do in cases of deliberate abandonment, with the added weight working against any residual buoyancy of the salvaged and breached hull. Many of the sites visited during the archaeological site survey component of this research have been noted as filled up with rocks, cement, and gravel, something previously noted at the Mallows Bay Ships' Graveyard in Maryland. Amongst other archaeological studies of abandoned vessels, however, few acknowledge this as a factor in site formation. In some cases, archaeologists may interpret anomalous findings as vessel contents rather than as indicators of placement assurance methods. Researchers, for instance, identified the large amount of ballast stone found in the hull of the "wreck of stones," identified as the American vessel *Redemptora*, as atypical due to the amount of stone being "to the detriment of her carrying capacity."[56] Instead, it could be considered a measure taken for proper sinking and assured placement on the seabed, and hence a factor in the site's formation. This amount of stone, taken in consideration with the already mentioned use of fire on the vessel, means that it would have sunk faster as the structure burnt. These processes could have also ensured that the vessel stayed where it sank. Scholars have noted these activities in relation to the sites of *Jhelum* (Port Stanley) and the Cypress Landing shipwreck (North Carolina).

Overseas studies also illustrate the inclination of researchers to disregard hull contents as indicators of potential deliberate discard. Illsley and Roberts (1979), in their commentary on the bateaux-style slate carrying the "Padarn Boat" found in North Wales (believed to date between 1788 and

1824), acknowledge that the vessel is a shipwreck due to the in situ slate in the hold of the vessel.[57] The question one must ask is whether this is enough to prove a wrecking incident, especially in the case of a vessel such as this, which is in a remarkably good state of preservation and articulation. Is it reasonable to use the large amount of slate and non-site-specific historical documentation regarding the profitability of the slate industry at a particular time to determine the time of wrecking, or for identifying a wrecking incident?[58] Using other evidence in their work, which outlines the existence of a highly articulated hull that was not perforated or upturned but filled with heavy material, may alternatively suggest deliberate abandonment. According to this perspective, the slate ceases to be cargo and becomes evidence for placement assurance. This alternative view is not one I advocate but is an alternative hypothesis that may shed light on possible conceptual problems in how we view submerged vessel remains. This reiterates the importance concerning transparency in the interpretation of the archaeological remnants of vessel remains and the exploration of all possible alternatives in site formation. For instance, in the case of a site at Claflin Point, Wisconsin, Bradley Rodgers noted a large quantity of dolomitic limestone within the hold but concluded that it represented cargo and that the vessel was a wrecked rock transport barge and not a discarded watercraft.[59] Rodgers bases his conclusions, however, upon the stone's worth, and the way that people had packed the material, not upon assumptions about the nature of the vessel's deposition.

Archival sources also contain references to people filling vessels with trash in an attempt to weigh down the hull, but more important, as a method of rubbish disposal. The *West Australian*, for instance, cites the vessel *Premier* as "carrying a miscellaneous cargo, including broken up parts of motor vehicle bodies which, like herself, had reached the end of their useful life."[60]

Piles

There is much evidence of people using networks of sunken piles in relation to the abandoned hulls of watercraft. We find these in three separate instances: the delineation of disposal areas, in associated jetties, and with placement assurance activities.

At the Garden Island Ships' Graveyard, authorities purposefully placed piles to outline the abandonment area. At the Jervois Basin Ships' Graveyard, an area delineated with piles as a log pool later became a useful area

Figure 45. Jetties at North Stockton, New South Wales, adjacent to remains of the abandoned watercraft *Kate Tatham* and *Sylvan*. Photo by Nathan Richards.

to abandon vessels safely without impeding navigation. At Homebush Bay (New South Wales), people used the piles for the primary purpose of facilitating safe navigation while restricting access to the ship-breaking area.

At two sites, the Otago Bay Ships' Graveyard (Tasmania) and at the North Stockton Ships' Graveyard (New South Wales), jetty piles associated with makeshift jetties are adjacent to the remains of abandoned watercraft, apparently used in association with salvage activities (fig. 45).

Piles were also used in the pinning down of at least one vessel, the paddle steamer *Jupiter*, at the Mutton Cove Ships' Graveyard (South Australia) (fig. 46) and may have once fixed the remains of the *Fides* at the Jervois Basin Ships' Graveyard to underlying substrate. In all cases, piles relate to placement assurance activities, whether directly associated with ensuring that a vessel would stay where it was discarded (as with the driving of piles through its hull) or through their association with hull-reduction strategies (salvage), aimed at least partially at reducing the residual buoyancy of a ship's hull. Both strategies relate to the need to reduce threats to navigation through the accidental refloating of abandoned hulls.

Figure 46. Remains of the *Jupiter*, Mutton Cove Ships' Graveyard (Port Adelaide, South Australia) showing a pile driven through the bow of the vessel. Photo by Nathan Richards.

Appropriate Abandonment Environment

The appropriate environment of abandonment is a crucial factor in ensuring the placement assurance of deliberately beached vessels. Certain environmental conditions, for instance, may adversely affect hull treatment procedures designed to ensure discard. At beached abandonment locations, if the salvager does not thoroughly breach a hull, be it with the use of explosives or some other procedure, or if they do not adequately weigh it down, the vessel may float off or move. Numerous environmental conditions affect the final stages of abandonment. These are usually limited to two factors: substrate and tide. The method of beaching, and the speed at which salvager runs the vessel, in turn plays a role.

Substrates

Nicholls's Seamanship and Nautical Knowledge indicates that in the case of the beaching of a vessel in the context of imminent undesired sinking, the "beach should, preferably, be of sand or gravel and free from rocks."[61]

Although this may occur because of a desire to minimize damage to a vessel when beaching it for future refloating, the situation when beaching for discard purposes is significantly different. The first trend seems to be beaching in a silty substrate. Although this means that the vessels will not suffer much damage during beaching, it means that the hull can settle into the substrate and will be less likely to float away.[62] This has been noticed in many cases, such as the ships' graveyards at Port Adelaide, South Australia (see figure 47), and from descriptions of the Bishop Island Ships' Graveyard in Brisbane. Other ships' graveyards, such as that at Witts Island, Tea Gardens, New South Wales (fig. 48), and Bulwer, Moreton Island, Queensland, have been deposited on a sand substrate, but this is also due to the use of the vessels in the creation of a small boat harbor, in addition to placement assurance considerations. Indeed, in this case, people had salvaged these beached vessels substantially—and to the point that they would not float, irrespective of the underlying substrate. In the case of wooden vessels, the examination of the substrate at the East Arm burning beach (which contained at one time the remains of at least six Indonesian fishing vessels) suggests that running vessels ashore on a rocky shore allowed damage to be inflicted that would affect seaworthiness. This also allowed for the maxi-

Figure 47. Muddy substrate at the Mutton Cove Ships' Graveyard (Port Adelaide, South Australia) showing remains of the *Excelsior* sinking. Photo by Nathan Richards.

Figure 48. Sandy riverine substrate at the Witts Island Ships' Graveyard (Port Stephens, New South Wales) showing remains of the *Federal*. Photo by Nathan Richards.

Figure 49. Rock substrate at the "East Arm Burning Beach" (Darwin Harbor, Northern Territory) showing solid footing and the effects of burning. Photo by Nathan Richards.

mum amount of material to be destroyed if the remains were set on fire (fig. 49). In this way, the substrate of the ships' graveyard, or abandonment area, may also provide clues about the perception of the hull and the expectation of what salvage behaviors individuals would need to carry out on specific hull types in postdepositional contexts.

Tide Height and Tidal Variation

Nicholls's Seamanship and Nautical Knowledge also suggests that when beaching a vessel,

> if there is an appreciable range of tide it will be best to beach the ship on the falling tide, just after high water, to give as much time as possible to secure the vessel before the tide rises to the same level again, and to give more opportunity to effect repairs.[63]

Although it is not the case that repairs would need to be carried out on the deliberately abandoned vessels that make up a part of this study, tidal variation may have been a factor that allowed the abandoners enough time to ensure placement or carry out more modifications to ensure the vessel remained where it lay. Although tide is not a concern with submerged hulls, which once sunk will never float again, it is a concern at beached abandonment sites where extensive salvage has occurred. Donald Shomette, for instance, has noted that the use of fire to reduce a hull will decrease that hull's weight and therefore increase its buoyancy.[64] If salvagers did not weigh the hull with enough stone, and if a tidal variation was large enough, the remains would likely leave its location of disposal. Although this also relates to ferrous-hulled vessels, the inherent buoyancy of wood under the right conditions may make an abandoned wooden hull act in a raftlike way despite its manner of breaching. Hence, the most probable hypothesis is that people endeavored to beach vessels at high tide in order to get their ship as far as possible on land, and then carried out further hull minimization at low tide. In the case of the Garden Island Ships' Graveyard, historical research provided five separate abandonment events between 1927 and 1935 where there were known dates and times of abandonment. This allowed for an assessment of this hypothesis by examining when watercraft were abandoned in relation to the height of the tide (see figure 50). For this site, it shows conclusively that tidal height was a consideration in planning abandonment, with all five events occurring at, or just before, the daily tidal maxima on each occasion. Delgado has also noted this practice of high-tide beaching for low-tide salvage in the case of the ship-breaking activities of

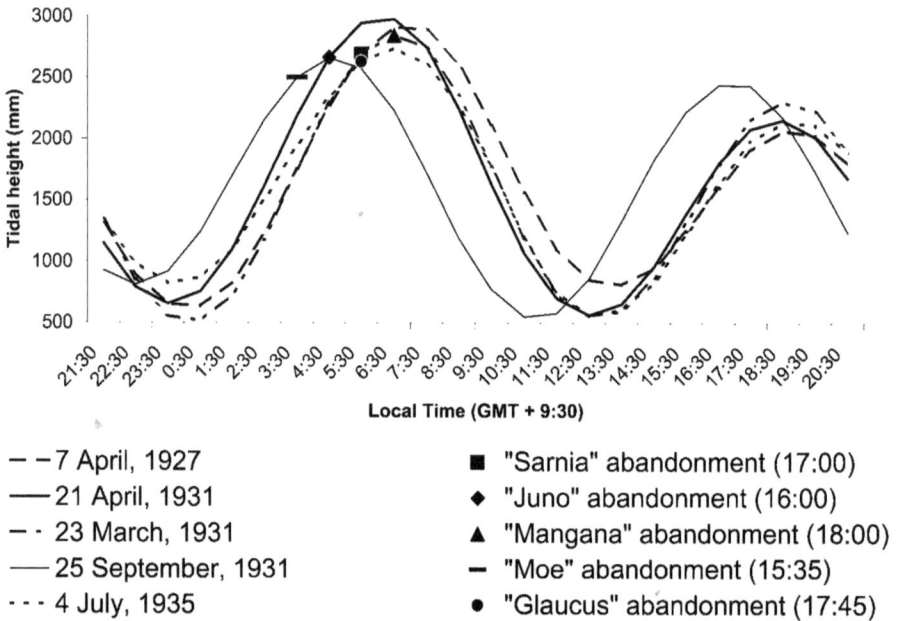

Figure 50. Sea levels for select vessels at the Garden Island Ships' Graveyard showing sea-level change in association with abandonment event. Sea levels for Port Adelaide (inner harbor) are supplied by the National Tidal Facility, Flinders University of South Australia. Copyright reserved.

salvager Charles Hare at South Beach and Rincon Point, San Francisco, in the 1850s during the California Gold Rush.[65]

Speed and Orientation

On the issue of speed, sources note that low speeds and a right angle to shore are important factors in maximizing refloating potential.[66] Previous work by Richards has addressed the issue of the angle of beaching at the Garden Island Ships' Graveyard, noting that people beached vessels between a forty-five- and ninety-degree angle or parallel with the shore.[67] However, this research also indicates that ship abandoners placed smaller, flatter bottom vessels parallel to shore and larger watercraft at an angle closer to perpendicular. This may have been due to spatial constraints at the site, which is within a tidal inlet rather than exposed beach. Nevertheless, in these cases it may be that people ran vessels aground at as high a speed as manageable in order to make the most of the space at hand, place the vessel as high up on the beach as possible, and inflict the maximum amount of damage to the hull as possible. Archival research, however, discovered no sources confirming the desirability of high speeds when "running aground" vessels.

Conclusion

Although the use of explosives in the sinking of a vessel is a common method of ship discard, such an activity does not typify the whole abandonment process. Deliberate abandonment events relate to the systematic processes associated with placement assurance, hull reduction, and salvage activities. In the consideration of any one of these processes, it is important to bear in mind that they are as much technologically dependent as the construction and modification of watercraft. These practices also represent the interaction of human decisions in relation to technological and economic conditions, as well as environmental restraints.

The decision to scuttle or destroy depends on a number of factors, such as the cost and ease of disassembly (related to the type of vessel) and the regulatory protocols in relation to discard. Logistical issues associated with all of these processes are important to understand, in order to appreciate the causes and consequences of discard activities.

In the case of ship discard, three stages of salvage exist. Although not all of these stages may exist at a particular site, in many cases archaeologists can detect them. Understanding the varied catalysts of these stages is important because they illustrate the socioeconomics of, and responsibilities associated with, ship owning. Additionally, the circumstances behind salvage can be read from the archaeological record, and salvage can be seen as a cause of abandonment (when prices for materials are high), as well as a consequence of abandonment (when economies are at a low ebb). Although salvage activities tend to be processes of reduction, the signatures of each type of salvage, with the differences in method and variations of the sections of the vessel being broken up, may leave behind vastly different signatures that relate to the method used and hence the socioeconomic status of the group that carried out these activities. These processes are more than just events in a vessel's life or their archaeological transformation. They are evidence for the assessment of the behaviors relating to the use and disposal of watercraft, clues about the reasons for abandonment, and insights into the perception of a vessel as a salvageable item.

8

Conclusion

We have stern keepers to trust her glory to—the fire and the worm. Never more shall sunset lay golden robes on her, nor starlight tremble on the waves that part at her gliding. Perhaps, where the low gate opens to some cottage-garden, the tired traveler may ask, idly, why the moss grows so green on its rugged wood; and even the sailor's child may not answer, nor know, that the night-dew lies deep in the war-rents of the wood of the old Temeraire.

—John Ruskin, *The Works of John Ruskin*

Shipbuilders construct watercraft to particular technological standards within the economic parameters dictated by their owner. They exist within a flux of diverse, changing conditions that see them pass through an array of systemic, techno-economic reassignments. As tools of commerce, they invariably came to their end within a causal and behavioral spectrum, at one end catastrophically lost, at the other end deliberately discarded. This research suggests a number of things. First, discarded vessels are not shipwrecks, noncatastrophically made a part of the archaeological record. The array of decision-making processes that define acts of abandonment makes discarded watercraft a reflection of changing techno-economic circumstances within maritime communities.

For this reason, researchers can use discarded watercraft as a mirror of the events and processes that brought about their disposal, and they are an extremely rich database that sheds light on the effect of technological and economic change and on economic and social circumstances. The analytic potential of abandoned watercraft relates to how we view discard behaviors. On one level, we can see discard as a process, with a myriad of interconnected causes, and on another, we can see discard as an event that culminates in a number of consequences for the use and reuse of watercraft.

Discard as Process

The process of discard appears in the rate of abandonment through time—the discard trend. This research has indicated that discard trends on national levels are indicative of a myriad of economic changes brought about by economic rise, decline, warfare, and the aftermath of war.

The relevance of warfare in relation to the deliberate abandonment of watercraft is that war creates economic incentives for industrial expansion and research and development. This occurs through a dramatic increase in demand for goods and services for a range of uses (such as munitions). It has a particular effect on ship construction due to fears of shipping shortages by dramatically increasing ship construction. The inevitable effects of this are that such sectors emerge in a "glut" of surplus capacity following the conflict, which brings about a decrease in the availability of trade and the disposal of vessels. These programs of tonnage sterilization normally commence with older or obsolete watercraft sold at cheap prices and eventually discarded. In such situations, the only alternative to disposal behavior is stockpiling behavior. Other studies on watercraft abandonment have noted this.

Although there would appear to be a link between economic expansion and a decrease in discard behaviors, and the opposite during times of financial hardship, this is not always the case. Regional analyses express the scope and nature of particular economic boom times in many different ways. This illustrates the degree to which discard sites are the sensitive indicators of trade conditions. Indeed, the abandonment trend itself is a historically unique signature of economic and technological change within nations and regions.

Other important aspects of discard behavior are the alterations to vessels that occur while they are still functional. The lateral cycling and reuse of ships have discernible effects on their use-life. These modifications and conversions are also relatable to the nature of changing trade conditions, and they reflect the tendency to dispose of watercraft, as they occur at times when economic and technological circumstances are changing rapidly. Indeed, discarded watercraft as a category are defined by their prolonged lives and the number of mercantile and support functions that many fulfilled over prolonged periods of time.

Other contributing factors to the discard trend are cultural constraints that predetermine the kinds of vessels that shipowners will abandon. Regulatory and legislative controls play a pivotal role in dictating the type of ships operating, the nations that merchants trade with, and the technological and economic standards in shipping. The abandoned watercraft record reflects this with the types of vessels abandoned over time and the nationality of these vessels. Similar cultural constraints also control the processes of discard itself. Federal sea dumping and environmental protection, as well as state ports and harbors legislation, have played a major role in controlling the methods involved in the disposal of unwanted or unusable watercraft. They also play an important role in the location of areas for abandonment.

Discard as Event

The discard processes within this research also have an influence on the nature of discard as an event. The discard event culminates in the beaching, scuttling, or demolition of watercraft. A number of standard behaviors relate to the varied processes leading to discard events, all of which leave behind their own archaeological signatures. Hull-reduction strategies, including salvage, are processes that aim to extensively diminish a vessel, weighing requirements for subsequent "safe" abandonment with the economic costs of dismantling and transport. Placement assurance techniques are those that facilitate the final placement of a vessel at an intended location, and the methods that ensure that it stays permanently disposed of, and will not become a future hazard to navigation. These two processes are the most fundamentally important discard activities that facilitate the transformation of a vessel from its systemic context to an archaeological one. They can, however, also be seen in certain instances as mechanisms that bring about the continued use of watercraft. In the case of postabandonment use, abandoned watercraft have their function as floating vessels discarded, and they become objects with other purposes, such as bathhouses, breakwaters, or artificial reefs. Over time, these final functions are abandoned, and barring their rebuilding and reuse, they cease to be in a systemic context.

Research has suggested that researchers can more substantially link the signatures of use and discard to temporal factors. The placement assurance, hull reduction and salvage mechanisms that archaeologists can detect from the examination of archaeological remains are as technologically dependent as the processes of ship construction. It is important to remember that the abandoned watercraft resource has much potential to fill in many of our historical gaps concerning ship technology. Although this research does not assert that the abandoned watercraft resource is as good a representation of technological innovation as the shipwreck resource is, its findings do indicate that it is a good indicator of technological change. We can see this reflected in the small number of vessels that have undergone major technological transformations through their use life. Certain processes that act on watercraft while in a systemic context, such as conversion and modification activities, have a direct influence on their passing into an archaeological context by artificially extending their use-life. In this way, we can see certain technologies as flexibly interrelated with economic, in that they are more open to amendment and use-life extension.

Indeed, the fates of all of the abandoned vessels mentioned here were the direct consequence of the type of vessel they were. Whether in the context of military campaigns or changing economic and technological circumstances, at their most fundamental level, discarded ships are a reflection of *choice*. Moreover, as the embodiment of human decision-making processes, these watercraft can be seen as a reflection of the consequences of economic, historic, and technological pressures. By considering the interaction between vessel design (a mirror of technological and economic development and change) and particular historical contexts (itself a reflection of these same processes), such discard sites have the potential to expose to us the social histories of humans at particular times in history, and even throughout periods of human history.

An understanding of the nature of abandoned watercraft in the past is beneficial in the analysis of that same resource in the present. Although on one hand it provides a framework within which we can clearly see that there has been a transition in the types of abandonment sites that have formed, we can more specifically understand that there are the same underlying issues revolving around the sacrifice of watercraft. Moreover, it becomes clearer that there is a high level of continuity within the political, technological, and economic causes and consequences of such discard behavior in relation to old, obsolete, or unwanted watercraft. From here, we can begin to see that unwanted vessels *are not just abandoned*; their owners abandon them for a range of reasons that tell us much about the people who used them. As has been demonstrated, the benefit of archaeological methods and assumptions coupled with the wealth of historical literature on the Australian experiences of deliberate vessel abandonment will serve to confirm the potential of this resource.

The Analysis of Abandonment

By seeing discard as a reflection of economically driven and technologically derived trade that can be discerned from the archaeological record, two assumptions previously communicated in maritime archaeology can be merged: watercraft are artifacts imbued with cultural norms and they are an "extraordinary database for anthropologically oriented archaeologists."[1]

The comparative methods used in this research, which entail the dissection of useful historical and archaeological data, its categorization into meaningful classificatory schema, and reassembly into relational aggregates, are an extension of methods used in shipwreck-based studies. The procedures used here have really been no different from any number of other archaeological studies, whether concentrating on artifact types, use-wear analysis, or geographical distribution. However, these methods have not been widely used within maritime archaeology, despite being a helpful way of carrying out comparative analysis. The application of these methods would be undoubtedly useful for any number of other types of sites and is simply dependent on the possibilities of their classification. Many other aspects of the seascape/landscape, especially when they have a major technologically derived aspect, are perfectly suited to being classified and can similarly be used as indices related to technological and economic trends.

The analyses in this book have used a resource of which two-thirds were unrecorded in the Australian Historic Shipwrecks Database. Although we do not currently know what percentage of the ANAVD translates to real archaeological sites for management, this research has made a case for the significance of discarded watercraft through its analysis.

Asking questions such as Was this vessel wrecked? or Was this vessel deliberately discarded? have huge ramifications for how we identify sites and how we come to understand them. This in turn contributes to the interpretive potential of watercraft in the archaeological record, irrespective of how they came to be at a particular location.

Indeed, the discard trends communicated in this work, although admittedly open to further refinement and analysis, are themselves an interpretive tool. An understanding of the peaks and troughs in these trends illuminates potential new interpretations for many shipwrecks, especially when seen in relation to the correlations between historic events and maritime fraud.

Potential Research Directions

There are many potential directions for research into the discard of watercraft and discard in general. From one perspective, the innumerable directions evident at the conclusion of this study represent the failings of the research. In hindsight, it may have made more sense to undertake a comparative analysis on a regional or statewide level. Such a study would have been able to make a detailed examination of the economic, technological, political, and geographic factors dictating discard trends in relative isolation and with minimal confusion from the myriad of factors at play within the many regions of a very large landmass. And such a study would have been undoubtedly easier. However, the challenge in exposing the significance of the entire abandoned vessel resource in a meaningful and broad-reaching way was too great to ignore.

Nevertheless, this has meant that there are many potential research directions emerging from the need to refine the abandoned vessel data set and more comprehensively establish, dismiss, and discuss any number of discard trend correlates. In particular, the concentration on watercraft discard on regional levels is an area that was only really touched on in this study. Indeed, the subject of the use of discard correlates on a regional level remains open to any number of similar studies. These studies, focusing on statewide or port-focused discard trends and their relationship to historical events, may help to communicate the causes and consequences of discard events and the causal relationships among economic, technological, and social processes.[2] This is not only limited to watercraft discard. Large amounts of data also are available concerning the official and illicit discard of any number of other types of material culture, including munitions, chemicals, dredge spoil, car bodies, scrap metal, medical supplies, aircraft, and other assorted equipment and refuse in the seas and oceans off Australia. This data may serve to reinforce or reappraise the findings contained in this work as well as communicate the history of the use of the sea as a dumping ground. Indeed, there are probably many site types that could have some light shed on them from the application of a generalist framework similar to the one espoused here.

Additionally, any number of studies, on local, regional, national, and even international levels, focusing on any aspect of the technological development of ships and shipping are likely to add to how we view the diffusion of technologies, or indeed, the role of watercraft as vectors of technological change. With an appropriate system of classification, and data set, diachronic analyses can contribute to the way we see archaeological methods as reinforcing or redefining the causal relationships in technological and economic models, and history in general.

Finally, similar examinations of discard behaviors in other countries may illustrate the common features or stark differences in separate trends. This in itself may contribute to how we understand the interaction of national economies, the causes and consequence of the shifts in economic and political power, and the degree to which researchers may discern the effects of global economic phenomena from archaeological remains.

Notes

Chapter 1. Introduction

1. Richards, "Deep Structures"; see also Richards and Staniforth, "Abandoned Ships Project."

2. Andrews, "Hulks"; Australian Government, Coastal and Marine Pollution home page; Australian Government, National Shipwreck Database home page; Lawes, "More Hulks"; Martin, "Hulks"; Thomas, "Clarence River"; Loney, *Jack Loney's Maritime Australia*; Loney, *Australian Shipwrecks Update Volume 5*; Stone and Loney, *High and Dry*; Parsons and Plunkett, *Scuttled and Abandoned Ships*; Smith, *Sailing Ships Hulked at Port Adelaide*; Glassford, "Fleet of Hulks"; Plunkett, *Sea Dumping in Australia*.

3. These institutions include state cultural heritage management agencies, archives (state and national branches), libraries, historical societies, universities, and museums in all states and territories of Australia: the Museum and Art Gallery of the Northern Territory; Maritime Museum of Tasmania; Tasmanian Museum and Art Gallery; Queensland Maritime Museum; Museum of Tropical North Queensland; Australian National Maritime Museums; Western Australian Maritime Museum; National Trust offices (Northern Territory); state and territory archives and records offices (Tasmania, South Australia, Northern Territory); state and territory heritage branches (Queensland, Tasmania, South Australia, Northern Territory, New South Wales, Victoria); state and territory libraries (South Australia, Northern Territory, Queensland); Newcastle Regional Library; state and territory offices of the National Archives (Adelaide, South Australia; Hobart, Tasmania); university archaeology and history departments (Flinders University, James Cook University); historical and maritime archaeological societies (Port Adelaide Historical Society, Society for Underwater Historical Research, Maritime Archaeological Association of Queensland, Cairns Historical Society); local museums (Morgan Museum, South Australia; Penneshaw Maritime and Folk Museum, South Australia; Kingscote Museum, South Australia; Newcastle Regional Maritime Museum, New South Wales, Queenscliffe Maritime Museum, Victoria; Geelong Maritime Museum, Victoria; Port Albert Maritime Museum, Victoria; Portland Maritime Museum, Victoria; Warrnambool Maritime Museum, Victoria; Polly Woodside Museum, Victoria); university libraries (University of Queensland, Flinders University, Northern Territory University); and port authority archives (Cairns).

4. Milne, McKewan, and Goodburn, *Nautical Archaeology on the Foreshore*.

5. See, for example, Attenborough and Roberts, "Sunbeam"; Baker, "Report of Hulk"; Dalgairns and Peterson, "Garthneill"; Darkin, "Gem"; Ford, "Unidentified Shipwreck D"; Foster, "Unidentified Ketch"; Nash, "Sunbeam"; Stevenson, "Comparative Study of the Garthneill and Enterprise Hulks."

6. McCarthy, "Salvage Archaeology," 291.

7. See Dumas, "Ancient Wrecks," 32; Green, *Australia's Oldest Wreck*; Muckelroy, *Maritime Archaeology*, 60; McGrail, "Prehistoric Water Transport in N. W. Europe," 12; Baker, "Technical Importance of Shipwreck Archaeology," 17–18.

8. Rathje, "Manifesto for Modern Material-Culture Studies," 51.

9. Delgado, "Erosion Exposed Shipwreck Remains"; Delgado, "Skeleton in the Sand"; Delgado, "Documentation and Identification of the Two-Masted Schooner *Neptune*"; Bright, "Beached Shipwreck Dynamics"; Fontenoy, "A Discussion of Maritime Archaeology," 47; McCarthy, "Black Cats," 217.

10. See, for instance, Gould, "Looking Below the Surface," 3–4, and Gould, *Archaeology and the Social History of Ships*, 11, which were later supported in subsequent projects such as Gould, "H.M.S. Vixen," "Archaeology of HMS Vixen"; Souza, *Persistence of Sail in the Age of Steam*.

11. McCarthy, *Iron Ships and Steam Shipwrecks*.

12. McCarthy, "SS Xantho," 21–23.

13. Henderson, "Archaeological Value of Iron Vessels and Steamships," 11.

14. Brouwer, *International Register of Historic Ships*.

15. See McCarthy, "Introduction," 7, and McCarthy, "SS Xantho," 21–22.

16. For a full list of sources see Richards, "Archaeological Examination of Watercraft Abandonment in Australia."

17. MacLeod, "Report on the Corrosion of Iron Shipwrecks in South Australia," 1–10; Kenderdine, *Historic Shipping on the River Murray*, 274–76; Kentish, *Stabilisation of Santiago*; McCarthy, "SS Xantho," 204–5, 347; O'Reilly, "Assessment of Australian Built Wooden Sailing Vessels."

18. Richards, "History and Archaeology of the Garden Island Ships' Graveyard"; Richards, "Inferences from the Study of Iron and Steamship Abandonment"; Richards, "Garden Island Ships' Graveyard"; Richards, "Deep Structures"; Richards, "Role of Isolation in Cultural Site Formation"; Richards, "Role of Geo-politics in Cultural Site Formation"; Doyle, "Examination of Associations"; Richards and Nash, "Unfit for Further Use."

19. Such as Jeffery, "Development of Maritime Archaeology in South Australia," 85.

20. Simpson and Weiner, *Oxford English Dictionary* 15:280.

21. See Stevens, *Dictionary of Shipping Terms and Phrases*, 6, 64; Holman, *Handy Book for Shipowners and Masters*, 45, 53–54; Lloyd's of London, *Lloyd's Calendar: 1973*, 423; Lloyd's of London, *Lloyd's Nautical Year Book: 1981*, 488, 500–501; Lloyd's of London, *Lloyd's Nautical Year Book: 1991*, 370, 380.

22. Shomette, *Tidewater Time Capsule*, 6–7; and see also Babits and Corbin-Kjorness, "Final Report on an Archaeological Survey of the Western Shore of the Pungo River," 38–39.

23. Ballard and Archbold, *Discovery of the Titanic*; Gesner, *Pandora*, xi, 13, 14; Gesner, "HMS Pandora Project," 1; Harris and Adams, "Sea Venture," 365–66.

24. See Lloyd's of London, *Lloyd's Calendar: 1973*, 425, and Lloyd's of London, *Lloyd's Nautical Year Book: 1981*, 493.

25. Matthews, *American Merchant Ships, 1850–1900: Series 2*, 135.

26. See Strachan, *History and Archaeology of the Sydney Cove Shipwreck*, 1; Nash, "Sydney Cove Historic Shipwreck," 11; Nash, *Cargo for the Colony*, 22.

27. See Duncan, "Signposts in the Sea"; Souza, *Persistence of Sail in the Age of Steam*; Murphy, "Shipwrecks as a Data Base for Human Behavioral Studies."

28. Parsons, *Pioneer Australian Steamship Company*, 66; Parsons and Plunkett, *Scuttled and Abandoned Ships*, 3; Stone and Loney, *High and Dry*, 16, 58.

29. Richards, "History and Archaeology of the Garden Island Ships' Graveyard," 71; South Australian Government, *Government Record Group 51*, file 170/622/1934.

30. Moore, "Boneyard Below the Bridge," 3.

31. Richards, *Shipwreck Heritage of the Richmond River*, sec. 13.

32. See Parsons, *Century of Wrecks of Steamships in NSW*.

33. Richards, *Shipwreck Heritage of the Richmond River*.

34. See, for instance, Richards, *Shipwreck Heritage of the Clarence River*, 54.

35. See the case of the *Westralian*, cited in its final Customs House Register (*British Register of Australian Shipping*, Hobart 4/1923) as "no longer in existence (wrecked)," despite the remains of this vessel existing in the Otago Bay Ships' Graveyard (Tasmania, Australia) and confirmed with measurements taken during archaeological inspection.

36. Nutley and Smith, *Maritime Archaeology of Myall Lakes/Tea Gardens*, 20.

37. Dundon, *Shipbuilders of Brisbane Water NSW*, 239.

38. Phillips, *River Boat Days*, 128.

39. Johnstone, *Archaeology of Ships*, 10, 13; Crumlin-Pedersen, "Ship Types and Sizes, AD 800–1400," 72; Brouwer, *International Register of Historic Ships*, 44–45; Gifford and Gifford, "Sailing Characteristics of Saxon Ships."

40. Gould, "H.M.S. Vixen"; Gould, "Archaeology of HMS Vixen"; Gould, "HMS Vixen."

41. See, for instance, Barfield, *Dictionary of Anthropology*, 289–93. Used in maritime archaeology for the first time by Gould, "Looking Below the Surface," 6–8, to describe the potential of shipwrecks to produce generalizations about human behavior.

42. As noted by McCarthy, *Jervoise Bay Shipwrecks*, 1.

43. COIITC, *Technological Change in Australia* 2:17.

44. Bach, "Sea Transport in Australia," 7.

Chapter 2. Abandoned Watercraft in History and Archaeology

1. See Bruce-Mitford, *Aspects of Anglo-Saxon Archaeology*, 1–5, 17–73, 81–82, 114–19; Johnstone, *Archaeology of Ships*, 68–70, 102–12; Fenwick, *Graveney Boat*, 195, 197; Christensen, "Scandinavian Ships from Earliest Times to the Vikings," 166, 168; Christensen, *Guide to the Viking Ship Museum*, 6, 20–22, 27; Evans, "Com-

ing of the Anglo-Saxons," 114; Evans, "Kingly Burial," 116; Evans, "Snape Boat"; Evans, "Sutton Hoo"; Martin, "Swans of the Sea God," 122, 124; Christensen, "Oseberg Ship"; Christensen, "Gokstad Ship"; Brouwer, *International Register of Historic Ships*, 163–65; Gould, *Archaeology and the Social History of Ships*, 174–75; Muller-Wille, "Boat-Graves in Northern Europe," 187.

2. Johnstone, *Archaeology of Ships*, 80.

3. Christensen, "Scandinavian Ships from Earliest Times to the Vikings," 162, 167; Christensen, *Guide to the Viking Ship Museum*, 86, 114; Randsborg, "Seafaring and Society," 16; Delgado, "Hjortspring Boat," 193; Gould, *Archaeology and the Social History of Ships*, 111.

4. Bruce-Mitford, *Aspects of Anglo-Saxon Archaeology*, 1.

5. Randsborg, "Seafaring and Society," 21.

6. Meaney, *Gazetteer of Early Ango-Saxon Burial Sites*, 171; Fenwick, *Graveney Boat*, 197.

7. Jenkins, *Boat Beneath the Pyramids*, 158.

8. Ibid; Throckmorton, "Shipwright's Art," 92; El-Baz, "Finding a Pharaoh's Funeral Bark"; Miller, "Riddle of the Pyramid Boats"; Patch and Haldane, *Pharoah's Boat at the Carnegie*; Haldane, "Lisht Timbers"; Haldane, "Khufu Ships"; Jones, *Egyptian Bookshelf*; Gould, *Archaeology and the Social History of Ships*, 104, 122–25.

9. Johnstone, *Archaeology of Ships*, 9–16; Jenkins, *Boat Beneath the Pyramids*, 161; Lipke, *Royal Ship of Cheops*, 1; Lipke, "Retrospective on the Royal Ship of Cheops," 19, 30; Kadry, "Solar Boat of Cheops," 123–24; Miller, "Riddle of the Pyramid Boats," 545; Haldane, "Lisht Timbers," 103; Haldane, "Khufu Ships," 223; Jones, *Egyptian Bookshelf*, 18–19, 27.

10. See Meiggs, *Roman Ostia*, 155; Johnstone, *Archaeology of Ships*, 100–101; Marsden, *Ships of the Port of London: First to Eleventh Centuries*, 11, 97, 104; Lemee, Schiellerup, and Gothche, "Ships and Shipyards in Copenhagen"; Delgado, "County Hall Ship"; Delgado, "New Guys House Boat"; Lemee, "Ship Cemetery on the B&W Site"; Gould, *Archaeology and the Social History of Ships*, 115.

11. Marsden, *Ships of the Port of London: First to Eleventh Centuries*, 11, 109–29.

12. For discussions, see Merrifield, *London*, 201–2.

13. Ibid., 203; Marsden, *Ships of the Port of London: First to Eleventh Centuries*, 129.

14. Merrifield, *London*, 203.

15. Marsden, "Blackfriars Wreck 3," 130–32; Marsden, *Ships of the Port of London: First to Eleventh Centuries*, 33–108; Marsden, *Ships of the Port of London: Twelfth to Seventeenth Centuries*, 55–104; Delgado, "Blackfriars Wrecks."

16. Runestone Press, *Sunk!* 26; Reiss, "Ship Beneath Manhattan," 90; Reiss, "Ronson Ship," 349–50; Steffy, "Thirteen Colonies," 125–28.

17. Bullen, "Glimpse into Niantic's Hold," 326–27; Delgado, "No Longer a Buoyant Ship," 316–17; Delgado, "What Becomes of the Old Ships?" 8; Delgado, "Gold Rush Enterprise," 321; Delgado, "Niantic"; Parker, "Story of the Ship Niantic," 51; Lawson, "Egeria," 17–18; Edwin Fox Restoration Society, *Story of the Edwin Fox*; Johnston,

"End of the Age of Sail," 240, 242–43; Aldsworth, "Excavations at the Former Royal Naval Dockyard, Bermuda," 109—110, 128–29; Brouwer, *International Register of Historic Ships*, 152–53; O'Keefe, "Shipwreck Under the City"; O'Keefe, "Looking at the Ship Under the City."

18. Fisher, "Two Englands," 468–69.

19. Delgado, "No Longer a Buoyant Ship," 319; Delgado, "Gold Rush Enterprise," 322; Parker, "Story of the Ship Niantic," 51–52.

20. Christoffersen, "Iron Age Finds in Funen," 57.

21. Greenhill in White, "Putting People Back into Ships," 1.

22. Ibid.

23. Hockmann, "Mainz Boats," 255–56; Hockmann, "Late Roman Rhine Vessels from Mainz," 125.

24. Hockmann, "Late Roman Rhine Vessels from Mainz," 126, 133.

25. Christoffersen, "Iron Age Finds in Funen," 57.

26. Milne in Hammond, "Graveyard of Wooden Ships Found on Thames Foreshore," 4.

27. Ibid.

28. Steffy, "Kyrenia Ship," 94; Steffy, "Boat," 43–47; Wachsmann, "Galilee Boat," 81–82; Wachsmann, "Sea of Galilee Wreck," 364–65; Crumlin-Pedersen, "Medieval Ships in Danish Waters," 67–8; Crumlin-Pedersen, "Aspects of Wood Technology in Medieval Shipbuilding," 142.

29. As noted by Hutchinson, *Medieval Ships and Shipping*, 110.

30. Heal and Hutchinson, "Three Recently Found Logboats," 213.

31. Goodburn, "Fragments of an Early Carvel-Built Vessel From Camber, East Sussex, England," 332–33.

32. Ballard, "Transporting of the Obelisks at Karnak"; Ballard, "Queen Hatshepsut's Great Lighter"; Ballard, "Egyptian Shipping of About 1500 B.C."; Ballard, "Great Obelisk Lighter of 1550 B.C."; Ballard, "Egyptian Obelisk Lighter"; Solver, "Egyptian Obelisk-Ships"; Jenkins, *Boat Beneath the Pyramids*, 131; Ward-Haldane, "Boat Timbers from El-Lisht," 142; Wehausen et al., "Colossi of Memnon and Egyptian Barges," 295–96, 306; Patch and Haldane, *Pharoah's Boat at the Carnegie*, 28, 44; Haldane, "Lisht Timbers," 102–3, 241–42.

33. Richardson, "Excavations at Hungate, York," 67–69, 113; Tatton-Brown, "Excavations at the Customs House Site, City of London," 103, 109, 116; Hutchinson, "Plank Fragment from a Boat-Find," 29; Hutchinson, *Medieval Ships and Shipping*, 56, 65, 69, 105–6, 108–10; Friel, "Henry V's Grace Dieu and the Wreck in the R. Hamble," 11; Clarke et al., "Recent Work on the R. Hamble Wreck"; Marsden, *Ships of the Port of London: First to Eleventh Centuries*, 141, 152–59; Marsden, *Ships of the Port of London: Twelfth to Seventeenth Centuries*, 9, 22, 30, 41–54, 113–27, 136–44, 160–72, 175, 179, 181, 217–21; McGrail, *Ancient Boats in North-West Europe*, 41.

34. Stammers and Kearon, *Jhelum*, 109.

35. Throckmorton, *Shipwrecks and Archaeology*, vii; Bright, "Beached Shipwreck Dynamics."

36. See, for instance, Matthews, *American Merchant Ships 1850–1900: Series 1*, 52; Moore, *Last Days of Mast and Sail*, 3.

37. Arenhold, "Nydam Boat at Kiel"; Christensen, "Scandinavian Ships from Earliest Times to the Vikings," 162, 164; Johnstone, *Archaeology of Ships*, 74, 78, 80; Muckelroy, *Maritime Archaeology*, 11; Evans, "Coming of the Anglo-Saxons," 112, 114; Crumlin-Pedersen, "Wrecks in the North Sea and the Baltic," 69–70; Crumlin-Pedersen, "Maritime Aspects of the Archaeology of Roman and Migration-Period Denmark," 42, 45; Rieck, "Aspects of Coastal Defence in Denmark," 90–91; Rieck, "Nydam"; Rieck, "Maritime Archaeology in Denmark," 84; Cederlund, "Baltic Sea," 50; Delgado, "Nydam Boat"; Gould, *Archaeology and the Social History of Ships*, 112–13; Akerlund, *Fartygsfynden in den Forna Hamnen i Kalmar*; Linder and Raban, *Marine Archaeology*, 48; Martin, "Viking World," 130; Martin, "North Sea Traders," 134, 136; Marsden et al., "Late Saxon Logboat from Clapton," 89, 95, 99, 109–10; Bill, "Skuldelev Ships," 388–89; Einarrson, "Kalmar Harbour Wrecks," 219–20; Hutchinson, *Medieval Ships and Shipping*, 4–5; Springmann, "Mukran Wreck," 120–23.

38. Warner, *Navy*, 50–51, 54–55, 58.

39. Dugan, *Man Explores the Sea*, 250–51; Still, "Confederate Naval Strategy"; Still, *Iron Afloat*; Wood, "Battle Was a Drawn One," 98; Mayhew, "Defense"; Baker, Anuskiewicz, and Garrison, "Mapping and Site Characterization in Zero Visibility"; Broadwater, "York River Shipwreck Project"; Broadwater, "Shipwreck in a Swimming Pool"; Broadwater, "In the Shadow of Wooden Walls"; Broadwater, "HMS Charon"; Broadwater, "Yorktown Shipwrecks"; Switzer, "Interpretation of the Stern Area of the Privateer Defence"; Switzer, "Nautical Archaeology in Penobscot Bay"; Switzer, "Recovery and Initial Interpretation of the Shot Locker and Bilge Pump Well"; Switzer, "Maritime Archaeology in the United States"; Switzer, "Defence Project"; Switzer, "Privateers, Not Pirates"; Switzer, "Defence" (1997); Switzer, "Defence" (1998); Wyman, "Developing the Plans for the Revolutionary War Privateer Defence"; Hazzard, "Yorktown Shipwreck Archaeology Project"; Shomette, *Shipwrecks on the Chesapeake*; Shomette, *Tidewater Time Capsule*; Shomette, "Chesapeake Flotilla," 98–99; Leone, "Land and Water, Urban Life, and Boats," 175; Sands, *Yorktown's Captive Fleet*; Sands, "Gunboats and Warships of the American Revolution"; Bryce, *Weaponry from the Machault*; Zacharchuk and Waddell, *Excavation of the Machault*; Broadwater, Adams, and Renner, "Yorktown Shipwreck Archaeological Project"; Howe and Matthews, *American Clipper Ships* 2:405–6, 588, 656, 743; Sullivan, *Legacy of the Machault*; Matthews, *American Merchant Ships, 1850–1900: Series 1*, 274; Mattews, *American Merchant Ships, 1850–1900: Series 2*, 127, 214; Beattie and Pothier, *Battle of the Restigouche*; Cassavoy and Crisman, "War of 1812"; Crisman, "Struggle for a Continent"; Crisman, "Boscawen"; Watts, "Civil War at Sea," 226; Cussler and Dirgo, *Sea Hunters*, 183, 358, 367; Garrison, "CSS Georgia"; Johnston, "Cornwallis Cave Wreck"; Stevens, "Machault"; Zarzynski, "Wiawaka Bateaux Cluster"; Stephenson, "Physical Processes at the CSS Chattahoochee Wreck Site"; Abbass, "Newport and Captain Cook's Ships."

40. Cousteau, *Silent World*, 33, 35; Canby, *History of Ships and Seafaring*, 102–3; Lloyd's of London, *Lloyd's Calendar: 1965*, 653–54; Lloyd's of London, *Lloyd's Calendar: 1973*, 418; Kemp, *Oxford Companion to Ships and the Sea*, 755; Broeze, *Island Nation*, 48; Van Der Vat, *Grand Scuttle*; Smith, *Project AE2*, 23.

41. Randsborg, "Seafaring and Society," 17.

42. Porter, "Our Cake Is All Dough," 128; Simmons, "Steamboats on Inland Waterways," 199; Van Der Vat, *Grand Scuttle*, 12.

43. Taylor in Howe and Matthews, *American Clipper Ships* 2:557.

44. Kemp, *Campaign of the Spanish Armada*, 112.

45. Warner, *Navy*, 37, 52; Blackburn, *Illustrated Encyclopedia*, 142; Gould, "Archaeology of War," 121; Stenuit, "Wreck of the Pink Evstafi," 320.

46. Broadwater, "Yorktown Shipwreck Archaeological Project," 812.

47. Crumlin-Pedersen, "Ship Types and Sizes, AD 800–1400," 75.

48. Broadwater, "Yorktown Shipwreck Archaeological Project," 806, 810.

49. Crisman, "Struggle for a Continent," 143.

50. Ibid., 143–44, 146.

51. Gould, "H.M.S. Vixen," 43, 45, 66–67; Gould, "Archaeology of HMS Vixen," 144; Gould, "HMS Vixen"; Gould, *Archaeology and the Social History of Ships*, 281–89.

52. Gould, "H.M.S. Vixen," 53, 64; Gould, "Archaeology of HMS Vixen," 145.

53. Gould, "H.M.S. Vixen," 69–70; Gould, "Archaeology of HMS Vixen," 146.

54. Lenihan, "From Pearl to Bikini," 294.

55. See, for instance, the work on *Ticonderoga* and *Eagle* by Crisman, "Coffins of the Brave," 4–8; Cassavoy and Crisman, "War of 1812," 177, 179, 185–86.

56. Delgado, *Ghost Fleet*, 18.

57. Paine, *Down East*, 115–16.

58. Eliot, "Bikini's Nuclear Graveyard"; Weisgall, *Operation Crossroads*; Delgado, *Ghost Fleet*; Askins, "Crossroads Wrecks"; Lenihan, "From Pearl to Bikini."

59. Delgado, *Ghost Fleet*, 21–22.

60. Colton, "Colorado River Steamboat 'Charles H. Spencer,'" 6–7; Rusho, "Charles Spencer and His Wonderful Steamboat," 37, 39; Gesner, *Pandora*, 1; Simmons, "Steamboats on Inland Waterways," 197, 199; Carrell, "Charles H. Spencer," 96–97; Cussler and Dirgo, *Sea Hunters*, 42; Mackay, *Lady of the Lake*, 12, 13.

61. Johnstone, *Archaeology of Ships*, 112–14; Fenwick, "Graveney Boat"; Johnstone, *Graveney Boat*, 181, 183, 193, 223, "Graveney Boat," 175–76; Gould, *Archaeology and the Social History of Ships*, 113–14.

62. Claesson, "Annabella," 16–17.

63. Merriman, *Cypress Landing Shipwreck of Chocowinity Bay*, 1, 10.

64. La Roche, "Small Boat Finds," 108–10; Crisman, "Struggle for a Continent," 132–33; Delgado, "Quebec Bateaux," 332.

65. Moore, "Kingston Inner Harbour Survey"; Moore, "Boneyard Below the Bridge."

66. Watson, "Wreck Rescue," 7; Wood, "Hulk Survey, Kidwelly, Dyfed," 6–7; Emery, "Successful Search for Sunken Boats," 4; Milne, McKewan, and Goodburn, *Nautical Archaeology on the Foreshore.*

67. Dobson, "Maritime Fife Completes Phase 2," 3.

68. Devendra, "Remains of Riverine Craft," 22.

69. Leone, "Land and Water, Urban Life, and Boats," 177.

70. Ellis, "Africa's Sahel," 164–65.

71. Throckmorton, "American Heritage in the Falklands," 35; Throckmorton, "Bones on a Beach," 211; Dean and Miller, "Story of the St Mary," 35; Smith, *Condemned at Stanley,* 3; Southby-Tailyour, *Falkland Island Shores,* 9; Dean, "Falklands Wrecks and Hulks," 148–50.

72. Jackson, *Quail Island,* 81–85.

73. Lellman, "Hulks at Stanley Harbour"; Goold-Adams, *Return of the Great Britain*; Throckmorton, "Shipwright's Art," 98–100; Low and Throckmorton, "First and Last Voyage of the St. Mary"; Wilson, "Wreck of the 'Lady Elizabeth'"; Cumming and Carter, "Earl of Abergavenny"; Bound, "Hulk Jhelum"; Bound, "Iron Bean-End Fastenings"; Stammers and Kearon, "Jhelum"; Stammers and Baker, "Fell's Patent Knees"; Dean, "Charles Cooper"; Dean, "Egeria"; Dean, "Falklands Wrecks and Hulks"; Dean, "Snow Squall"; Delgado, "Earl of Abergavenny"; Delgado, "Vicar of Bray"; Stammers, "Jhelum."

74. Stammers and Kearon, *Jhelum,* 109.

75. Merriman, *Cypress Landing Shipwreck of Chocowinity Bay,* 12.

76. Lawson, "Egeria," 17.

77. Throckmorton, "American Heritage in the Falklands," 39; Smith, *Condemned at Stanley,* 25; Lawson, "Egeria," 18; Dean, "Actaeon," 18.

78. Southby-Tailyour, *Falkland Island Shores,* 10.

79. Throckmorton, "American Heritage in the Falklands," 37.

80. Bayreuther and Hovrath, "Snowsquall Project," 104.

81. Bound, "Hulk Jhelum," 44.

82. Shomette, "Shipwrecks of Mallows Bay"; Shomette, "From Maritime Antiquarianism to Underwater Archaeology"; Shomette, *Ghost Fleet of Mallows Bay,* 201–338; Hopkins, "Final Anchorage"; Langley, "Mallows Bay"; see also Mattox, *Building the Emergency Fleet,* and Webb, "United States Wooden Steamship Program During World War 1."

83. Shomette, "Shipwrecks of Mallows Bay," 63, 73, 79, 82, 84, 100; Shomette, *Ghost Fleet of Mallows Bay,* 234, 237, 254, 283; Hopkins, "Final Anchorage," 75.

84. Shomette, "Shipwrecks of Mallows Bay," 83, 95; Shomette, *Ghost Fleet of Mallows Bay,* 256, 259, 262–63, 271, 275.

85. Shomette, *Ghost Fleet of Mallows Bay,* 283.

86. Peterson, *Steamboating on the Upper Mississippi,* 300.

87. Ibid., 463.

88. Hunter, *Steamboats of the Western Rivers,* 179, 181, 218, 484–88, 504, 585–606.

89. Paine, *Down East*, 113.

Chapter 3. The Abandonment Process and Archaeological Theory

1. Barfield, *Dictionary of Anthropology*, 237.

2. In McCarthy, "Australian Maritime Archaeology," 33, citing Green, *Maritime Archaeology*, 235.

3. Such as Bass, "Plea for Historical Particularism in Nautical Archaeology"; Veth and McCarthy, "Types of Explanation in Maritime Archeology," 12; McCarthy, *Iron and Steamship Archaeology* 1:191–92.

4. Babits and Van Tilburg, "Introduction," 2.

5. Staniforth, "Future for Australian Maritime Archaeology?" 90.

6. Veth and McCarthy, "Types of Explanation in Maritime Archeology," 12.

7. McCarthy, *Iron and Steamship Archaeology*, 1; Martin, "De-Particularizing the Particular."

8. Martin, "De-Particularizing the Particular," 383–84.

9. See, for example, the works of the "Behavioralists," or "Behavioral Archaeologists," in Schiffer, "Preliminary Consideration of Behavioral Change"; Schiffer, *Behavioral Archaeology*; Schiffer, "Some Relationships between Behavioral and Evolutionary Archaeologies"; Schiffer, "Explanation of Long-Term Technological Change"; and Schiffer and Skibo, "Explanation of Artifact Variability." Hosty and Stuart, in "Maritime Archaeology Over the Last Twenty Years," 16, note Gould and Muckelroy as prominent anthropologically inclined archaeological researchers.

10. Such as McCarthy, "SS Xantho"; Staniforth, "Archaeology of the Event"; Staniforth, "Dependent Colonies"; Richards, "History and Archaeology of the Garden Island Ships' Graveyard"; O'Reilly, "Assessment of Australian Built Wooden Sailing Vessels"; Veth and McCarthy, "Types of Explanation in Maritime Archeology"; Doyle, "Examination of Associations"; Duncan, "Signposts in the Sea"; Gibbs, "Maritime Archaeology and Behaviour during Crisis"; Gibbs, "Archaeology of Crisis."

11. Souza, *Persistence of Sail in the Age of Steam*; Corbin, *Material Culture of Steamboat Passengers*.

12. Foster, *Port Phillip Shipwrecks Stage 1*; Foster, *Port Phillip Shipwrecks Stage 2*; Foster, *Port Phillip Shipwrecks Stage 3*; Foster, *Port Phillip Shipwrecks Stage 4*. Also see studies such as Jordan, *East Coast Shipwrecks*; Kenderdine, *Shipwrecks 1656–1942*; Coroneos and McKinnon, *Shipwrecks of Investigator Strait and the Lower Yorke Peninsula*; Coroneos, *Shipwrecks of Encounter Bay and Backstairs Passage*.

13. Jeffery, "Research into Australian-built Coastal Vessels," 54.

14. Jeffery, "Maritime Archaeological Investigations into Australian-Built Vessels."

15. Coroneos, "One Interpretation," 7.

16. Ibid., 9.

17. See Coroneos, *Shipwrecks of Encounter Bay and Backstairs Passage*, 101–11; Coroneos and McKinnon, *Shipwrecks of Investigator Strait and the Lower Yorke Peninsula*, 95–102.

18. O'Reilly, "Assessment of Australian Built Wooden Sailing Vessels."

19. Duncan, "Signposts in the Sea"; Doyle, "Examination of Associations."

20. Doyle, "Examination of Associations," 170.

21. As noted by Edmonds et al., *Historic Shipwrecks National Research Plan*, 70.

22. Hodder, *Archaeological Process*, 19.

23. Staniforth, "Archaeology of the Event," 159; Staniforth, "Dependent Colonies."

24. Murphy, "Shipwrecks as a Data Base for Human Behavioral Studies," 69.

25. As noted by Hodder, *Archaeological Process*, 2–3, 5.

26. Veth and McCarthy, "Types of Explanation in Maritime Archeology," 12.

27. Hodder, *Archaeological Process*, 60.

28. Ibid., 5.

29. Gould, "Looking Below the Surface," 6.

30. Hodder, *Archaeological Process*, 14.

31. Watson, "Method and Theory in Shipwreck Archaeology," 36.

32. Gould, *Archaeology and the Social History of Ships*, 13.

33. Watson, "Method and Theory in Shipwreck Archaeology," 31.

34. Gould, *Archaeology and the Social History of Ships*, 13.

35. Bach, *Maritime History of Australia*, 2.

36. Valdaliso, "Diffusion of Technological Change in the Spanish Merchant Fleet," 95.

37. Muckelroy, *Maritime Archaeology*; see also Lenihan, "Rethinking Shipwreck Archaeology," 49; Lenihan and Murphy, "Considerations for Research Designs in Shipwreck Archaeology," 235.

38. Lenihan, "Rethinking Shipwreck Archaeology," 50.

39. Gibbins and Adams, "Shipwrecks and Maritime Archaeology," 281.

40. Murphy, "Shipwrecks as a Data Base for Human Behavioural Studies," 75.

41. McCarthy, "SS Xantho," 22.

42. Throckmorton, *Shipwrecks and Archaeology*, 31–32.

43. Throckmorton, "Bones on a Beach," 211; Lenihan, "Rethinking Shipwreck Archaeology," 53; Murphy, "Shipwrecks as a Data Base for Human Behavioural Studies," 70–71; Shomette, *Tidewater Time Capsule*, 6–7; Martin, "De-Particularizing the Particular," 393.

44. Watson, "Method and Theory in Shipwreck Archaeology," 31.

45. Martin, "De-Particularizing the Particular," 383.

46. Trigger, *History of Archaeological Thought*, 148. Indeed, Johnson, *Archaeological Theory*, 163, considers it an archaeological metanarrative.

47. Trigger, *History of Archaeological Thought*, 290, 323.

48. Ibid., 291–94.

49. Ibid., 250.

50. Ibid., 254.

51. Eighmy, "Use of Material Culture in Diachronic Anthropology," 35.

52. Gould, *Archaeology and the Social History of Ships*, 18.

53. Trigger, *History of Archaeological Thought*, 15.

54. See Miller, *Material Culture and Mass Consumption*; Spencer-Wood, *Consumer Choice in Historical Archaeology*; Henry, "Consumers, Commodities, and Choices"; Purser, "Consumption as Communication"; Gibb, *Archaeology of Wealth*.

55. Such as that proposed by Henry, "Consumers, Commodities, and Choices," 5.

56. Johnston, "End of the Age of Sail," 231.

57. COIITC, *Technological Change in Australia* 2:318.

58. Murphy, "Shipwrecks as a Data Base for Human Behavioural Studies," 65.

59. For an overview of these processes see COIITC, *Technological Change in Australia*, vol. 1; Kasper, "Technological Change and Economic Growth"; Mokyr, *Lever of Riches*; Volti, *Society and Technological Change*. Also see case studies such as Graham, "Transition from Paddle-Wheel to Screw Propeller"; Musson and Robinson, "Early Growth of Steam Power"; Guthrie, *History of Marine Engineering*, 37, 43, 46; Mak and Walton, "Persistence of Old Techniques"; Hutchins, "History and Development of the Shipbuilding Industry in the United States," 42; Fletcher, "From Coal to Oil in British Shipping"; Tann and Breckin, "International Diffusion of the Watt Engine"; Goldrick, "Problems of Modern Naval History," 20; Griffiths, "British Shipping and the Diesel Engine"; Jervis, "Navies, Politics, and Political Science," 48–49, 58; Thompson, "Some Mild and Radical Observations on Desiderata," 104; Armstrong, "Crewing of British Coastal Colliers," 76; Robinson, "Early Diffusion of Steam Power"; Weski, "German Windships at the Beginning of the 20th Century," 19.

60. See Schiffer, *Portable Radio in American Life*; Schiffer, "Cultural Imperatives and Product Development"; Schiffer, "Studying Technological Differentiation"; COIITC, *Technological Change in Australia* 1:8.

61. COIITC, *Technological Change in Australia* 1:25.

62. Ibid., 1, 66, 69, 166; Kasper, "Technological Change and Economic Growth," 246.

63. COIITC, *Technological Change in Australia* 1:67.

64. Kasper, "Technological Change and Economic Growth," 242.

65. Eyres, *Ship Construction*, 3.

66. Ojala, "Productivity and Technological Change in Eighteenth and Nineteenth Century Sea Transport"; Henning and Henning, "Technological Change from Sail to Steam."

67. COIITC, *Technological Change in Australia* 1:66.

68. Pearce, "On Some Results of Recent Improvements in Naval Architecture," 1; Hurd, *Triumph of the Tramp Ship*, 163; Fletcher, "Suez Canal and World Shipping," 556, 558–60; Parkinson, *Economics of Shipbuilding in the United Kingdom*, 6; Palmer, *Ships and Shipping*, 39; Fisher, *Australians*, 144, 177; COIITC, *Technological Change in Australia* 2:351–52.

69. Wood, "Battle Was a Drawn One," 97–98; Robertson, *Evolution of Naval Armament*, 262; Kemp, *Campaign of the Spanish Armada*, 113; Gould, "H.M.S. Vixen," 44; Bound, "British Sea Power," 19–20; Van Der Vat, *Grand Scuttle*, 46.

70. Millar, "On the Rise and Progress of Steam Navigation," 130; Robertson, *Evolution of Naval Armament*, 3, 35, 249; Harley, "Shift from Sailing Ships to Steamships," 215–16; Hunter, *Steamboats of the Western Rivers*, 124.

71. Basch, "Ancient Wrecks and the Archaeology of Ships," 9.

72. Lenihan, "Rethinking Shipwreck Archaeology," 54–56.

73. Ibid., 55.

74. Murphy, "Shipwrecks as a Data Base for Human Behavioral Studies," 71, 83–84.

75. Gould, *Archaeology and the Social History of Ships*, 18, 249.

76. Murphy, "Shipwrecks as a Data Base for Human Behavioral Studies," 71.

77. Leone, "Land and Water, Urban Life, and Boats," 174; Murphy, "Shipwrecks as a Data Base for Human Behavioral Studies," 85.

78. Hodder, *Archaeological Process*, 27.

79. Oxley, "Environment of Historic Shipwreck Sites," 48.

80. Ibid., 46.

81. Cameron, "Structure Abandonment in Villages"; Cameron and Tomka, *Abandonment of Settlements and Regions*.

82. Schiffer, "Archaeological Context and Systemic Context"; Schiffer, *Formation Processes of the Archaeological Record*; and Schiffer, Downing, and McCarthy, "Waste Not, Want Not"; Muckelroy, *Maritime Archaeology*.

83. Lenihan and Murphy, "Considerations for Research Designs in Shipwreck Archaeology," 234–35.

84. Ward, Larcombe, and Veth, "Towards New Process-Oriented Models for Describing Wreck Disintegration"; Ward, Larcombe, and Veth, "New Process-Based Model for Wreck Site Formation."

85. See Simpson, "Historical Salvage and Maritime Archaeology," 4.

86. See Schiffer, Butts, and Grimm, *Taking Charge*; Schiffer, Hollenback, and Bell, *Draw the Lightning Down*; Schiffer, *Technological Perspectives on Behavioral Change*; Schiffer, "Explanation of Long-Term Technological Change"; Schiffer and Miller, *Material Life of Human Beings*; Schiffer and Miller, "Behavioral Theory of Meaning"; Schiffer and Skibo, "Theory and Experiment in the Study of Technological Change."

87. Schiffer, *Formation Processes of the Archaeological Record*, 3–4, 7.

88. Ibid., 141–261.

89. Gould, *Archaeology and the Social History of Ships*, 9.

90. See, for instance, Guthrie et al., "Wrecks and Marine Microbiology"; Anuskiewicz, "Technology, Theory and Analysis"; Ward, Larcombe, and Veth, "Towards New Process-Oriented Models for Describing Wreck Disintegration"; Randell, "Effects of Material Type on Concretion Formation."

91. Schiffer, "Archaeological Context and Systemic Context," 156.

92. Lenihan and Murphy, "Considerations for Research Designs in Shipwreck Ar-

chaeology," 237; see also Murphy, "Shipwrecks as a Data Base for Human Behavioral Studies," 66; particular reference is to the work of Basch, "Ancient Wrecks and the Archaeology of Ships," and Muckelroy, *Maritime Archaeology.*

93. Murphy, "Shipwrecks as a Data Base for Human Behavioral Studies," 85.

94. Gould, *Archaeology and the Social History of Ships*, 3–4; Gould, "Wreck of the Barque *North Carolina.*"

95. Gould, "Archaeology of War."

96. Gould, "Bird Key Wreck," 9.

97. Ibid., 12.

98. Gould, "Bird Key Harbor Brick Wreck," 336.

99. McCarthy, "SS Xantho," 139; McCarthy, *Iron and Steamship Archaeology*, 56–58.

100. Babits and Corbin-Kjorness, "Final Report on an Archaeological Survey of the Western Shore of the Pungo River," 34.

101. Hodder, *Archaeological Process*, 28.

102. Ibid.

103. Trigger, *History of Archaeological Thought*, 36.

104. Oxley, "Environment of Historic Shipwreck Sites," 89.

105. Schiffer, *Formation Processes of the Archaeological Record*, 281.

106. Ibid., 25–140.

107. Ibid., 14.

108. Schiffer, Downing, and McCarthy, "Waste Not, Want Not," 68; Schiffer, *Formation Processes of the Archaeological Record*, 28, 36.

109. Schiffer, "Archaeological Context and Systemic Context," 159; Schiffer, *Formation Processes of the Archaeological Record*, 29.

110. Schiffer, Downing, and McCarthy, "Waste Not, Want Not," 68; Schiffer, *Formation Processes of the Archaeological Record*, 29–30.

111. Schiffer, Downing, and McCarthy, "Waste Not, Want Not," 68; Schiffer, *Formation Processes of the Archaeological Record*, 30–32.

112. Schiffer, Downing, and McCarthy, "Waste Not, Want Not," 68; Schiffer, *Formation Processes of the Archaeological Record*, 32–35.

113. Schiffer, *Formation Processes of the Archaeological Record*, 89.

114. Ibid., 48.

115. Ibid., 17.

116. Ibid., 62.

117. Schiffer, "Archaeological Context and Systemic Context," 161–62; Schiffer, *Formation Processes of the Archaeological Record*, 58.

118. Schiffer, *Formation Processes of the Archaeological Record*, 64–69.

119. Ibid., 20–29.

120. Ibid., 89.

121. Ibid., 90–91.

122. Ibid., 90.

123. Ibid., 92.

124. Ibid., 99.
125. Ibid., 101.
126. Ibid., 106.
127. Ibid., 107.
128. Ibid., 109.
129. Ibid., 111–14.
130. Lenihan, "Rethinking Shipwreck Archaeology," 63.
131. Murphy, "Shipwrecks as a Data Base for Human Behavioral Studies," 84.
132. Ibid., 67.

Chapter 4. Watercraft Abandonment in Australia: National Perspectives

1. Loney, *Jack Loney's Maritime Australia*, 86.
2. Loney, *Australian Shipwrecks Update Volume 5*, 138.
3. See Blainey, *Causes of War*, 139; Rosenburg and Sumida, "Machines, Men, Manufacturing, Management and Money," 35.
4. Davies, "Shipping Freight Costs," 97.
5. Broxam, *Shipping Arrivals and Departures, Tasmania*, ix.
6. Gregory, "Overview," 1.
7. Broxam, *Shipping Arrivals and Departures, Tasmania*, ix.
8. Ibid.
9. Ibid.
10. Bach, *Maritime History of Australia*, 187.
11. Ibid., 56.
12. Thomson, *England in the Nineteenth Century*, 138; Pollard and Robertson, *British Shipbuilding Industry*, 9.
13. Broeze, "Cost of Distance," 583.
14. Bach, *Maritime History of Australia*, 117.
15. Which Kennedy, "Great Britain's Maritime Strength and the British Mercantile Marine," 66, notes was itself dependant on the power of its merchant marine.
16. Pollard, "Laissez-Faire and Shipbuilding," 98; Thomson, *England in the Nineteenth Century*, 142.
17. Bach, *Maritime History of Australia*, 134, 139.
18. Parkinson, *Economics of Shipbuilding in the United Kingdom*, 3; Thomson, *England in the Nineteenth Century*, 142; Slaven, "British Shipbuilders," 37–38.
19. ANMA, *Australian Shipping*, 100.
20. Varns, *Blue Peter*, 4.
21. Broeze, "Private Enterprise and Public Policy," 20.
22. Commonwealth Government, *Shipbuilding Industry*, 15; Broeze, *Island Nation*, 103.
23. Pollard and Robertson, *British Shipbuilding Industry*, 9, 12–13; Cage, "Structure and Profitability of Tramp Shipping," 3.
24. Culliton, "Economics and Shipbuilding," 8, 12; Hutchins, "History and Development of the Shipbuilding Industry in the United States," 56.

25. Culliton, "Economics and Shipbuilding," 8.

26. Bach, *Maritime History of Australia*, 352.

27. Shaw, *Story of Australia*, 278–79.

28. Tull, *Community Enterprise*, 70.

29. Ibid., 71.

30. Jose, *History of Australasia*, 114–17; Cotter, "Golden Decade," 113; Fitzpatrick, *British Empire in Australia*, 80; Palmer, *Ships and Shipping*, 38; Clark, *History of Australia* 4:5.

31. See Fitzpatrick, *British Empire in Australia*, 121; Ward, *Empire in the Antipodes*, 4, 31, 110; Ward, *Australia*, 75, 78; Shann, *Economic History of Australia*, 185; Palmer, *Ships and Shipping*, 38; Bach, *Maritime History of Australia*, 96; Clark, *History of Australia* 4:8; Broeze, "Private Enterprise and Public Policy," 14.

32. Cotter, "Golden Decade," 125.

33. Fitchett, *Vanished Fleet*, 1.

34. Clark, *History of Australia* 4:23.

35. Clark, *Short History of Australia*, 135.

36. Loney, *Jack Loney's Maritime Australia*, 50.

37. Cotter, "Golden Decade," 113.

38. Ward, *Empire in the Antipodes*, 23, 30.

39. Jose, *History of Australasia*, 128; Parsons, *Southern Passages*, 51.

40. Castles and Harris, *Lawmakers and Wayward Whigs*, 95; Clark, *Short History of Australia*, 135–36; Roberts, *History of Australian Land Settlement*, 228.

41. Kok, *Pictorial History of Strahan*, 19.

42. Broxam, *Shipping Arrivals and Departures, Tasmania*, ix. This is supported by Clark, *Short History of Australia*, 135–36.

43. Clark, *Short History of Australia*, 120.

44. Bach, "Sea Transport in Australia," 7.

45. Clark, *History of Australia* 3:188, 190, 197, 293–95, 359; Clark, *Select Documents in Australian History*, 292; Clark, *Short History of Australia*, 103.

46. Clark, *Short History of Australia*, 110.

47. Clark, *History of Australia* 3:295.

48. Bach, *Maritime History of Australia*, 142.

49. Ibid., 134, 142; cf. Rostrow, "Investment and the Great Depression," 136, and Aldcroft, "Depression in British Shipping," 14, who cite this period as 1873–96.

50. Ward, *Australia*, 108–9; Bach, *Maritime History of Australia*, 201; Clark, *History of Australia* 5:56, 85, 111; Castles and Harris, *Lawmakers and Wayward Whigs*, 232.

51. ANMA, *Australian Shipping*, 101.

52. Shann, *Economic History of Australia*, 328; Clark, *Short History of Australia*, 169, 171.

53. Cage, "Structure and Profitability of Tramp Shipping," 7.

54. Bach, *Maritime History of Australia*, 143.

55. Ibid., 143.

56. Louis and Turner, *Depression of the 1930s*, 1.

57. Gazeley and Rice, "Wages and Employment in Britain Between the Wars," 298.

58. Dyos and Aldcroft, *British Transport*, 320–21; Gazeley and Rice, "Wages and Employment in Britain Between the Wars," 296.

59. Southgate, *English Economic History*, 268–69.

60. Dyos and Aldcroft, *British Transport*, 301.

61. Hutchins, "History and Development of the Shipbuilding Industry in the United States," 56.

62. Called by Shaw, *Story of Australia*, 233, an "unhealthy boom."

63. Southgate, *English Economic History*, 268–69.

64. Dyos and Aldcroft, *British Transport*, 320–21.

65. Ibid.; Hudspeth and Scripps, *Capital Port*, 194.

66. Watt, *Stewart Island's Kaipipi Shipyard and the Ross Sea Whalers*, 215, 220.

67. Bach, *Maritime History of Australia*, 317–19.

68. Hutchins, "History and Development of the Shipbuilding Industry in the United States," 55.

69. Slaven, "British Shipbuilders," 38–39.

70. Dyos and Aldcroft, *British Transport*, 320–21.

71. Clark, *Short History of Australia*, 224; Clark, *History of Australia* 6:308.

72. Harvey, "Last Voyage of the 'Macdhui,'" 19.

73. Horne, *Lucky Country*, 193.

74. Ward, *Australia*, 139; Moss, *Sound of Trumpets*, 296.

75. As described by Clark, *History of Australia* 6:322.

76. See Broadus, *Depression Decade*, 3–24; Louis and Turner, *Depression of the 1930s*, 1.

77. Crowley, "1901–14," 416.

78. Cotter, "War, Boom and Depression," 262; Dyos and Aldroft, *British Transport*, 299–301; Dickey, *Rations, Residence, Resources*, 174; Louis and Turner, *Depression of the 1930s*, 1.

79. Morris, "1928 Marine Cooks' Strike," 109.

80. Foster, *Port Phillip Shipwrecks Stage 1*, 15.

81. Kerr, *Tasmanian Trading Ketch*, 21, 105.

82. Christopher, *South Australian Shipwrecks*, 78; Loney, *Australian Shipwrecks* 4:141; Loney, *Wrecks on the South Australian Coast*, 132–33; Parsons and Plunkett, *Scuttled and Abandoned Ships*, 43; Arnott, *Investigator Strait Maritime Heritage Trail*, 18–20.

83. Richards, "Role of Geo-politics in Cultural Site Formation."

84. Blainey, *Causes of War*.

85. Ward, *Australia*, 28, 127; Buxton, "1870–90," 200; Crowley, "1901–14," 270–71; de Garis, "1890–1900," 254; Robertson, "1930–1939," 452.

86. Clark, *History of Australia* 4:84.

87. Bach, *Maritime History of Australia*, 95, 103.

88. Hutchins, "History and Development of the Shipbuilding Industry in the United States," 52; Clark, *Short History of Australia*, 208.

89. Henderson in Sledge, "Wreck Inspection North Coast."

90. Tull, *Community Enterprise*, 63.

91. Similarly noted by Hughes, *Australian Iron and Steel Industry*, 132, and in the United States by Hutchins, "History and Development of the Shipbuilding Industry in the United States," 15.

92. Hughes, *Australian Iron and Steel Industry*, 15; Shaw, *Story of Australia*, 271, 278; Bolton, "1930–1939," 488; Clark, *Short History of Australia*, 256; Hudson, "1951–72," 522, 527, 533.

93. Foster, "Defence and Victorian Shipwrecks," 22.

94. Bach, *Maritime History of Australia*, 103.

95. Noted by Tull, "Shipping, Ports and the Marketing of Australia's Wheat," 46.

96. Culliton, "Economics and Shipbuilding," 12.

97. Davies, "Shipping Freight Costs," 97.

98. Culliton, "Economics and Shipbuilding," 9.

99. Ibid., 11.

100. Hutchins, "History and Development of the Shipbuilding Industry in the United States," 55.

101. Bach, *Maritime History of Australia*, 57.

102. Ibid., 288–89.

103. Ibid., 286, 315; Tull, "Shipping, Ports and the Marketing of Australia's Wheat," 45–46.

104. Bach, *Maritime History of Australia*, 286.

105. Southgate, *English Economic History*, 268–69; Kennedy, "Great Britain's Maritime Strength and the British Mercantile Marine," 67.

106. Kennedy, "Great Britain's Maritime Strength and the British Mercantile Marine," 68.

107. Matthews, *American Merchant Ships 1850–1900: Series 1*, 275–76.

108. Graeme-Evans and Wilson, *Built to Last*, 81.

109. Bach, *Maritime History of Australia*, 249.

110. Kerr and McDermott, *Huon Pine Story*, 97.

111. Pemberton, "Historical Geography of Australian Coastal Shipping," 169; Bach, *Maritime History of Australia*, 351, 370; Barsness, "Maritime Activity and Port Development in the United States Since 1900," 169.

112. Graeme-Evans and Wilson, *Built to Last*, 81.

113. Milne, McKewan, and Goodburn, *Nautical Archaeology on the Foreshore*, 8.

114. See Paine, *Down East*, 150.

115. Fassett, "Foreword," vii–viii.

116. Bach, *Maritime History of Australia*, 346, 351.

Chapter 5. Watercraft Abandonment in Australia: Environmental and Regional Perspectives

1. Kenderdine, "When the River Runs Clear," 2.

2. See Parsons, *Century of Wrecks of Steamships in NSW*, 8–9, 11, 44, 51; Christopher, *Divers' Guide to South Australia*,11–12, for examples.

3. See Portnoy, "Microarchaeological View of Human Settlement Space and Function," 213; Hohman in Rathje, "Manifesto for Modern Material-Culture Studies," 52.

4. McCarthy, "Shipwrecks in Jervoise Bay," 354; see also McCarthy, *Jervoise Bay Shipwrecks*, 20.

5. Hudspeth and Scripps, *Capital Port*, 128.

6. Bird, *Seaport Gateways of Australia*, 3; Bach, *Maritime History of Australia*, 25.

7. Tull, *Community Enterprise*, 73.

8. Ibid., 1

9. Broeze, "Private Enterprise and Public Policy," 14; Tull, "Shipping, Ports and the Marketing of Australia's Wheat," 47; Riley, "Steam on the Rim," 28.

10. Kerr, *Tasmanian Trading Ketch*, 35, 37, 125.

11. Orme, "Shipbuilding in Northern Tasmania," 31.

12. Richards, "Deep Structures"; Richards, "Archaeological Examination of Watercraft Abandonment in Australia."

13. Commonwealth Government, *Beaches, Fishing Ground and Sea Routes Protection Act 1932.*

14. Ibid.

15. Tull, *Community Enterprise*, 75.

16. Commonwealth Government, *Beaches, Fishing Ground and Sea Routes Protection Act 1932*, 99.

17. Broeze, *Island Nation*, 6.

18. Noted by Tull, "Shipping, Ports and the Marketing of Australia's Wheat," 49.

19. Kenderdine, "Revelations About River Boats and 'Rotten Rows,'" 22–23.

20. Babits and Corbin-Kjorness, "Final Report on an Archaeological Survey of the Western Shore of the Pungo River," 28, 76, 78.

21. See, for example, references to the potential of other abandoned vessels in, Kenderdine, "Revelations About River Boats and 'Rotten Rows,'" 21; Kenderdine, *Historic Shipping on the Murray River*, 76–77; Learmouth, *Story of a Port: Portland, Victoria*, 66.

22. Clark, *History of Australia* 4:409.

23. Shaw, *Economic Development of Australia*, 30, 40, 48, *Story of Australia*, 84; Clark, *History of Australia* 3:143–50, 263; Clark, *Select Documents in Australian History*, 291.

24. Clark, *History of Australia* 4:256; Clark, *Select Documents in Australian History*, 291; Clark, *History of Australia* 5:96.

25. Mudie, *Riverboats*, 233–34.

26. Clark, *History of Australia* 4:190, 244, 312; Gibson-Wilde, *Gateway to a Golden Land*, 114.

27. Clark, *History of Australia* 4:406–7.

28. Ibid. 4:196, 5:184.

29. Shann, *Economic History of Australia*, 342, 386–88; Shaw, *Economic Development of Australia*, 110; Shaw, *Story of Australia*, 208.

30. Shann, *Economic History of Australia*, 389; Shaw, *Economic Development of Australia*, 132; Shaw, *Story of Australia*, 261, 279, 300.

31. Gibson-Wilde, *Gateway to a Golden Land*, 103.

32. Tull, *Community Enterprise*, 1.

33. Ibid., 3.

34. Ibid., 12.

35. Dickey, *Rations, Residence, Resources*, 14; Parsons, *Southern Passages*, 41; Castles and Harris, *Lawmakers and Wayward Whigs*, 77;

36. Bolton, *Thousand Miles Away*, 39, 78, 144, 192, 257.

37. Tull, *Community Enterprise*, 70.

38. Hudspeth and Scripps, *Capital Port*, xvii.

39. Shaw, *Economic Development of Australia*, 13, 30, 49.

40. Graeme-Evans and Wilson, *Built to Last*, 8; Hudspeth and Scripps, *Capital Port*, xvii, 11, 32, 42.

41. Shaw, *Economic Development of Australia*, 49, 50; Dyster, "Port of Launceston Before 1851," 104; Broeze, "Private Enterprise and Public Policy," 14.

42. Hudspeth and Scripps, *Capital Port*, 41.

43. Hartwell, *Economic Development of Van Diemen's Land*, 190; Morrissey, "Pastoral Economy," 64.

44. Hartwell, *Economic Development of Van Diemen's Land*, 187, 190.

45. Gibson-Wilde, *Gateway to a Golden Land*, 113; Tull, *Community Enterprise*, 66.

46. Hudspeth and Scripps, *Capital Port*, 106–7.

47. Matthews, "North Arm Ships' Graveyard, Port Adelaide, South Australia," 30.

48. Hudspeth and Scripps, *Capital Port*, 163–64, 171, 193–95, 199.

49. Broomhill, "Port in the Great Depression," 9; Clark, *Short History of Australia*, 224; Dickey, *Rations, Residence, Resources*, 183; De Rooy, "Taking the Rough with the Smooth," 25; Probert, "South Australia and the Great Depression," 122; Tregenza, *Le Messuriers of Port Adelaide*, 80, 83, 90; Walter, "70 Years of Progress," 11.

50. Morrissey, "Pastoral Economy," 65; Shann, *Economic History of Australia*, 104, 189; Shaw, *Economic Development of Australia*, 29, 39, 48; Broeze, "Private Enterprise and Public Policy," 10.

51. Dickey, *Rations, Residence, Resources*, 14; Castles and Harris, *Lawmakers and Wayward Whigs*, 77; O'Reilly, "Assessment of Australian Built Wooden Sailing Vessels," 57.

52. Bolton, *Thousand Miles Away*, 14, 21, 37, 44–45, 47–48, 91, 127, 139–40, 156, 278; Gibson-Wilde, *Gateway to a Golden Land*, 80.

53. Shaw, *Economic Development of Australia*, 115; Tull, "Shipping, Ports and the Marketing of Australia's Wheat," 36, *Community Enterprise*, 14, 23, 56.

54. Roberts, *History of Australian Land Settlement*, 291; Shaw, *Economic Development of Australia*, 5.

55. Shann, *Economic History of Australia*, 102, 104, 189; Shaw, *Story of Australia*, 94.

56. Bolton, *Thousand Miles Away*, 221.

57. Hudspeth and Scripps, *Capital Port*, 153–55, 158–59.

58. Bolton, *Thousand Miles Away*, 296; Dickey, *Rations, Residence, Resources*, 122; Castles and Harris, *Lawmakers and Wayward Whigs*, 203.

59. Hudspeth and Scripps, *Capital Port*, 242, 256.

60. Aldcroft, "Eclipse of British Coastal Shipping," 27, 29; Broeze, "Private Enterprise and Public Policy," 21; Devendra, "Remains of Riverine Craft," 22; Simmons, "Steamboats on Inland Waterways," 206.

61. Parsons, *Southern Passages*, 99.

62. Barsness, "Maritime Activity and Port Development in the United States Since 1900," 170; Clark, *History of Australia* 5:29.

63. Dyos and Aldcroft, *British Transport*, 299; Bach, *Maritime History of Australia*, 188–89; Bolton, *Thousand Miles Away*, 162–63.

64. Bach, "Sea Transport in Australia," 7.

65. Bach, *Maritime History of Australia*, 386.

66. Kerr, *Tasmanian Trading Ketch*, 105.

67. Bolton, *Thousand Miles Away*, 162, 192, 263.

68. Matthews, "North Arm Ships' Graveyard, Port Adelaide, South Australia," 85.

69. Clark, *History of Australia* 5:46; Parsons, *Southern Passages*, 227.

70. Bach, *Maritime History of Australia*, 236.

71. Bach, "Sea Transport in Australia," 7; Purtell, *Mosquito Fleet*, 2–3.

72. Hughes, *Australian Iron and Steel Industry*, 29; Tull, *Community Enterprise*, 53–54.

73. Parsons, *Australian Coastal Passenger Ships*, 9.

74. Hudspeth and Scripps, *Capital Port*, 333.

75. Tull, *Community Enterprise*, 78.

76. Bach, *Maritime History of Australia*, 252.

77. Mudie, *Riverboats*, 124.

78. Castles and Harris, *Lawmakers and Wayward Whigs*, 227.

79. Kenderdine, "Revelations About River Boats and 'Rotten Rows,'" 23; see also Kenderdine, *Historic Shipping on the Murray River*, 70.

80. Moore, *Last Days of Mast and Sail*, 238.

81. Hunter, *Steamboats of the Western Rivers*, 4.

82. Tull, *Community Enterprise*, 61.

83. South Australian Government, *South Australian Parliamentary Papers*, 8.

84. Parsons, *Australian Shipowners and Their Fleets* 1:6.

85. Kerr, *Tasmanian Trading Ketch*, 105; Hudspeth and Scripps, *Capital Port*, 171, 193.

86. Purtell, *Mosquito Fleet*, 2–3; Curby, "Richmond River Maritime History Survey," 8, 23.

87. Workman, in Belle, "Ketches and Ketchmen," 12.

88. Tregenza, *Le Messuriers of Port Adelaide*, 133.

89. Ibid.

90. Kerr, *Tasmanian Trading Ketch*, 126, 127.

91. Jacques, *Dive Tasmania*, 51.

92. Graeme-Evans and Wilson, *Built to Last*, 46.

93. Bach, *Maritime History of Australia*, 352.

94. Baty, *Ships that Passed*, 9.

95. COIITC, *Technological Change in Australia* 2:318–19.

96. Ibid. 2:319–20.

97. Hudspeth and Scripps, *Capital Port*, 45.

98. Souter, *Archaeological Watching Brief for New Maritime Museum Site*, 2.

99. Tull, *Community Enterprise*, 21–22.

100. Bach, *Maritime History of Australia*, 404.

101. COIITC, *Technological Change in Australia* 2:325.

102. Lenihan, "Rethinking Shipwreck Archaeology," 54.

103. Bach, *Maritime History of Australia*, 342.

104. Barsness, "Maritime Activity and Port Development in the United States Since 1900," 167.

105. COIITC, *Technological Change in Australia* 2:325; Tull, *Community Enterprise*, 39.

106. Bach, *Maritime History of Australia*, 361.

107. Ibid., 355, 404.

108. Ibid., 354.

109. Hudspeth and Scripps, *Capital Port*, 291, 301.

110. Eyres, *Ship Construction*, 4.

111. O'Reilly, "Assessment of Australian Built Wooden Sailing Vessels," 35–36, 38–40.

112. Bach, *Maritime History of Australia*, 256.

113. Ibid., 268.

114. Ibid., 404.

115. Tull, *Community Enterprise*, 2.

116. Richards, "Role of Geo-politics in Cultural Site Formation."

Chapter 6. Archaeological Signatures of Use

1. Kenderdine, "Revelations About River Boats and 'Rotten Rows,'" 20.

2. Still, "Confederate Naval Strategy," 339.

3. Kenderdine, "Revelations About River Boats and 'Rotten Rows,'" 93.

4. Culliton, "Economics and Shipbuilding," 6.

5. See Paine, *Down East*, 107.

6. Graeme-Evans and Wilson, *Built to Last*, 31.

7. Bathgate, "History, Topography and Search of Jervoise Bay," 39.

8. Glassford, "Fleet of Hulks," 222.

9. Paine, *Down East*, 89.

10. Gerr, "Suitability of the Big Wooden Schooner," 399–400.

11. Howe and Matthews, *American Clipper Ships* 2:386–87; Matthews, *American Merchant Ships, 1850–1900: Series 1*, 128, 137, 239; Matthews, *American Merchant Ships, 1850–1900: Series 2*, 272–73.

12. See Matthews, *American Merchant Ships, 1850–1900: Series 1*.

13. Mudie, *Riverboats*, 59.

14. Glassford, "Fleet of Hulks," 218.

15. Stone and Loney, *High and Dry*, 9; Cairns and Henderson, *Unfinished Voyages*, 179.

16. Glassford, "Fleet of Hulks," 252.

17. *Argus*, 12 December 1933; Parsons, *Australian Shipowners and Their Fleets* 10:259.

18. Glassford, "Fleet of Hulks," 218.

19. Hudspeth and Scripps, *Capital Port*, 127–28, 166, 219, 243.

20. Parsons, *Ships of Burns, Philp and Company*, 8.

21. Parsons, *Ketches of South Australia*, 5.

22. Glassford, "Fleet of Hulks," 230.

23. Wanklyn, "Floating Circus," 31; Rimes, "Old Liner Becomes Alaskan Hotel," 10.

24. Warne, "Marmion Beach Wreck," 46.

25. Halls, "Tale of Two Coal Hulks," 9.

26. Bathgate, "History, Topography and Search of Jervoise Bay," 39.

27. Culliton, "Economics and Shipbuilding," 5.

28. Richards, "History and Archaeology of the Garden Island Ships' Graveyard," 110.

29. Jacques, *Dive Tasmania*, 71–72.

30. Loney, *Australian Shipwrecks Update Volume 5*, 138; Stone and Loney, *High and Dry*, 9.

31. *South Australian Register*, 31 May 1912, 6f.

32. Watt, *Stewart Island's Kaipipi Shipyard and the Ross Sea Whalers*, 179, 181.

33. *News*, 24 June 1949.

34. Flynn, *North Australian Fishing Maps*, 69.

35. Arnold et al., *Texas Liberty Ships*.

36. Ibid., 87.

37. Ibid., 88, 94.

38. *Times-Colonist*, 15 August 1992, A8; *Providence*, 28 August 1992; *Vancouver Sun*, 3 September 1992.

39. *West Australian*, 13 July 1996, 33.

40. Jordan, *East Coast Shipwrecks*, 177.

41. Fisheries Division, *Darwin's Artificial Reefs*, 3.

42. Ibid., 1.

43. Sandilands, "Swansong," 6.

44. Hooper and Ramm, "Preliminary Report on Artificial Reefs in the Vicinity of Darwin Harbor," 23.

45. Sandilands, "Swansong," 6.

46. Hooper and Ramm, "Preliminary Report on Artificial Reefs in the Vicinity of Darwin Harbor," 2, 23.

47. *Times-Colonist*, 15 August 1992, A8.

48. Norty, "Environmental Considerations of Artificial Reefs," 9–11.

49. Ibid., 11.

50. Sandilands, "Swansong," 5.

51. See Commonwealth Government, *Senate Report*, 6 December 1994.

52. *Sound Telegraph*, 28 September 1994.

53. Weaver, "HMAS Perth Decommissioned," 3–4.

54. *Sound Telegraph*, 28 September 1994.

55. *Sound Telegraph*, 14 December 1994, 3, 3 July 1996, 3, 9 October 1996, 23; *Sunday Times*, 28 January 1996, 21; *West Australian*, 13 July 1996.

56. *Busselton-Dunsborough Mail*, 17 December 1997, 1.

Chapter 7. The Signatures of Discard

1. Smith, Arnold, and Oertling, "Investigation of a Civil War Anti-Torpedo Raft," 150.

2. Kenderdine, "Revelations About River Boats and 'Rotten Rows,'" 22; see also Kenderdine, *Historic Shipping on the Murray River*, 64.

3. Kenderdine, *Historic Shipping on the Murray River*, 64.

4. Parsons, *Ketches of South Australia*, 1.

5. Casson, *Ancient Mariners*, 88–89.

6. Bound, "Hulk Jhelum," 43.

7. Also noted by Matthews, "North Arm Ships' Graveyard, Port Adelaide, South Australia," 96.

8. O'May, *Wrecks in Tasmanian Waters*, 201.

9. McCarthy, "Salvage Archaeology," 1.

10. *Hobart Community Express*, 4 February 1967.

11. Coroneos, "Myall Lakes Shipwrecks Study," 45.

12. *West Australian*, 7 March 1938, 16a.

13. Ingram-Brown, *"Scrap Now before Prices Collapse Further,"* 302–3.

14. Such as at the shipwreck of *Victoria*; see Coroneos, *Shipwrecks of Encounter Bay and Backstairs Passage*, 91–92.

15. Lloyd's of London, *Lloyd's Calendar: 1938*, 581–82.

16. Burn, "Recent Trends in the History of the Steel Industry," 99.

17. Buxton, "1870–90," 111.

18. Watt, *Stewart Island's Kaipipi Shipyard and the Ross Sea Whalers*, 220.

19. Cree, "Port's Scrap Heap," 17.

20. Loney, *Australian Shipwrecks Update Volume 5*, 138.

21. Baty, *Ships that Passed*; see also Parsons, *Australian Coastal Passenger Ships*, 15, 19, 35, 37–38, 45.

22. As noted by Clark, *History of Australia* 6:336.

23. Broomhill, "Port in the Great Depression," 10, 11, *Unemployed Workers*, 105–6.

24. Graeme-Evans and Wilson, *Built to Last*, 83.

25. *News*, 5 February 1931, 17 February 1931, 4 March 1932; *Advertiser*, 2 August 1930, 6 March 1931, 30 April 1931, 3 February 1932; *South Australian Register*, 15 January 1930, 24 February 1930, 3 July 1930.

26. Gould, "H.M.S. Vixen," 71.

27. McCarthy, "SS Xantho," 157, 213.

28. Stammers and Kearon, *Jhelum*, 108.

29. McCarthy, "Shipwrecks in Jervoise Bay," 361.

30. Marshall and Miners, "Wreck of Stones," 13.

31. Kimpton and Henderson, "Last Voyage of the Day Dawn Wreck," 25; see also McCarthy, "Black Cats," 124.

32. Matthews, *American Merchant Ships, 1850–1900: Series 1*, 160, 231; Matthews, *American Merchant Ships, 1850–1900: Series 2*, 151, 186, 229, 301, 332.

33. Matthews, *American Merchant Ships, 1850–1900: Series 2*, 151–52.

34. Shomette, *Ghost Fleet of Mallows Bay*, 247–52; Delgado, "What Becomes of the Old Ships?" 2, 6; *Courier Mail*, 4 July 1986, 1, 30.

35. McCarthy, *Excavation of the Barque Day Dawn*, 8.

36. Moore, "Kingston Inner Harbor Survey," 86.

37. Nutley and Smith, *Maritime Archaeology of Myall Lakes/Tea Gardens*, 14, 19.

38. Jordan, *East Coast Shipwrecks*, 115.

39. See Letter to the Chief Harbor Master from the Secretary, 11 August 1923, Western Australian Maritime Museum, File 193/79/2: Richard McKenna Notes.

40. Loney, *Jack Loney's Maritime Australia*, 86; Loney, *Wrecks on the Western Australian Coast*, 186–87.

41. Loney, *Jack Loney's Maritime Australia*, 87.

42. McCarthy, "Black Cats," 5.

43. Howe and Matthews, *American Clipper Ships* 2:673.

44. Hopkins, "Final Anchorage," 74.

45. Cited by Richards, "History and Archaeology of the Garden Island Ships' Graveyard," 59–60.

46. Richards, "Garden Island Ships' Graveyard," 16.

47. South Australian Government, *Government Record Group 51*, files 32/5 HB 887/31:199, 235, 51/170/887/1931, 51/170/901/1937; *News*, 29 November 1935, 3;

Loney, *Australian Shipwrecks Update Volume 5*, 138; Richards, "History and Archaeology of the Garden Island Ships' Graveyard," 66–67, 70, 90.

48. Lords Commissioners of the Admiralty, *Manual of Seamanship* 2:329–30.

49. Jacques, *Dive Tasmania*, 52.

50. *West Australian*, 21 June 1968, 1.

51. *Bussleton-Dunsborough Mail*, 17 December 1997, 1.

52. *West Australian*, 13 July 1996, 33.

53. *Courier Mail*, 1 August 1963; Davenport, *Harbors and Marine*, 703.

54. Watt, *Stewart Island's Kaipipi Shipyard and the Ross Sea Whalers*, 186.

55. Cockcroft, *Nicholls's Seamanship and Nautical Knowledge*, 200.

56. McCarthy, "Shipwrecks in Jervoise Bay," 364.

57. Illsley and Roberts, "18th Century Boat in Lake Padarn."

58. Ibid., 55.

59. Rodgers, *1995 Predisturbance Wreck Site Investigation at Claflin Point*, 15, 28.

60. *West Australian*, 30 March 1938, 16a.

61. Cockcroft, *Nicholls's Seamanship and Nautical Knowledge*, 200.

62. As noted by Babits and Kjorness-Corbin, "Final Report on an Archaeological Survey of the Western Shore of the Pungo River," 3.

63. Cockroft, *Nicholls's Seamanship and Nautical Knowledge*, 200.

64. Shomette, "Shipwrecks of Mallows Bay," 90; Shomette, *Ghost Fleet of Mallows Bay*, 267.

65. Delgado, "What Becomes of the Old Ships?" 4.

66. Cockcroft, *Nicholls's Seamanship and Nautical Knowledge*, 200.

67. Richards, "History and Archaeology of the Garden Island Ships' Graveyard," 89.

Chapter 8. Conclusion

1. Lenihan, "Rethinking Shipwreck Archaeology," 63.

2. For an example of a good study of a regional study that considered discard correlates, see Doyle, "Examination of Associations."

Bibliography

Abbass, D. K. "Newport and Captain Cook's Ships." *Great Circle* 23, no. 1 (2003): 3–20.

Advertiser (Adelaide, South Australia). 1930–32.

Akerlund, H. *Fartygsfynden in den Forna Hamnen i Kalmar* (Shipfinds in the ancient harbor in Kalmar). Stockholm: Almqvist & Wiksells Bokt, 1951.

Aldcroft, D. H. "The Eclipse of British Coastal Shipping, 1913–21." *Journal of Transport History* 5, no. 1 (1963): 24–38.

———. "The Depression in British Shipping." *Journal of Transport History* 7, no. 1 (1965): 14–24.

Aldsworth, F. G. "Excavations at the Former Royal Naval Dockyard, Bermuda: A Nineteenth Century Slave Hulk." *Bermuda Journal of Archaeology and Maritime History* 1 (1989): 109–30.

Andrews, G. K. "Hulks." *Australian Sea Heritage* 13, Autumn (1987): 17–18.

ANMA (Australian National Maritime Association). *Australian Shipping: Structure, History and Future.* Melbourne: Australian National Maritime Association, 1989.

Anuskiewicz, R. J. "Technology, Theory and Analysis: Using Remote Sensing as a Tool for Middle-Range Theory Building in Maritime and Nautical Archaeology." In *Maritime Archaeology: A Reader of Substantive and Theoretical Contributions*, edited by Lawrence Babits and Hans Van Tilburg, 223–31. New York: Plenum Press, 1998.

Arenhold, L. "The Nydam Boat at Kiel." *Mariner's Mirror* 4, no.6 (1916): 182–85.

Argus (Adelaide, South Australia). 1933.

Armstrong, J. "The Crewing of British Coastal Colliers, 1870–1914." *Great Circle* 20, no. 2 (1998): 73–89.

Arnold, J. B., III, J. L. Goloboy, A. W. Hall, R. A. Hall, and J. D. Shively. *Texas Liberty Ships: From World War II Working-Class Heroes to Artificial Reefs.* Texas: Texas Parks and Wildlife, 1998.

Arnott, T. K. "Torpedo Boat—Queenscliffe." In *Maritime Archaeology Association of Victoria: Project Reports 1984.* Melbourne: Maritime Archaeology Association of Victoria, 1984.

———. *Investigator Strait Maritime Heritage Trail.* Adelaide: State Heritage Branch, Department of Environment and Natural Resources, 1996.

Askins, A. "Crossroads Wrecks." In *Encyclopedia of Underwater and Maritime Archaeology*, edited by James P. Delgado, 117–19. London: British Museum Press, 1997.

Attenborough, D., and R. Roberts. "The Sunbeam." Unpublished wreck inspection report, Flinders University, Adelaide, Aus., 1997.

Australian Government. Department of Environment and Heritage. Coastal and Marine Pollution home page, http://www.deh.gov.au/coasts/pollution/dumping/index.html. Accessed 10 June 2002.

———. National Shipwreck Database home page, http://www.environment.gov.au/cgi-bin/heritage/nsd/nsd_list.pl. Accessed 24 June 2002.

Babits, L. E., and A. Corbin-Kjorness. "Final Report on an Archaeological Survey of the Western Shore of the Pungo River from Wades Point to Woodstock Point." Unpublished report, East Carolina University, Greenville, N.C., 1995.

Babits, L. E., and H. Van Tilburg. "Introduction." In *Maritime Archaeology: A Reader of Substantive and Theoretical Contributions,* edited by Lawrence Babits and Hans Van Tilburg, 1–3. New York: Plenum Press, 1998.

Bach, J. "Sea Transport in Australia: The Rise and Fall of the Intrastate Shipping Industry of New South Wales." In *Maritime History,* vol. 2, edited by Robert Craig, 5–30. Newton Abbot, UK: David and Charles, 1973.

———. *A Maritime History of Australia.* Sydney: Thomas Nelson, 1976.

Baker, J. G., R. J. Anuskiewicz, and E. G. Garrison. "Mapping and Site Characterization in Zero Visibility: The C.S.S. Georgia." *Underwater Archaeology: The Challenge Before Us: The Proceedings of the Twelfth Conference on Underwater Archaeology* (1981): 10–20.

Baker, M. "Report of Hulk." Unpublished wreck inspection report, Flinders University, Adelaide, Aus., 1997.

Baker, W. A. "The Technical Importance of Shipwreck Archaeology." In *Maritime Archaeology: A Reader of Substantive and Theoretical Contributions,* edited by Lawrence E. Babits and Hans Van Tilburg, 17–23. New York: Plenum Press, 1998.

Ballard, G. A. "The Transporting of the Obelisks at Karnak." *Mariner's Mirror* 6 (1920): 264–73, 307–14.

———. "Queen Hatshepsut's Great Lighter." *Mariner's Mirror* 12 (1926): 221–23.

———. "Egyptian Shipping of About 1500 B.C." *Mariner's Mirror* 23 (1937): 103–5.

———. "The Great Obelisk Lighter of 1550 B.C." *Mariner's Mirror* 27 (1941): 290–306.

———. "The Egyptian Obelisk Lighter." *Mariner's Mirror* 33 (1947): 158–64.

Ballard, R. D., R. Archbold. *The Discovery of the Titanic: Exploring the Greatest of All Lost Ships.* Toronto: Madison, 1995.

Barfield, T., ed. *The Dictionary of Anthropology.* Oxford: Blackwell, 1997.

Barsness, R. W. "Maritime Activity and Port Development in the United States Since 1900: A Survey." *Journal of Transport History* 2, no. 3 (1974): 167–84.

Basch, L. "Ancient Wrecks and the Archaeology of Ships." *International Journal of Nautical Archaeology and Underwater Exploration* 1 (1972): 1–58.

Bass, G. F. "A Plea for Historical Particularism in Nautical Archaeology." In *Shipwreck Anthropology,* edited by Richard A. Gould, 91–104. Albuquerque: University of New Mexico Press, 1983.

Bathgate, D. "The History, Topography and Search of Jervoise Bay." In *Jervoise Bay*

Shipwrecks, by Michael McCarthy. Perth: Department of Maritime Archaeology, Western Australian Museum, 1979.

Baty, S. *Ships that Passed*. Frenchs Forest, Aus.: Reed Books, 1984.

Bayreuther, W. A., and M. J. Hovrath. "The Snowsquall Project: Saving the Last Yankee Clipper Ship." *Bermuda Journal of Archaeology and Maritime History* 5(1993): 99–109.

Beattie, J., and B. Pothier. *The Battle of the Restigouche*. Quebec: Canadian Heritage, 1996.

Belle, J. "Ketches and Ketchmen—Mr. Workman's Talk on 20/7/77." *Portonian* 5, no. 3 (1977): 10–12.

Bill, J. "Skuldelev Ships." In *Encyclopedia of Underwater and Maritime Archaeology*, edited by James P. Delgado, 388–89. London: British Museum Press, 1997.

Bird, J. *Seaport Gateways of Australia*. Melbourne: Oxford University Press, 1968.

Blackburn, G. J. *The Illustrated Encyclopedia of Ships, Boats, Vessels and Other Water-Borne Craft*. London: John Murray, 1978.

Blainey, G. *The Causes of War*. Bungay, UK: Macmillan, 1973.

Bolton, G. C. *A Thousand Miles Away: A History of North Queensland to 1920*. Canberra: Australian National University Press, 1972.

———. "1930–1939." In *A New History of Australia*, edited by Frank Crowley, 458–503. Melbourne: William Heinemann, 1980.

Bound, M. "The Hulk Jhelum: A Derivative Expression of Late British Indiaman Ship-Building." *International Journal of Nautical Archaeology and Underwater Exploration* 19, no. 1 (1990): 43–47.

———. "Iron Bean-End Fastenings: Fell's Patent No.8186, a Puzzle Resolved." *International Journal of Nautical Archaeology and Underwater Exploration* 79 (1993): 338–42.

———. "British Sea Power: Ships, Armament, Strategy and Tactics." In *Excavating Ships of War*, edited by Mensun Bound, 8–30. Oswestry, UK: Anthony Nelson, 1998.

Bright, L. "Beached Shipwreck Dynamics." In *Underwater Archaeology Proceedings*. Society for Historical Archaeology Conference, Kansas City, Mo., 1993.

British Register of Australian Shipping, Australian Archives, Adelaide, South Australia.

Broadus, M. *Depression Decade: From New Era Through New Deal 1929–1941*. Vol. 9 of *The Economic History of the United States*. New York: Holt, Rinehart and Winston, 1964.

Broadwater, J. D. "The York River Shipwreck Project: Results from the 1978 Survey." In *The Realms of Gold: The Proceedings of the 10th Conference on Underwater Archaeology* (1981): 33–44.

———. "Yorktown Shipwreck." *National Geographic* 173, no.6 (1988): 802–23.

———. "Shipwreck in a Swimming Pool: An Assessment of the Methodology and Technology Utilized on the Yorktown Shipwreck Archaeological Project." *Historical Archaeology Special Issue* 4 (1992): 36–46.

———. "In the Shadow of Wooden Walls: Naval Transports During the American War of Independence." In *The Archaeology of Ships of War*, edited by Mensun Bound, 58–63. Owestry, UK: Anthony Nelson, 1995.

———. "HMS Charon." In *Encyclopedia of Underwater and Maritime Archaeology*, edited by James P. Delgado, 97. London: British Museum Press, 1997.

———. "Yorktown Shipwrecks." In *Encyclopedia of Underwater and Maritime Archaeology*, edited by James P. Delgado, 471–72. London: British Museum Press, 1997.

Broadwater, J. D., R. M. Adams, and M. Renner. "The Yorktown Shipwreck Archaeological Project: An Interim Report on the Excavation of Shipwreck 44T088." *International Journal of Nautical Archaeology and Underwater Exploration* 14, no. 4 (1985): 301–45.

Broeze, F. J. A. "The Cost of Distance: Shipping and the Early Australian Economy, 1788–1850." *Economic History Review* 28, no. 4 (1975): 582–97.

———. "Private Enterprise and Public Policy: Merchant Shipping in Australia and New Zealand, 1788–1992." In *Land and Sea: The Role of Shipping in Australasian Economic Development*, edited by G. D. Snooks and J. J. Pincus, 8–32. Melbourne: Oxford University Press and the Economic History Society of Australia and New Zealand, 1992.

———. *Island Nation: A History of Australians and the Sea*. St. Leonards, N.S.W.: Allen & Unwin, 1998.

Broomhill, R. "The Port in the Great Depression." *Portonian* 1, no. 3 (1973): 9–11.

———. *Unemployed Workers: A Social History of the Great Depression in Adelaide*. St. Lucia, Queensland: University of Queensland Press, 1978.

Brouwer, N. *International Register of Historic Ships*. 2nd ed. New York: Sea History Press, 1993.

Broxam, G. *Shipping Arrivals and Departures, Tasmania*. Vol. 3, *1843–1850*. Melbourne: Navarine, 1998.

Bruce-Mitford, R. *Aspects of Anglo-Saxon Archaeology*. London: Victor Gollancz, 1974.

Bryce, D. *Weaponry from the Machault: An 18th-Century French Frigate*. Quebec: Environment Canada, 1984.

Bullen, I. "A Glimpse into Niantic's Hold." *California History* 63, no. 4 (1979): 326–33.

Burn, D. L. "Recent Trends in the History of the Steel Industry." *Economic History Review* 17, no. 2 (1947): 95–102.

Busselton-Dunsborough Mail. Western Australian Maritime Museum, Fremantle, 1997.

Buxton, G. L. "1870–90." In *A New History of Australia*, edited by Frank Crowley, 165–215. Melbourne: William Heinemann, 1980.

Byron, T. *Scuba Divers Guide: Australia's Southern Great Barrier Reef*. Padstow Heights, Aus.: Aqua Sports Publications, 1987.

Cage, R. A. "The Structure and Profitability of Tramp Shipping, 1850–1920: Some Evidence from Four Glasgow Based Firms." *Great Circle* 17, no. 1 (1995): 1–21.

Cairns, L., and G. Henderson. *Unfinished Voyages: Western Australian Shipwrecks 1881–1900.* Nedlands: University of Western Australia Press, 1995.

Cameron, C. M. "Structure Abandonment in Villages." *Archaeological Method and Theory* 3 (1991): 155–94.

Cameron, C. M., and S. Tomka, eds. *Abandonment of Settlements and Regions: Ethnoarchaeological and Archaeological Approaches.* New York: Cambridge University Press, 1993.

Canby, C. *A History of Ships and Seafaring.* London: Leisure Arts, 1965.

Carrell, T. L. "Charles H. Spencer." In *Encyclopedia of Underwater and Maritime Archaeology,* edited by James P. Delgado, 96–97. London: British Museum Press, 1997.

Cassavoy, K. A., and K. J. Crisman. "The War of 1812: Battle for the Great Lakes." In *Ships and Shipwrecks of the Americas: A History Based on Underewater Archaeology,* edited by George F. Bass, 169–88. London: Thames and Hudson, 1996.

Casson, L. *The Ancient Mariners.* Princeton: Princeton University Press, 1991.

Castles, A. C., and M. C. Harris. *Lawmakers and Wayward Whigs: Governmental Law in South Australia 1836–1986.* Netley, Aus.: Wakefield Press, 1987.

Cederlund, C. O. "Baltic Sea." In *Encyclopedia of Underwater and Maritime Archaeology,* edited by James P. Delgado, 48–53. London: British Museum Press, 1997.

Christensen, A. E. "Scandinavian Ships from Earliest Times to the Vikings." In *A History of Seafaring Based on Underwater Archaeology,* edited by George F. Bass, 159–180. New York: Thames and Hudson, 1972.

———. *Guide to the Viking Ship Museum.* Oslo: Universitetets Oldsaksamling, 1987.

———. "Gokstad Ship." In *Encyclopedia of Underwater and Maritime Archaeology,* edited by James P. Delgado, 172–74. London: British Museum Press, 1997.

———. "Oseberg Ship." In *Encyclopedia of Underwater and Maritime Archaeology,* edited by James P. Delgado, 302–3. London: British Museum Press, 1997.

Christoffersen, J. "Iron Age Finds in Funen (Fyn)—Some Archaeological Problems of Defining Maritime Sites." In *Aspects of Maritime Scandinavia AD 200–1200,* edited by Ole Crumlin-Pederson, 55–66. Roskilde, Den.: Viking Ship Museum, 1991.

Christopher, P. *Divers' Guide to South Australia.* Adelaide: Published by the author, 1988.

———. *South Australian Shipwrecks: A Database.* Adelaide: Society for Underwater Historical Research, 1990.

Claesson, S. "Annabella: The Excavation of a Nineteenth-Century Coasting Schooner in Cape Neddick, Maine." *INA Quarterly* 23, no. 2 (1996): 16–21.

Clark, C. M. H. *A History of Australia.* Vol. 3, *The Beginning of an Australian Civilization, 1824–1851.* Victoria: Melbourne University Press, 1978.

———. *A History of Australia*. Vol. 4, *The Earth Abideth For Ever, 1851–1888*. Victoria: Melbourne University Press, 1978.

———. *Select Documents in Australian History, 1788–1850*. Sydney: Angus and Robertson, 1980.

———. *A Short History of Australia*. 2nd ed. New York: Mentor Books, 1980.

———. *A History of Australia*. Vol. 5, *The People Make Laws 1888–1915*. Victoria: Melbourne University Press, 1981.

———. *A History of Australia*. Vol. 6, *"The Old Dead Tree and the Young Green Tree," 1916–1935*. Victoria: Melbourne University Press, 1987.

Clarke, R., M. Dean, G. Hutchinson, S. McGrail, and J. Squirrel. "Recent Work on the R. Hamble Wreck Near Bursledon, Hampshire." *International Journal of Nautical Archaeology and Underwater Exploration* 22, no. 1 (1993): 21–44.

Cockcroft, A. N. *Nicholls's Seamanship and Nautical Knowledge*. 25th ed. Glasgow: Brown, Son and Ferguson, 1983.

Cockrell, W. A. "A Trial Model for the Analysis of Shipwrecks." In *Shipwreck Anthropology*, edited by Richard A. Gould, 207–19. Albuquerque: University of New Mexico Press, 1983.

COIITC (Committee of Inquiry into Technological Change in Australia). *Technological Change in Australia*. Vol. 1, *Technological Change and Its Consequences, Including Discussions of Processes of Change, Conclusions, and Recommendations for Maximising Benefits and Minimising Adverse Consequences*. Canberra: Australian Government Publishing Service, 1980.

———. *Technological Change in Australia*. Vol. 2, *Technological Change in Industry, Likely Technologies and Applications in Australia*. Canberra: Australian Government Publishing Service, 1980.

Colton, H. S. "The Colorado River Steamboat 'Charles H. Spencer.'" *Steamboat Bill: Journal of the Steamship Historical Society of America* 61, no.7 (1957): 6–7.

Commonwealth Government. *Beaches, Fishing Ground and Sea Routes Protection Act 1932*, Flinders University, South Australia.

———. House of Representatives. *The Shipbuilding Industry: In the Wake of the Bounty*. Canberra: Australian Government Publishing Services, 1992.

———. *Senate Report*, 6 December 1994.

Corbin, A. *The Material Culture of Steamboat Passengers: Archaeological Evidence from the Missouri River*. New York: Kluwer Academic/Plenum, 2000.

Coroneos, C. "One Interpretation for the Short Working Lives of Early Australian Wooden Sailing Vessels in Victorian Waters." *Bulletin of the Australian Institute for Maritime Archaeology* 15, no. 2 (1991): 7–14.

———. *Shipwrecks of Encounter Bay and Backstairs Passage*. Adelaide: Australian Institute for Maritime Archaeology and Australian National Centre of Excellence for Maritime Archaeology, 1997.

———. "Myall Lakes Shipwrecks Study." Report to New South Wales State Heritage Office, Maroubra, Aus., 1998.

Coroneos, C., and R. McKinnon. *Shipwrecks of Investigator Strait and the Lower*

Yorke Peninsula. Adelaide: Australian Institute for Maritime Archaeology and Australian National Centre of Excellence for Maritime Archaeology, 1997.

Cotter, R. "The Golden Decade." In *Essays in Economic History of Australia: 1788–1939*, edited by James Griffith, 113–34. Brisbane: Jacaranda Press, 1967.

———. "War, Boom and Depression." In *Essays in Economic History of Australia: 1788–1939*, edited by James Griffith, 244–82. Brisbane: Jacaranda Press, 1967.

Courier Mail (Brisbane, Queensland). 1963–1986.

Cousteau, J. *The Silent World*. London: Penguin Books, 1958.

Cree, N. "Port's Scrap Heap." *Australasian Ships and Ports Magazine* 1, no. 12 (1989): 17.

Crisman, K. J. "'Coffins of the Brave': A Return to Lake Champlain's War of 1812 Ship Graveyard." *INA Quarterly* 22, no. 1 (1995): 4–8.

———. "Struggle for a Continent: Naval Battles of the French and Indian Wars." In *Ships and Shipwrecks of the Americas: A History Based on Underwater Archaeology*, edited by George F. Bass, 129–48. London: Thames and Hudson, 1996.

———. "Boscawen." In *Encyclopedia of Underwater and Maritime Archaeology*, edited by James P. Delgado, 69–70. London: British Museum Press, 1997.

Crowley, F. "1901–14." In *A New History of Australia*, edited by Frank Crowley, 260–311. Melbourne: William Heinemann, 1980.

Crumlin-Pedersen, O. "Wrecks in the North Sea and the Baltic." In *Underwater Archaeology: A Nascent Discipline*, 65–75. Paris: United Nations Educational, Scientific and Cultural Organization, 1972.

———. "Aspects of Wood Technology in Medieval Shipbuilding." In *Sailing into the Past*, edited by Ole Crumlin-Pederson and M. Vinner, 138–149. Roskilde, Den.: Viking Ship Museum, 1986.

———. "Introduction." In *Aspects of Maritime Scandinavia AD 200–1200*, edited by Ole Crumlin-Pederson, 7–9. Roskilde, Den.: Viking Ship Museum, 1991.

———. "Maritime Aspects of the Archaeology of Roman and Migration-Period Denmark." In *Aspects of Maritime Scandinavia AD 200–1200*, edited by Ole Crumlin-Pederson, 41–53. Roskilde, Den.: Viking Ship Museum, 1991.

———. "Ship Types and Sizes, AD 800–1400." In *Aspects of Maritime Scandinavia AD 200–1200*, edited by Ole Crumlin-Pederson, 69–82. Roskilde, Den.: Viking Ship Museum, 1991.

———. "Medieval Ships in Danish Waters." In *Crossroads in Ancient Shipbuilding*, edited by Christer Westerdahl, 65–72. Oxford: Oxbow Books, 1994.

Culliton, J. W. "Economics and Shipbuilding." In *The Shipbuilding Business in the United States of America*, vol. 1, edited by F. G. Fassett Jr., 1–13. New York: Macdonald and Jane's, 1974.

Cumming, E. M., and D. J. Carter. "The Earl of Abergavenny (1805), an Outward Bound English East Indiaman." *International Journal of Nautical Archaeology and Underwater Exploration* 19, no. 1 (1990): 31–33.

Cunningham, T. J. "About Docks that Are Closed and Ships that Have Gone: Reminiscences of Thomas James Cunningham." *Portonian* 16, no. 4 (1988): 3–8.

Curby, P. "Richmond River Maritime History Survey—1840–1960: Part A." Unpublished report for the Richmond River Shire Council, Cronulla, Aus., 1997.

Cussler, C., and C. Dirgo. *The Sea Hunters*. New York: Pocket Star Books, 1997.

Dalgairns, S., and A. Peterson. "The Garthneill." Unpublished ARCH 3005 field report, Flinders University, Adelaide, Aus., 1997.

Darkin, G. "Gem." Unpublished ARCH 3005 field report, Flinders University, Adelaide, Aus., 1997.

Davenport, W., comp. *Harbours and Marine: Port and Harbour Developments in Queensland from 1824–1985*. Brisbane: Department of Harbours and Marine, 1986.

Davies, M. "Shipping Freight Costs: South Australian Copper and Copper-Ore Cargoes, 1845–1870." *Great Circle* 20, no. 2 (1998): 90–119.

Dean, M., and S. Miller. "The Story of the St Mary." *Falkland Islands Journal* (1979): 35–41.

Dean, N. "Actaeon." In *Encyclopedia of Underwater and Maritime Archaeology*, edited by James P. Delgado, 18. London: British Museum Press, 1997.

———. "Charles Cooper." In *Encyclopedia of Underwater and Maritime Archaeology*, edited by James P. Delgado, 95–96. London: British Museum Press, 1997.

———. "Egeria." In *Encyclopedia of Underwater and Maritime Archaeology*, edited by James P. Delgado, 138. London: British Museum Press, 1997.

———. "Falklands Wrecks and Hulks." In *Encyclopedia of Underwater and Maritime Archaeology*, edited by James P. Delgado, 148–50. London: British Museum Press, 1997.

———. "Snow Squall." In *Encyclopedia of Underwater and Maritime Archaeology*, edited by James P. Delgado, 392–93. London: British Museum Press, 1997.

de Garis, B. K. "1890–1900." In *A New History of Australia*, edited by Frank Crowley, 216–59. Melbourne: William Heinemann, 1980.

Delgado, J. P. "No Longer a Buoyant Ship: Unearthing the Gold Rush Storeship Niantic." *California History* 63, no. 4 (1979): 316–25.

———. "'What Becomes of the Old Ships?' Dismantling the Gold Rush Fleet of San Francisco." *Pacific Historian* 25, no. 4 (1981): 1–9.

———. "A Gold Rush Enterprise: Sam Ward, Charles Mersch, and the Storeship Niantic." *Huntington Library Quarterly* 46 (1983): 321–30.

———. "Erosion Exposed Shipwreck Remains: Winter 1982." In *Submerged Cultural Resources Survey: Portions of Point Reyes National Marine Sanctuary*, edited by Larry E. Murphy, 179–85. Santa Fe: Submerged Cultural Resources Unit, National Parks Service, 1984.

———. "Skeleton in the Sand: Documentation of the Environmentally Exposed 1856 Ship *King Phillip*, San Francisco." *Proceedings of the Sixteenth Annual Conference on Underwater Archaeology* (1985): 30–36.

———. "Documentation and Identification of the Two-Masted Schooner *Neptune*." *Historical Archaeology* 20 (1986): 95–108.

———. *Ghost Fleet: The Sunken Ships of Bikini Atoll.* Honululu: University of Hawai'i Press, 1996.

———. "Blackfriars Wrecks." In *Encyclopedia of Underwater and Maritime Archaeology,* edited by James P. Delgado, 64–66. London: British Museum Press, 1997.

———. "County Hall Ship." In *Encyclopedia of Underwater and Maritime Archaeology,* edited by James P. Delgado, 115–16. London: British Museum Press, 1997.

———. "Earl of Abergavenny." In *Encyclopedia of Underwater and Maritime Archaeology,* edited by James P. Delgado, 136–37. London: British Museum Press, 1997.

———. "Hjortspring Boat." In *Encyclopedia of Underwater and Maritime Archaeology,* edited by James P. Delgado, 193. London: British Museum Press, 1997.

———. "New Guys House Boat." In *Encyclopedia of Underwater and Maritime Archaeology,* edited by James P. Delgado, 295–96. London: British Museum Press, 1997.

———. "Niantic." In *Encyclopedia of Underwater and Maritime Archaeology,* edited by James P. Delgado, 297. London: British Museum Press, 1997.

———. "Nydam Boat." In *Encyclopedia of Underwater and Maritime Archaeology,* edited by James P. Delgado, 300–301. London: British Museum Press, 1997.

———. "Quebec Bateaux." In *Encyclopedia of Underwater and Maritime Archaeology,* edited by James P. Delgado, 332–33. London: British Museum Press, 1997.

———. "Vicar of Bray." In *Encyclopedia of Underwater and Maritime Archaeology,* edited by James P. Delgado, 457–58. London: British Museum Press, 1997.

De Rooy, M. "Taking the Rough with the Smooth: The Depression Experience in Port Adelaide, 1929–1931." History honors thesis, Adelaide University, South Australia, 1987.

Devendra, S. "Remains of Riverine Craft: Material for Ecological and Community Studies." *Bulletin of the Australian Institute for Maritime Archaeology* 17, no. 2 (1993): 17–24.

Dickey, B. *Rations, Residence, Resources.* Netley, Aus.: Wakefield Press, 1986.

Dobson, N. "Maritime Fife Completes Phase 2." *Nautical Archaeology: Society Newsletter for the World of Underwater, Foreshore, Ship and Boat Archaeology,* Spring 1997, 1–3.

Doyle, C. "An Examination of Associations Between Significant Historic Events and the Loss and Discard of Vessels in the Townsville Catchment, 1865–1981." Master's thesis, James Cook University, Townsville, Aus., 2000.

Dugan, J. *Man Explores the Sea.* London: Penguin Books, 1960.

Dumas, F. "Ancient Wrecks." In *Underwater Archaeology: A Nascent Discipline.* Paris: United Nations Educational, Scientific and Cultural Organization, 1972.

Duncan, B. "Signposts in the Sea: An Investigation of the Shipwreck Patterning and Cultural Seascapes of the Gippsland Region, Victoria." Honors thesis, James Cook University, Townsville, Aus., 2000.

Dundon, G. *The Shipbuilders of Brisbane Water NSW: Including 500 Named Vessels Built Between 1829 and 1953.* Adelaide: Openbook, 1997.

Dyos, H. J., and D. H. Aldcroft. *British Transport: An Economic Survey from the*

Seventeenth Century to the Twentieth. Leicester, UK: Leicester University Press, 1969.

Dyster, B. "The Port of Launceston Before 1851." *Great Circle* 3, no. 2(1981): 103–24.

Edmonds, L., S. Kenderdine, G. Nayton, and M. Staniforth. *Historic Shipwrecks National Research Plan*. Canberra: Department of Communication and the Arts, 1995.

Edwin Fox Restoration Society, Inc. *The Story of the Edwin Fox*. 2nd ed. Picton, N.Z.: Toneden Promotions, 1987.

Eighmy, J. L. "The Use of Material Culture in Diachronic Anthropology." In *Modern Material Culture: The Archaeology of Us*, edited by Richard A. Gould and Michael B. Schiffer, 31–50. New York: Academic Press, 1981.

Einarsson, L. "Kalmar Harbour Wrecks." In Encyclopedia of Underwater and Maritime Archaeology, edited by James P. Delgado, 219–20. London: British Museum Press, 1997.

El-Baz, F. "Finding a Pharaoh's Funeral Bark." *National Geographic* 173, no. 4 (1988): 513–33.

Eliot, J. E. "Bikini's Nuclear Graveyard." *National Geographic* 181, no. 6 (1992): 70–83.

Ellis, W. S. "Africa's Sahel: The Stricken Land." *National Geographic* 172, no. 2 (1987): 140–179.

Emery, M. "Successful Search for Sunken Boats." *Nautical Archaeology: Society Newsletter for the World of Underwater, Foreshore, Ship and Boat Archaeology*, Spring 1997, 4.

Evans, A. C. "The Coming of the Anglo-Saxons." In *History from Beneath the Sea: Shipwrecks and Archaeology*, edited by Peter Throckmorton, 112–15. Melbourne: RD Press, 1987.

———. "A Kingly Burial." In *History from Beneath the Sea: Shipwrecks and Archaeology*, edited by Peter Throckmorton, 116–22. Melbourne: RD Press, 1987.

———. "Snape Boat." In *Encyclopedia of Underwater and Maritime Archaeology*, edited by James P. Delgado, 392. London: British Museum Press, 1997.

———. "Sutton Hoo." In *Encyclopedia of Underwater and Maritime Archaeology*, edited by James P. Delgado, 411–13. London: British Museum Press, 1997.

Eyres, D. J. *Ship Construction*. 2nd ed. London: Heinemann, 1980.

Fassett, F. G., Jr. "Foreword." In *The Shipbuilding Business in the United States of America*, vol. 1, edited by F. G. Fassett Jr., vii–ix. New York: Macdonald and Jane's, 1974.

Fenwick, V. H. "The Graveney Boat: A Pre-Conquest Discovery in Kent." *International Journal of Nautical Archaeology and Underwater Exploration* 1 (1972): 119–29.

———. "Graveney Boat." In *Encyclopedia of Underwater and Maritime Archaeology*, edited by James P. Delgado, 175–76. London: British Museum Press, 1997.

———, ed. *The Graveney Boat: a Tenth-Century Find From Kent, Excavation and Recording; Interpretation of the Boat Remains and the Environment; Reconstruction and Other Research; Conservation and Display.* British Archaeological Reports, International Series, no. 53. Oxford, 1978.

Ferrall, R. A. *The Story of the Port of Launceston.* Launceston, Aus.: Port of Launceston Authority, 1983.

Fisher, A. C., Jr. "Two Englands." *National Geographic* 156, no. 4 (1979): 442–81.

Fisher, J. *The Australians: From 1788 to Modern Times.* London: Seal Books, 1977.

Fisheries Division. *Darwin's Artificial Reefs.* Darwin, Aus.: Department of Primary Industries and Fisheries, 1992.

Fitchett, T. K. *The Vanished Fleet: Australian Coastal Passenger Ships, 1910–1960.* Melbourne: Rigby, 1976.

Fitzpatrick, B. *The British Empire in Australia: An Economic History, 1834–1939.* South Melbourne: Macmillan of Australia, 1969.

Fletcher, M. E. "The Suez Canal and World Shipping, 1869–1914." *Journal of Economic History* 18, no. 4 (1958): 556–73.

———. "From Coal to Oil in British Shipping." *Journal of Transport History* 3, no. 2 (1975): 1–19.

Flynn, M., ed. *North Australian Fishing Maps: Fish Finder.* Darwin, Aus.: Editor's Office, 2000.

Fontenoy, P. "A Discussion of Maritime Archaeology." In *Maritime Archaeology: A Reader of Substantive and Theoretical Contributions,* edited by Lawrence E. Babits and Hans Van Tilburg, 47–52. New York: Plenum Press, 1994.

Ford, J. "Unidentified Shipwreck D." Unpublished ARCH 3005 field report, Flinders University, Adelaide, Aus., 1997.

Foster, L. *Port Phillip Shipwrecks Stage 1: An Historical Survey.* Melbourne: Victoria Archaeological Survey, 1987.

———. *Port Phillip Shipwrecks Stage 2: An Historical Survey.* Melbourne: Victoria Archaeological Survey, 1988.

———. "Defence and Victorian Shipwrecks." *Bulletin of the Australian Institute for Maritime Archaeology* 13, no. 1 (1989): 19–27.

———. *Port Phillip Shipwrecks Stage 3: An Historical Survey.* Melbourne: Victoria Archaeological Survey, 1989.

———. *Port Phillip Shipwrecks Stage 4: An Historical Survey.* Melbourne: Victoria Archaeological Survey, 1990.

Foster, M. "Unidentified Ketch." Unpublished ARCH 3005 field report, Flinders University, Adelaide, Aus., 1996.

Friel, I. "Henry V's Grace Dieu and the Wreck in the R. Hamble Near Bursledon, Hampshire." *International Journal of Nautical Archaeology and Underwater Exploration* 22, no. 1 (1993): 3–19.

Garrison, E. "CSS Georgia." In *Encyclopedia of Underwater and Maritime Archaeology,* edited by James P. Delgado, 168–69. London: British Museum Press, 1997.

Gazeley, I., and P. Rice. "Wages and Employment in Britain Between the Wars: Quarterly Evidence from the Shipbuilding Industry." *Explorations in Economic History* 33 (1996): 296–318.

Gerr, S. "The Suitability of the Big Wooden Schooner for Long-Distance Deep-Sea Trading." *Mariner's Mirror* 61, no. 4 (1975): 399–403.

Gesner, P. *Pandora: An Archaeological Perspective*. Brisbane: Queensland Museum, 1991.

———. "HMS Pandora Project—A Report on Stage 1: Five Seasons of Excavation." *Memoirs of the Queensland Museum: Cultural Heritage Series* 2 1 (2000): 1–52.

Gibb, J. B. *The Archaeology of Wealth: Consumer Behaviour in English America*. New York: Plenum Press, 1996.

Gibbins, D., and J. Adams. "Shipwrecks and Maritime Archaeology." *World Archaeology* 32, no. 3 (2001): 279–91.

Gibbs, M. "Maritime Archaeology and Behaviour during Crisis: The Wreck of the VOC Ship Batavia (1629)." In *Natural Disasters, Catastrophism and Cultural Change*, edited by J. Grattan and R. Torrence, 128–45. London: One World Archaeology, Routledge, 2002.

———. "The Archaeology of Crisis: Shipwreck Survivor Camps in Australasia." *Historical Archaeology* 37, no. 1 (2003): 128–45.

Gibson-Wilde, D. *Gateway to a Golden Land: Townsville to 1884*. Townsville, Aus.: History Department, James Cook University, 1984.

Gifford, E., and J. Gifford. "The Sailing Characteristics of Saxon Ships as Derived from Half-Scale Working Models with Special Reference to the Sutton Hoo Ship." *International Journal of Nautical Archaeology and Underwater Exploration* 24, no. 2 (1995): 121–31.

Glassford, R. W. "A Fleet of Hulks." *Royal Australian Historical Society Journal and Proceedings* 39, no. 5 (1953): 217–52.

Goldrick, J. "The Problems of Modern Naval History." In *Doing Naval History: Essays Toward Improvement*, edited by John B. Hattendorf, 11–23. Newport, R. I.: Naval War College Press, 1995.

Goodburn, D. "Fragments of an Early Carvel-Built Vessel from Camber, East Sussex, England." *International Journal of Nautical Archaeology and Underwater Exploration* 19, no. 4 (1990): 327–34.

Goold-Adams, R. *The Return of the Great Britain*. London: Weidenfeld and Nicolson, 1976.

Gould, R. A. "The Archaeology of War: Wrecks of the Spanish Armada of 1588 and the Battle of Britain, 1940." In *Shipwreck Anthropology*, edited by Richard A. Gould, 105–42. Albuquerque: University of New Mexico Press, 1983.

———. "Looking Below the Surface: Shipwreck Archaeology as Anthropology." In *Shipwreck Anthropology*, edited by Richard A. Gould, 3–22. Albuquerque: University of New Mexico Press, 1983.

———. "H.M.S. Vixen: An Early Ironclad Ram at Bermuda." *Bermuda Journal of Archaeology and Maritime History* 1 (1989): 43–80.

———. "The Archaeology of HMS Vixen, an Early Ironclad Ram in Bermuda." *International Journal of Nautical Archaeology and Underwater Exploration* 20, no. 1 (1991): 141–53.

——. "Bird Key Harbor Brick Wreck (FOJE 029) 1990 Fieldwork." In *Dry Tortugas National Park: Submerged Cultural Resources Assessment*, edited by Larry E. Murphy, 333–351. Santa Fe: Submerged Cultural Resources Unit, National Parks and Wildlife Service, 1993.

——. "The Bird Key Wreck, Dry Tortugas National Park, Florida." *Bulletin of the Australian Institute for Maritime Archaeology* 19, no. 2 (1995): 7–16.

——. "HMS Vixen." In *Encyclopedia of Underwater and Maritime Archaeology*, edited by James P. Delgado, 459–60. London: British Museum Press, 1997.

——. *Archaeology and the Social History of Ships*. Cambridge: Cambridge University Press, 2000.

——. "The Wreck of the Barque *North Carolina*, Bermuda, 1880: An Underwater Crime Scene?" *American Antiquity* 70, no. 1 (2005): 107–28.

Graeme-Evans, A., and P. Wilson. *Built to Last: The Story of the Shipwrights of Port Cygnet, Tasmania, and Their Boats 1863–1997*. 2nd ed. Woodbridge, Aus.: Tasbook, 1996.

Graham, G. S. "The Transition from Paddle-Wheel to Screw Propeller." *Mariner's Mirror* 44, no. 1 (1958): 35–48.

Green, J. N. *Australia's Oldest Wreck: The Loss of the Trial, 1622*. Supplementary Series, 27. Oxford, 1977.

——. *Maritime Archaeology: A Technical Handbook*. London: Academic Press, 1990.

Greenhill, B., and J. Morrison. *The Archaeology of Boats and Ships*. Annapolis: Naval Institute Press, 1995.

Gregory, R. G. "An Overview." In *Recovery from the Depression: Australia and the World Economy in the 1930s*, edited by R. G. Gregory and N. G. Butlin, 1–32. Melbourne: Cambridge University Press, 1988.

Griffiths, D. "British Shipping and the Diesel Engine: The Early Years." *Mariner's Mirror* 81, no. 3 (1995): 313–31.

Guthrie, J. *A History of Marine Engineering*. London: Hutchinson Educational, 1971.

Guthrie, J. N., L. L. Blackall, D. J. W. Moriarty, and P. Gesner. "Wrecks and Marine Microbiology: Case Study from the Pandora." *Bulletin of the Australian Institute for Maritime Archaeology* 18, no. 2 (1994): 19–24.

Haldane, C. "The Lisht Timbers: A Preliminary Report." In *The Pyramid Complex of Senwosret I at Lisht: Metropolitan Museum of Art Egyptian Expedition XXV, The Southern Cemeteries at Lisht III*, edited by D. Arnold, 102–12 and plates. New York: Metropolitan Museum of Art, 1992.

——. "Dashur Boats." In *Encyclopedia of Underwater and Maritime Archaeology*, edited by James P. Delgado, 122–23. London: British Museum Press, 1997.

——. "Khufu Ships." In *Encyclopedia of Underwater and Maritime Archaeology*, edited by James P. Delgado, 222–23. London: British Museum Press, 1997.

——. "Lisht Timbers." In *Encyclopedia of Underwater and Maritime Archaeology*, edited by James P. Delgado, 241–42. London: British Museum Press, 1997.

Halls, C. "A Tale of Two Coal Hulks." *Port of Fremantle Quarterly* Summer (1975): 8–10.

Hammond, N. "Graveyard of Wooden Ships Found on Thames Foreshore." *Nautical Archaeology: Society Newsletter for the World of Underwater, Foreshore, Ship and Boat Archaeology*, Autumn 1995, 4.

Harley, C. K. "The Shift from Sailing Ships to Steamships 1850–1890: A Study in Technological Change and Its Diffusion." In *Essays on a Mature Economy: Britain After 1840*, edited by Donald N. McClosky, 215–31. London: Methuen, 1971.

Harris, E. C., and J. R. Adams. "Sea Venture." In *Encyclopedia of Underwater and Maritime Archaeology*, edited by James P. Delgado, 365–366. London: British Museum Press, 1997.

Hartwell, R. M. *The Economic Development of Van Diemen's Land 1820–1850*. Carlton, Aus.: Melbourne University Press, 1954.

Harvey, F. R. "The Last Voyage of the "Macdhui" 6–18 June, 1942: Unrecognized Sacrifice by Merchant Fleets During World War II." *Great Circle* 22, no. 1 (2000): 17–29.

Hazzard, D. K. "The Yorktown Shipwreck Archaeology Project." *Underwater Archaeology: The Proceedings of the 11th Conference on Underwater Archaeology* (1982): 39–44.

Heal, S. V. E., and G. Hutchinson. "Three Recently Found Logboats." *International Journal of Nautical Archaeology and Underwater Exploration* 15, no. 3 (1986): 205–13.

Henderson, G. "The Archaeological Value of Iron Vessels and Steamships." In *Iron Ships and Steam Shipwrecks: Papers from the First Australian Seminar on the Management of Iron Vessels and Steam Shipwrecks*, edited by Michael McCarthy, 10–12. Fremantle: Western Australian Maritime Museum, 1988.

Henning, G. R., and M. Henning. "Technological Change from Sail to Steam: Export Lumber Shipments from the Pacific Northwest, 1898–1913." *International Journal of Maritime History* 2, no. 2 (1990): 133–45.

Henry, S. L. "Consumers, Commodities, and Choices: A General Model of Consumer Behavior." *Historical Archaeology* 25, no. 2 (1991): 3–14.

Hobart Community Express. (Hobart, Tasmania). 1967.

Hockmann, O. "Late Roman Rhine Vessels from Mainz, Germany." *International Journal of Nautical Archaeology and Underwater Exploration* 22, no. 2 (1993): 125–35.

———. "Mainz Boats." In *Encyclopedia of Underwater and Maritime Archaeology*, edited by James P. Delgado, 255–56. London: British Museum Press, 1997.

Hodder, I. *The Archaeological Process: An Introduction*. Oxford: Blackwell, 1999.

Holdcamper, F. R. "Biography of the List of Merchant Vessels of the United States." *American Neptune* 24, no. 2 (1964): 119–23.

Holman, M. R. *A Handy Book for Shipowners and Masters*. 15th ed. London: Commercial Printing and Stationery, 1953.

Hooper, J. N. A., and D. C. Ramm. "Preliminary Report on Artificial Reefs in the

Vicinity of Darwin Harbour, and Recommendations for the Design and Establishment of Further Reef Structures." Unpublished report by the Northern Territory Museum of Arts and Sciences and the Department of Primary Industry and Fisheries, Darwin, Aus., 1989.

Hopkins, F. "The Final Anchorage: The WW1 Emergency Fleet Wrecks at Mallow's Bay." *Underwater Archaeology Proceedings from the Society for Historical Archaeology Conference*, 1995, 72–76.

Horne, D. *The Lucky Country*. Adelaide: Penguin Books, 1971.

Hosty, K., and I. Stuart. "Maritime Archaeology Over the Last Twenty Years." *Australian Archaeology* 39 (1994): 9–19.

Howe, O. T., and F. C. Matthews. *American Clipper Ships, 1833–1858*. Vol. 2, *Malay–Young Mechanic*. New York: Dover, 1986.

Hudson, W. J. "1951–72." In *A New History of Australia*, edited by Frank Crowley, 504–551. Melbourne: William Heinemann, 1980.

Hudspeth, A., and L. Scripps. *Capital Port: A History of the Marine Board of Hobart 1858–1997*. Hobart, Aus.: Hobart Ports, 2000.

Hughes, H. *The Australian Iron and Steel Industry, 1848–1962*. Melbourne: Melbourne University Press, 1964.

Hunter, L. C. *Steamboats of the Western Rivers: An Economic and Technological History*. New York: Dover, 1993.

Hurd, A. *The Triumph of the Tramp Ship*. London: Cassell, 1922.

Hutchins, J. G. B. "History and Development of the Shipbuilding Industry in the United States." In *The Shipbuilding Business in the United States of America*, vol. 1, edited by F. G. Fassett Jr., 14–60. New York: Macdonald and Jane's, 1974.

Hutchinson, G. "A Plank Fragment from a Boat-Find from the River Usk at Newport." *International Journal of Nautical Archaeology and Underwater Exploration* 13, no. 1 (1984): 27–32.

———. *Medieval Ships and Shipping*. Leicester, UK: Leicester University Press, 1998.

Illsley, J. S., and O. T. P. Roberts. "An 18th Century Boat in Lake Padarn, North Wales." *International Journal of Nautical Archaeology and Underwater Exploration* 8, no. 1 (1979): 45–67.

Ingram-Brown, L. "Scrap Now before Prices Collapse Further." *Nautical Magazine* 227, no. 5 (1982): 302–3.

Jackson, P. *Quail Island: A Link with the Past*. Christchurch: Department of Conservation, 1990.

Jacques, M. *Dive Tasmania: Including Bass Strait and Macquarie Island*. Hobart, Aus.: Gemini, 1997.

Jeffery, W. "Santiago." *Annual Report of the Society for Underwater Historical Research* (1979): 24.

———. "The Development of Maritime Archaeology in South Australia." In *Proceedings of the Second Southern Hemisphere Conference on Maritime Archaeology*, edited by William Jeffery and J. Amess, 83–92. Adelaide: South Australian Department of Environment and Planning and the Commonwealth Department of Home Affairs and Environment, 1983.

———. "Research into Australian-built Coastal Vessels Wrecked in South Australia, 1840–1900." *Bulletin of the Australian Institute for Maritime Archaeology* 13, no. 2 (1989): 51–56.

———. "Maritime Archaeological Investigations into Australian-Built Vessels Wrecked in South Australia." *International Journal of Nautical Archaeology and Underwater Exploration* 21, no. 3 (1992): 209–19.

Jenkins, N. *Boat Beneath the Pyramids.* New York: Thames and Hudson Limited, 1980.

Jervis, R. "Navies, Politics, and Political Science." In *Doing Naval History: Essays Toward Improvement,* edited by John B. Hattendorf, 41–52. Newport, R.I.: Naval War College Press, 1995.

Johnson, M. *Archaeological Theory: An Introduction.* Oxford: Blackwell, 2000.

Johnston, P. F. "The End of the Age of Sail: Merchant Shipping in the Nineteenth Century." In *Ships and Shipwrecks of the Americas: A History Based on Underwater Archaeology,* edited by George F. Bass, 231–50. London: Thames and Hudson, 1996.

———. "Cornwallis Cave Wreck." In *Encyclopedia of Underwater and Maritime Archaeology,* edited by James P. Delgado, 110–111. London: British Museum Press, 1997.

Johnstone, P. *The Archaeology of Ships.* London: Bodley Head, 1974.

Jones, D. *Egyptian Bookshelf: Boats.* London: University of Texas Press, 1995.

Jordan, D. J. *East Coast Shipwrecks: A Thematic Historical Survey.* Victoria: Heritage Victoria, 1995.

Jordan, K. "The Pier 35 Wreck." Unpublished internal report, Maritime Heritage Unit, Heritage Victoria, 1997.

Jose, A. W. *History of Australasia.* Sydney: Angus and Robertson, 1913.

Kadry, A. "The Solar Boat of Cheops." *International Journal of Nautical Archaeology and Underwater Exploration* 15, no. 2 (1986): 123–31.

Kasper, W. "Technological Change and Economic Growth." In *Technological Change in Australia.* Vol. 4, *Selected Papers on Technological Change, Committee of Inquiry into Technological Change in Australia,* 237–60. Canberra: Australian Government Publishing Service, 1980.

Kemp, P. K., ed. *The Campaign of the Spanish Armada.* Oxford: Phaidon Press, 1988.

———. *The Oxford Companion to Ships and the Sea.* Oxford: Oxford University Press, 1988.

Kenderdine, S. "When the River Runs Clear: Interpretation of the River Murray Cultural Landscape." In *Muddy Waters: Proceedings of the First Conference on the Submerged and Terrestrial Archaeology of Historic Shipping on the River Murray, Echuca September 21–23 1992,* edited by Sarah Kenderdine and William Jeffery,

1–9. Adelaide: State Heritage Branch, Department of Environment and Natural Resources, 1992.

———. "Revelations About River Boats and 'Rotten Rows': A Guide to Wreck Sites of the River Murray." *Bulletin of the Australian Institute for Maritime Archaeology* 18, no. 1 (1994): 17–28.

———. *Historic Shipping on the Murray River: A Guide to the Terrestrial and Submerged Archaeological Sites in New South Wales and Victoria.* Sydney: New South Wales Government, Department of Planning, 1994.

———. *Historic Shipping on the River Murray: A Guide to the Terrestrial and Submerged Archaeological Sites in South Australia.* Adelaide: State Heritage Branch, Department of Environment and Land Management, 1995.

———. *Shipwrecks 1656–1942: A Guide to Historic Wrecksites of Perth.* Fremantle: Western Australia Maritime Museum, 1995.

Kennedy, G. C. "Great Britain's Maritime Strength and the British Mercantile Marine, 1922–1935." *Mariner's Mirror* 80, no. 1 (1994): 66–76.

Kentish, P. *Stabilisation of Santiago.* Report No. MET 1291, part 1. University of South Australia, Adelaide, 1995.

Kerr, G. *The Tasmanian Trading Ketch: An Illustrated Oral History.* 3rd ed. Portland, Aus.: Mainsail Books, 1998.

Kerr, G., and H. McDermott. *The Huon Pine Story: A History of Harvest and Use of a Unique Timber.* Portland, Aus: Mainsail Books, 1999.

Kimpton, G., and G. Henderson. "The Last Voyage of the Day Dawn Wreck." *Bulletin of the Australian Institute for Maritime Archaeology* 15, no. 2 (1991): 25–28.

Kok, A. *A Pictorial History of Strahan: The Story of Strahan and the Macquarie Harbour Region of West Coast Tasmania.* Hobart, Aus.: Hindsight, n.d.

Langley, S. B. M. "Mallows Bay." In *Encyclopedia of Underwater and Maritime Archaeology,* edited by James P. Delgado, 257–58. London: British Museum Press, 1997.

La Roche, D. "The Small Boat Finds at the 'Musee Da La Civilisation' in Quebec City." *Underwater Archaeology Proceedings from the Society for Historical Archaeology Conference,* 1987, 108–13.

Lawes, D. "More Hulks." *Australian Sea Heritage* 14 (Spring 1987): 3.

Lawson, E. "Egeria: The Nineteenth Century Canadian Built Sailing Ship at Port Stanley." *Falkland Islands Journal* (1986): 15–19.

Learmouth, N. F. *The Story of a Port: Portland, Victoria.* Melbourne: Portland Harbor Trust, 1960.

LeLeu, L. W. "My Life Amongst the Ketches as a Shipwright 1912–1963, Part 3." *Portonian* 5, no. 4 (1977): 8–11.

Lellman, K. V. "The Hulks at Stanley Harbour." *Sea Breezes* 16 (1933): 270–71.

Lemee, C. "A Ship Cemetery on the B&W Site in Christianshavn." *Maritime Archaeology Newsletter from Roskilde, Denmark* 9 (December 1997): 29–34.

Lemee, C., P. Schiellerup, and M. Gothche. "Ships and Shipyards in Copenhagen." *Maritime Archaeology Newsletter from Roskilde* 7 (December 1996): 16–20.

With Particular Reference to the River Murray." In *Muddy Waters: Proceedings of the First Conference on the Submerged and Terrestrial Archaeology of Historic Shipping on the River Murray*, Echuca, Aus., September 21–23 1992, edited by Sarah Kenderdine and William Jeffery, chap. 10, 1–14. Adelaide: State Heritage Branch, Department of Environment and Natural Resources, 1992.

Mak, J., and G. M. Walton. "The Persistence of Old Techniques: The Case of Flatboats." *Journal of Economic History* 33, no. 2 (1973): 444–52.

Marsden, P. "Blackfriars Wreck 3: A Preliminary Note." *International Journal of Nautical Archaeology and Underwater Exploration* 1 (1972): 130–32.

———. *Ships of the Port of London: First to Eleventh Centuries*. London: English Heritage, 1994.

———. *Ships of the Port of London: Twelfth to Seventeenth Centuries*. London: English Heritage, 1996.

Marsden, P., N. Branch, J. Evans, R. Gale, D. Goodburn, S. Juggins, S. McGrail, J. Rackham, I. Tyers, D. Vaughan, and D. Whipp. "A Late Saxon Logboat from Clapton, London Borough of Hackney." *International Journal of Nautical Archaeology and Underwater Exploration* 18, no. 2 (1989): 89–111.

Marshall, W., and R. Miners. "The Wreck of Stones." *Bulletin of the Australian Institute for Maritime Archaeology* 10, no. 1 (1986): 12–13.

Martin, C. "North Sea Traders." In *History from Beneath the Sea: Shipwrecks and Archaeology*, edited by Peter Throckmorton, 134–39. Melbourne: RD Press, 1987.

———. "Swans of the Sea God." In *History from Beneath the Sea: Shipwrecks and Archaeology*, edited by Peter Throckmorton, 122–28. Melbourne: RD Press, 1987.

———. "The Viking World." In *History from Beneath the Sea: Shipwrecks and Archaeology*, edited by Peter Throckmorton, 128–33. Melbourne: RD Press, 1987.

———. "De-Particularizing the Particular: Approaches to the Investigation of Well-Documented Post-Medieval Shipwrecks." *World Archaeology* 32, no. 3 (2001): 383–99.

Martin, T. "Hulks." *Australian Sea Heritage* 14 (Spring 1987): 2.

Matthews, F. C. *American Merchant Ships, 1850–1900: Series 1*. New York: Dover, 1987.

———. *American Merchant Ships, 1850–1900: Series 2*. New York: Dover, 1987.

Matthews, S. "The North Arm Ships' Graveyard, Port Adelaide, South Australia: Some Historical Perspectives of the Ships and Associated Maritime Activity and an Examination of the Artefact Assemblage." Archaeology honors thesis, Flinders University, Adelaide, Aus., 1998.

Mattox, W. C. *Building the Emergency Fleet*. New York: Macdonald and Jane's, 1970.

Mayhew, D. R. "The Defense: Search and Recovery, 1972–73." *International Journal of Nautical Archaeology and Underwater Exploration* 3, no. 2 (1974): 312–13.

McCarthy, M. *Jervoise Bay Shipwrecks*. Perth: Department of Maritime Archaeology, Western Australian Museum, 1979.

———. *Excavation of the Barque Day Dawn: The Excavation and Identification of the*

Lenihan, D. J. "Rethinking Shipwreck Archaeology: A History of Ideas and Considerations for New Directions." In *Shipwreck Anthropology*, edited by Richard A. Gould, 37–89. Albuquerque: University of New Mexico Press, 1983.

———. "From Pearl to Bikini: The Underwater Archaeology of World War II in the Pacific." In *Excavating Ships of War*, edited by Mensun Bound, 294–302. Oswestry, UK: Anthony Nelson, 1998.

Lenihan, D. J., and L. E. Murphy. "Considerations for Research Designs in Shipwreck Archaeology." In *Maritime Archaeology: A Reader of Substantive and Theoretical Contributions*, edited by Lawrence Babits and Hans Van Tilburg, 233–39. New York: Plenum Press, 1998.

Leone, M. P. "Land and Water, Urban Life, and Boats: Underwater Reconnaissance in the Patuxent River on Chesapeake Bay." In *Shipwreck Anthropology*, edited by Richard A. Gould, 173–88. Albuquerque: University of New Mexico Press, 1983.

Linder, E., and A. Raban. *Marine Archaeology*. London: Cassell, 1975.

Lipke, P. *The Royal Ship of Cheops*. British Archaeological Reports, International Series 225. Oxford, 1984.

———. "Retrospective on the Royal Ship of Cheops." In *Sewn Plank Boats*, edited by Sean McGrail and E. Kently, 19–34. British Archaeological Reports, International Series 275. Oxford, 1985.

Lloyd's of London. *Lloyd's Calendar: 1938*. London: Lloyd's of London, 1938.

———. *Lloyd's Calendar: 1965*. London: Lloyd's of London, 1965.

———. *Lloyd's Calendar: 1973*. London: Lloyd's of London, 1973.

———. *Lloyd's Nautical Year Book: 1981*. London: Lloyd's of London, 1981.

———. *Lloyd's Nautical Year Book: 1991*. London: Lloyd's of London, 1991.

Loney, J. K. *Jack Loney's Maritime Australia: Short Tales of Ships and Men*. Melbourne: Quadricolor, 1980.

———. *Australian Shipwrecks*. Vol. 3, *1871 to 1900*. Geelong, Aus.: List, 1982.

———. *Australian Shipwrecks*. Vol. 4, *1901 to 1986*. Portarlington, Aus.: Marine History Publications, 1987.

———. *Australian Shipwrecks Update Volume 5: 1622–1990*. Portarlington, Aus.: Marine History Publications, 1991.

———. *Wrecks on the South Australian Coast*. Mebourne: Lonestone Press, 1993.

———. *Wrecks on the Western Australian Coast*. Yarram, Aus.: Lonestone Press, 1994.

Lords Commissioners of the Admiralty. *Manual of Seamanship*. Vol. 2, *1932*. London: His Majesty's Stationery Office, 1932.

Louis, L. J., and I. Turner. *The Depression of the 1930s*. North Melbourne: Cassell Australia, 1974.

Low, S. H., and P. Throckmorton. "The First and Last Voyage of the St. Mary." *Sea History* 9(Fall 1977): 6–9.

Mackay, M. *Lady of the Lake: The TSS Earnslaw Story*. Queenstown, N.Z.: Malcolm Mackay, 1999.

MacLeod, I. D. "Report on the Corrosion of Iron Shipwrecks in South Australia:

Wreck of an Ex-American Whaler in Cockburn Sound by the Maritime Archaeological Association of Western Australia 1976–1977. Perth: Western Australian Museum, 1980.

———. "Shipwrecks in Jervoise Bay." *Records of the Western Australian Museum* 10, no. 4 (1983): 335–73.

———. "Salvage Archaeology: A Case Study." In *Proceedings of the Second Southern Hemisphere Conference on Maritime Archaeology,* edited by W. Jeffery and J. Amess, 283–91. Adelaide: South Australian Department of Environment and Planning and the Commonwealth Department of Home Affairs and Environment, 1983.

———. "Introduction." In *Iron Ships and Steam Shipwrecks: Papers from the First Australian Seminar on the Management of Iron Vessels and Steam Shipwrecks,* edited by Michael McCarthy, 7–8. Fremantle: Western Australian Maritime Museum, 1988.

———. *Iron Ships and Steam Shipwrecks: Papers from the First Australian Seminar on the Management of Iron Vessels and Steam Shipwrecks.* Fremantle: Western Australian Maritime Museum, 1988.

———. "SS Xantho: Towards a New Perspective. An Integrated Approach to the Maritime Archaeology and Conservation of an Iron Steamship Wreck." Ph.D. diss., James Cook University, Townsville, Aus., 1996.

———. "The 'Black Cats': Report into the Feasibility of Locating, Raising and Conserving One of the Four Catalina Flying Boats Scuttled Off Rottnest Island in the Years 1945–1946." Western Australia Maritime Museum Report No. 125. Fremantle: Department of Maritime Archaeology, 1997.

———. "Australian Maritime Archaeology: Changes, Their Antecedents and the Path Ahead." *Australian Archaeology* 47 (1998): 33–38.

———. *Iron and Steamship Archaeology: Success and Failure on the SS Xantho.* New York: Kluwer Academic/Plenum, 2000.

McGrail, S. "Prehistoric Water Transport in N. W. Europe." *Mariner's Mirror* 75, no. 4 (1989): 297–312.

———. *Ancient Boats in North-West Europe: The Archaeology of Water Transport to AD 1500.* New York: Addison Wesley Longman, 1998.

Meaney, A. *A Gazetteer of Early Ango-Saxon Burial Sites.* London: George Allen and Unwin, 1964.

Meiggs, R. *Roman Ostia.* Oxford: Oxford University Press, 1960.

Merrifield, R. *London: City of the Romans.* London: B. T. Batsford, 1983.

Merriman, A. M. *The Cypress Landing Shipwreck of Chocowinity Bay: A North Carolina Sail Flat, an Archaeological and Historical Study.* East Carolina University Research Report No.9. Greenville, N.C.: Program in Maritime History and Nautical Archaeology, 1997.

Millar, W. J. "On the Rise and Progress of Steam Navigation." In *Lectures on Naval Architecture and Engineering: With Catalogue of the Exhibition,* 129–46. Glasgow: William Collins, Sons, 1881.

Miller, D. *Material Culture and Mass Consumption.* London: Basil Blackwell, 1987.

Miller, P. "Riddle of the Pyramid Boats." *National Geographic* 173, no. 4 (1988): 534–50.

Milne, G., C. McKewan, and D. Goodburn. *Nautical Archaeology on the Foreshore: Hulk Recording on the Medway.* London: Royal Commission on the Historical Monuments of England, 1998.

Mokyr, J. *The Lever of Riches: Technological Creativity and Economic Progress.* New York: Oxford University Press, 1990.

Moore, A. *Last Days of Mast and Sail: An Essay in Nautical Comparative Anatomy.* Oxford: Clarendon Press, 1970.

Moore, J. "The Boneyard Below the Bridge." *Freshwater: A Journal of the Marine Museum of the Great Lakes of Kingston* 11, nos. 1–4 (1995): 3–28.

———. "Kingston Inner Harbour Survey: A Preliminary Archaeological Survey of Submerged and Partially Submerged Vessels (BbGc-29 to BbGc-42) in the Inner Harbour, Kingston, Ontario." Report for the Marine Museum of the Great Lakes at Kingston, 1995.

Morris, R. "The 1928 Marine Cooks' Strike and the Origin of the Transport Workers' Act." *Great Circle* 21, no. 2 (1999): 109–20.

Morrissey, S. "The Pastoral Economy, 1821–1850." In *Essays in Economic History of Australia: 1788–1939*, edited by James Griffith, 51–112. Brisbane: Jacaranda Press, 1967.

Moss, J. *Sound of Trumpets: History of the Labour Movement in South Australia.* Netley, Aus.: Wakefield Press, 1985.

Muckelroy, K. W. *Maritime Archaeology.* London: Cambridge University Press, 1978.

———. "Introducing Maritime Archaeology." In *Maritime Archaeology: A Reader of Substantive and Theoretical Contributions*, edited by Lawrence Babits and Hans Van Tilburg, 23–35. New York: Plenum Press, 1998.

Mudie, I. *Riverboats.* Melbourne: Sun Books, 1965.

Muller-Wille, M. "Boat-Graves in Northern Europe." *International Journal of Nautical Archaeology and Underwater Exploration* 3, no. 2 (1974): 187–204.

Murphy, L. E. "Shipwrecks as a Data Base for Human Behavioural Studies." In *Shipwreck Anthropology*, edited by Richard A. Gould, 65–90. Albuquerque: University of New Mexico Press, 1983.

Musson, A. E., and E. Robinson. "The Early Growth of Steam Power." *Economic History Review* 11, no. 3 (1959): 418–40.

Nash, D. "Sunbeam." Unpublished wreck inspection report, Flinders University, Adelaide, Aus., 1999.

Nash, M. "The Sydney Cove Historic Shipwreck (1797)." *Australian Sea Heritage* 32 (1992): 11–13.

———. *Cargo for the Colony: The Wreck of the Merchant Ship Sydney Cove.* Sydney: Braxus Press, 1996.

News. (Adelaide, South Australia) 1931–1949.

Norty, J. "Environmental Considerations of Artificial Reefs." *Marine Life Society of South Australia Newsletter* 276 (2001): 9–12.

Nutley, D., and T. Smith. *The Maritime Archaeology of Myall Lakes/Tea Gardens: Area Conservation Plan.* Sydney: New South Wales Heritage Office, 1999.

Ojala, J. "Productivity and Technological Change in Eighteenth and Nineteenth Century Sea Transport: A Case Study of Sailing Ship Efficiency in Kokkola, Finland, 1721–1913." *International Journal of Maritime History* 9, no. 1 (1997): 93–123.

O'Keefe, M. "The Shipwreck Under the City: The Inconstant, Wellington, New Zealand." *Bulletin of the Australian Institute for Maritime Archaeology* 23 (1999): 121–25.

———. "Looking at the Ship Under the City: The Inconstant and the ICOMOS Cultural Tourism Charter." *Bulletin of the Australian Institute for Maritime Archaeology* 25 (2001): 109–11.

O'May, H. *Wrecks in Tasmanian Waters 1797–1950.* Hobart, Aus.: Government Printer, 1985.

O'Reilly, R. "An Assessment of Australian Built Wooden Sailing Vessels (Constructed Between 18509–1899) Operating the South Australian Intrastate Trade: Methods and Materials." Archaeology honors thesis, Flinders University, Adelaide, Aus., 1999.

Orme, Z. K. "Shipbuilding in Northern Tasmania." *Bulletin of the Australian Institute for Maritime Archaeology* 12, no. 2 (1988): 27–32.

Oxley, I. "The Environment of Historic Shipwreck Sites: A Review of the Preservation of Materials, Site Formation and Site Environmental Assessment." Master's thesis, University of St. Andrews, St. Andrews, Scotland, 1998.

Paine, L. *Down East: A Maritime History of Maine.* Gardiner, Maine: Tilbury House, 2000.

Palmer, M. *Ships and Shipping.* London: B. T. Batsford, 1971.

Parker, J. "The Story of the Ship Niantic: Invincible Amphibian." *American West* 17, no. 6 (1980): 48–53.

Parkinson, J. R. 1960. *The Economics of Shipbuilding in the United Kingdom.* Cambridge: Cambridge University Press, 1960.

Parsons, R. H. *Australian Coastal Passenger Ships.* Adelaide: Published by the author, 1981.

———. *A Century of Wrecks of Steamships in NSW, 1836–1936.* Adelaide: Published by the author, 1982.

———. *Ketches of South Australia.* Adelaide: Published by the author, 1983.

———. *Australian Shipowners and Their Fleets.* Vol. 1, *Northern Rivers of New South Wales.* Adelaide: Published by the author, 1986.

———. *Southern Passages: A Maritime History of South Australia.* Adelaide: Wakefield Press, 1986.

———. *A Pioneer Australian Steamship Company: A History of the Hunter's River S.N.Co and the Australasian Steam Navigation Company.* Adelaide: Published by the author, 1990.

———. *Australian Shipowners and Their Fleets*. Vol. 10, *Melbourne Enrolments, 1839–1859, Part 3*. Adelaide: Published by the author, 1991.

———. *The Ships of Burns, Philp and Company*. Adelaide: Published by the author, 1992.

Parsons, R. H., and G. Plunkett. *Scuttled and Abandoned Ships in Australian Waters*. Adelaide: Published by the author, 1995.

Patch, D. C., and C. W. Haldane. *The Pharoah's Boat at the Carnegie*. Pittsburgh: Carnegie Museum of Natural History, 1990.

Pearce, W. M. "On Some Results of Recent Improvements in Naval Architecture." In *Lectures on Naval Architecture and Engineering: With Catalogue of the Exhibition*, 1–14. Glasgow: William Collins, Sons, 1881.

Pemberton, B. "The Historical Geography of Australian Coastal Shipping." Master's thesis, University of Melbourne, 1975.

Peterson, W. J. *Steamboating on the Upper Mississippi*. New York: Dover, 1968.

Phillips, P. J. *River Boat Days: On the Murray, Darling and Murrumbidgee*. Melbourne: Landsdowne Press, 1974.

Plunkett, G. *Sea Dumping in Australia: Historical and Contemporary Aspects*. Canberra: Commonwealth of Australia, 2003.

Pollard, S. "Laissez-Faire and Shipbuilding." *Economic History Review* 5, no. 1 (1952): 98–115.

Pollard, S., and P. Robertson. *The British Shipbuilding Industry, 1870–1914*. Cambridge: Harvard University Press, 1979.

Porter, D. D. "Our Cake Is All Dough: The Opening of the Lower Mississippi." In *Battles and Leaders of the Civil War*, edited by R. V. Johnson and C. C. Buel, 121–40. New York: Appleton-Century-Crofts, 1962.

Portnoy, A. W. "A Microarchaeological View of Human Settlement Space and Function." In *Modern Material Culture: The Archaeology of Us*, edited by Richard A. Gould and Michael B. Schiffer, 213–24. Academic Press: New York, 1981.

Probert, M. "South Australia and the Great Depression." *Cabbages and Kings: Select Issues in History and Australian Studies* 18 (1990): 112–22.

Providence. (Fremantle, Western Australia) 1992.

Purser, M. "Consumption as Communication in Nineteenth-Century Paradise Valley, Nevada." *Historical Archaeology* 26, no. 1 (1993): 105–16.

Purtell, J. *The Mosquito Fleet: Hawkesbury River Trade and Traders 1794–1994*. Berowra Heights, Aus.: Deerubbin Press, 1995.

Randell, S. "The Effects of Material Type on Concretion Formation: A Case Study of the HMS Pandora." *Bulletin of the Australian Institute for Maritime Archaeology* 23 (1999): 51–55.

Randsborg, K. "Seafaring and Society—In South Scandinavian and European Perspective." In *Aspects of Maritime Scandinavia AD 200–1200*, edited by Ole Crumlin-Pederson, 11–22. Roskilde, Den.: Viking Ship Museum, 1991.

Rathje, W. "A Manifesto for Modern Material-Culture Studies." In *Modern Material*

Culture: The Archaeology of Us, Richard A. Gould and Michael B. Schiffer, 51–66. New York: Academic Press, 1981.

Reiss, W. "The Ship Beneath Manhattan." In *History from Beneath the Sea: Shipwrecks and Archaeology*, edited by Peter Throckmorton, 185–87. Melbourne: RD Press, 1987.

———. "Ronson Ship." In *Encyclopedia of Underwater and Maritime Archaeology*, edited by James P. Delgado, 349–50. London: British Museum Press, 1997.

Richards, M. *Shipwreck Heritage of the Clarence River: A Survey Study*. Sydney: Heritage Office, 1996.

———. *Shipwreck Heritage of the Richmond River: A Survey Study*. Sydney: Heritage Office, 1997.

Richards, N. T. "The History and Archaeology of the Garden Island Ships' Graveyard, North Arm of the Port Adelaide River, Port Adelaide, South Australia." BA honors thesis, Flinders University, Adelaide, Aus., 1997.

———. "Inferences from the Study of Iron and Steamship Abandonment: A Case Study from the Garden Island Ships' Graveyard, South Australia." *Bulletin of the Australian Institute for Maritime Archaeology* 22 (1998): 75–80.

———. "The Garden Island Ships' Graveyard: Results and Findings of Archaeological Fieldwork 1996–1998." *Proceedings of the National Archaeology Students Conference (NASC), 1998* 1 (1999): 11–18.

———. "Deep Structures: An Examination of Deliberate Watercraft Abandonment in Australia." Ph.D. diss., Flinders University, Adelaide, Aus., 2002.

———. "The Role of Isolation in Cultural Site Formation: A Cast Study from Strahan, Tasmania." *Bulletin of the Australasian Institute for Maritime Archaeology* 27 (2003): 77–84.

———. "The Role of Geo-politics in Cultural Site Formation: A Cast Study from the Northern Territory." *Bulletin of the Australasian Institute for Maritime Archaeology* 28 (2004): 97–106.

———. "The Archaeological Examination of Watercraft Abandonment in Australia: A Retrospective." *Bulletin of the Australasian Institute for Maritime Archaeology* 29 (2005): 61–76.

Richards, N. T., and M. Nash. "Unfit for Further Use: Watercraft Discard in Tasmania (1808–1997)." *Australasian Institute for Maritime Archaeology* 29 (2005): 25–39.

Richards, N. T., and M. Staniforth. "The Abandoned Ships Project." *Historical Archaeology* 40 no. 4 (2006): 84–103.

Richardson, K. "Excavations at Hungate, York." *Archaeological Journal* 116 (1959): 51–114.

Rieck, F. "Aspects of Coastal Defence in Denmark." In *Aspects of Maritime Scandinavia AD 200–1200*, edited by Ole Crumlin-Pederson, 83–96. Roskilde, Den.: Viking Ship Museum, 1991.

———. "Nydam: A Wealth of Finds in a Dangerous Environment." *Maritime Archaeology Newsletter from Roskilde Denmark* 7 (December 1996): 5–6.

———. "Maritime Archaeology in Denmark, 1993–1998." In *Indian Ocean Week 1997: Proceedings*, edited by Graeme Henderson, 81–86. Fremantle: Western Australian Maritime Museum, 1998.

Riley, J. "Steam on the Rim: The Problem of Operating Early Steamships in the Pacific and the Modification of the Auckland Engines." *Bulletin of the Australian Institute for Maritime Archaeology* 23 (1999): 28–30.

Rimes, L. "Old Liner Becomes Alaskan Hotel." *Australasian Ships and Ports Magazine* 2, no. 4 (1990): 10.

Roberts, S. *History of Australian Land Settlement, 1788–1920*. South Melbourne: Macmillan of Australia, 1968.

Robertson, F. L. *The Evolution of Naval Armament*. London: Harold T. Storey, 1968.

Robertson, J. R. "1930–1939." In *A New History of Australia*, edited by Frank Crowley, 415–57. Melbourne: William Heinemann, 1980.

Robinson, E. H. "The Early Diffusion of Steam Power." *Journal of Economic History* 34, no. 1 (1974): 91–108.

Rodgers, B. A. *The 1995 Predisturbance Wreck Site Investigation at Claflin Point, Little Sturgeon Bay, Wisconsin*. Research Report No. 10. Greenville, N.C.: East Carolina University, 1995.

Rosenberg, D. A., and J. T. Sumida. "Machines, Men, Manufacturing, Management and Money: The Study of Navies as Complex Organisations and the Transformation of Twentieth Century Naval History." In *Doing Naval History: Essays Towards Improvement*, edited by John B. Hattendorf, 25–40. Newport, R.I.: Naval War College Press, 1995.

Rostrow, W. W. "Investment and the Great Depression." *Economic History Review* 8, no. 2 (1938): 136–58.

Runestone Press Geography Department. *Sunk! Exploring Underwater Archaeology*. New York: Runestone Press, 1994.

Rusho, W. J. "Charles Spencer and His Wonderful Steamboat." *Arizona Highways* 37, no. 8 (1962): 34–39.

Ruskin, J. *The Works of John Ruskin*. Vol. 13. London: George Allen, 1904.

Sandilands, J. "Swansong." *Community Link*, n.d., 5–7.

Sands, J. O. *Yorktown's Captive Fleet*. Charlottesville: University Press of Virginia, 1983.

———. "Gunboats and Warships of the American Revolution." In *Ships and Shipwrecks of the Americas: A History Based on Underwater Archaeology*, edited by George F. Bass, 149–68. London: Thames and Hudson, 1996.

Schiffer, M. B. "Archaeological Context and Systemic Context." *American Antiquity* 37 (1972): 156–65.

———. "A Preliminary Consideration of Behavioral Change." In *Transformations: Mathematical Approaches to Culture Change*, edited by C. Renfrew and K. L. Cooke, 353–68. New York: Academic Press, 1979.

———. *The Portable Radio in American Life*. Tucson: University of Arizona Press, 1992.

———. *Technological Perspectives on Behavioral Change*. Tucson: University of Arizona Press, 1993.

———. "Cultural Imperatives and Product Development: The Case of the Shirt-Pocket Radio." *Technology and Culture* 34, no. 1 (1994): 98–113.

———. *Behavioral Archaeology: First Principles*. Salt Lake City: University of Utah Press, 1995.

———. *Formation Processes of the Archaeological Record*. Salt Lake City: University of Utah Press, 1996.

———. "Some Relationships between Behavioral and Evolutionary Archaeologies." *American Antiquity* 61, no. 4 (1996): 643–62.

———. "The Explanation of Long-Term Technological Change." In *Anthropological Perspectives on Technology*, edited by M. B. Schiffer, 215–35. Albuquerque: University of New Mexico Press, 2001.

———. *Behavioral Archeology*. New York: Percheron Press, 2002.

———. "Studying Technological Differentiation: The Case of 18th-Century Electrical Technology." *American Anthropologist* 104, no. 4 (2002): 1148–61.

Schiffer, M. B., T. C. Butts, and K. Grimm. *Taking Charge: The Electric Automobile in America*. Washington, D.C.: Smithsonian Institution Press, 1995.

Schiffer, M. B., T. E. Downing, and M. McCarthy. "Waste Not, Want Not: An Ethnoarchaeological Study of Reuse in Tucson, Arizona." In *Modern Material Culture: The Archaeology of Us*, edited by Richard A. Gould and Michael B. Schiffer, 67–86. New York: Academic Press, 1981.

Schiffer, M. B., K. L. Hollenback, and C. Bell. *Draw the Lightning Down: Benjamin Franklin and Electrical Technology in the Age of Enlightenment*. Berkeley and Los Angeles: University of California Press, 2003.

Schiffer, M. B., and A. R. Miller. "A Behavioral Theory of Meaning." In *Pottery and People*, edited by J. M. Skibo and G. Feinman, 199–217. Salt Lake City: University of Utah Press, 1999.

———. *The Material Life of Human Beings: Artifacts, Behavior, and Communication*. London: Routledge, 1999.

Schiffer, M. B., and J. M. Skibo. "Theory and Experiment in the Study of Technological Change." *Current Anthropology* 28, no. 5 (1987): 595–622.

———. "The Explanation of Artifact Variability." *American Antiquity* 62, no. 1 (1997): 27–50.

Shann, E. *An Economic History of Australia*. Melbourne: Georgian House, 1967.

Shaw, A. G. L. *The Economic Development of Australia*. Croydon: Longmans of Australia, 1969.

———. *The Story of Australia*. Surrey: Faber and Faber, 1975.

Shomette, D. G. *Shipwrecks on the Chesapeake: Maritime Disasters on Chesapeake Bay and Its Tributaries, 1608–1978*. Centreville, Md.: Tidewater, 1982.

———. "The Shipwrecks of Mallows Bay: An Historic Overview." Report Prepared for the Maryland Historical Trust by the St. Clements Island-Potomac River Museum, Colton Point, Maryland. Centreville, Md., 1994.

———. "From Maritime Antiquarianism to Underwater Archaeology Along the Potomac Corridor, 1825–1994." In *Underwater Archaeology Proceedings from the Society for Historical Archaeology Conference; Washington, D.C., 1995*, edited by Paul Forsythe Johnston, 64–71. Tucson: Society for Historical Archaeology, 1995.

———. *Tidewater Time Capsule: History Beneath the Patuxent*. Centreville, Md.: Tidewater, 1995.

———. *Ghost Fleet of Mallows Bay: And Other Tales of the Lost Chesapeake*. Centreville, Md.: Tidewater, 1996.

———. "Chesapeake Flotilla." In *Encyclopedia of Underwater and Maritime Archaeology*, edited by James P. Delgado, 98–99. London: British Museum Press, 1997.

Simmons, J. J., III. "Steamboats on Inland Waterways: Prime Movers of Manifest Destiny." In *Ships and Shipwrecks of the Americas: A History Based on Underwater Archaeology*, edited by George F. Bass, 189–206. London: Thames and Hudson, 1996.

Simpson, G. D. "Historical Salvage and Maritime Archaeology." *Underwater Archaeology* (1999): 3–10.

Simpson, J. A., and E. S. C. Weiner, eds. *The Oxford English Dictionary*. Vol. 15, *Ser-Soosy*. 2nd ed. Oxford: Oxford University Press, 1989.

Slaven, A. "British Shipbuilders: Market Trends and Order Book Patterns Between the Wars." *Journal of Transport History* 3, no. 2 (1982): 37–62.

Sledge, S. "Wreck Inspection North Coast (WINC)." Unpublished report by the Maritime Archaeology Department, Western Australian Maritime Museum, Fremantle, 1978.

Smith, H. A., J. B. Arnold, and T. Oertling. "Investigation of a Civil War Anti-Torpedo Raft on Mustang Island, Texas." *International Journal of Nautical Archaeology and Underwater Exploration* 16, no. 2 (1987): 149–57.

Smith, J. *Condemned at Stanley: Notes and Sketches on the Hulks and Wrecks at Port Stanley, Falkland Islands*. Chippenham, UK: Picton Print, 1985.

Smith, T. *Project AE2: Investigation of the H.M.A. AE2 Submarine Wreck Site, Turkey, October, 1998*. Sydney: New South Wales Heritage Branch, 1999.

Smith, V. *Sailing Ships Hulked at Port Adelaide and Vessels Broken Up at Ships' Graveyard, North Arm (1953)*. North Arm File, South Australian Maritime Museum, Port Adelaide, South Australia.

Solver, C. V. "The Egyptian Obelisk-Ships." *Mariner's Mirror* 12 (1926): 237–56, 2 plates.

Sound Telegraph. Western Australian Maritime Museum, Fremantle, 1994.

Souter, C. *Archaeological Watching Brief for New Maritime Museum Site—Forrest Landing, Victoria Quay, Fremantle*. Department of Maritime Archaeology Report, No. 150. Fremantle: Western Australian Maritime Museum, 2000.

South Australian Government. *Government Record Group 51*. South Australian State Archives, Netley, South Australia.

———. *South Australian Parliamentary Papers*. Adelaide, South Australia, 1932.

South Australian Register. (Adelaide, South Australia) 1912–30.

Southby-Tailyour, E. *Falkland Island Shores*. London: Conway Maritime, 1985.

Southgate, G. W. *English Economic History*. London: J. M. Dent and Sons, 1965.

Souza, D. J. *The Persistence of Sail in the Age of Steam: Underwater Archaeological Evidence from the Dry Tortugas*. New York: Plenum Press, 1998.

Spencer-Wood, S., ed. *Consumer Choice in Historical Archaeology*. New York: Plenum Press, 1987.

Springmann, M.-J. "The Mukran Wreck, Sunk Off of the Isle of Rugen, Germany in 1565: A Preliminary Report." *International Journal of Nautical Archaeology and Underwater Exploration* 27, no. 2 (1998): 113–25.

Stammers, M. K. "Jhelum." In *Encyclopedia of Underwater and Maritime Archaeology*, edited by James P. Delgado, 218. London: British Museum Press, 1997.

Stammers, M. K., and J. Baker. "Fell's Patent Knees—Some Evidence of Their Use." *International Journal of Nautical Archaeology and Underwater Exploration* 80 (1994): 474–76.

Stammers, M. K., and J. Kearon. "The Jhelum—an East Indiaman?" *International Journal of Nautical Archaeology and Underwater Exploration* 20, no. 4 (1991): 351–53.

———. *The Jhelum: A Victorian Merchant Ship*. Stroud, UK: Sutton, 1992.

Staniforth, M. "The Archaeology of the Event—The Annales School and Maritime Archaeology." *Underwater Archaeology Proceedings from the Society for Historical Archaeology Conference 1997*, edited by Denise A. Lakey, 159–64. Tucson: Society for Historical Archaeology, 1997.

———. "Dependent Colonies: The Importation of Material Culture and the Establishment of a Consumer Society in Australia Before 1850." Ph.D. diss., Department of Archaeology, Flinders University, Adelaide, Aus., 1999.

———. "A Future for Australian Maritime Archaeology?" *Australian Archaeology* 50 (2000): 90–93.

Steffy, J. R. "The Kyrenia Ship: An Interim Report on Its Hull Construction" *American Journal of Archaeology* 89, no. 1 (1985): 71–101.

———. "The Boat: A Preliminary Study of Its Construction" In *The Excavation of an Ancient Boat in the Sea of Galilee (Lake Kinneret)*, edited by S. Waschmann, 29–47. Jerusalem: Israel Antiquities Authority, 1990.

———. "The Thirteen Colonies: English Settlers and Seafarers." In *Ships and Shipwrecks of the Americas: A History Based on Underwater Archaeology*, edited by George F. Bass, 107–28. London: Thames and Hudson, 1996.

Stenuit, R. "The Wreck of the Pink Evstafi: A Transport of the Imperial Russian Navy, Lost Off Shetland in 1780." *International Journal of Nautical Archaeology and Underwater Exploration* 5, no. 4 (1976): 317–31.

Stephenson, R. "Physical Processes at the CSS Chattahoochee Wreck Site." In *Maritime Archaeology: A Reader of Substantive and Theoretical Contributions*, edited by Lawrence E. Babits and Hans Van Tilburg, 261–66. New York: Plenum Press, 1998.

Stevens, E. F. *Dictionary of Shipping Terms and Phrases.* London: Sir Isaac Pitman and Sons, 1947.

Stevens, W. "Machault." In *Encyclopedia of Underwater and Maritime Archaeology,* edited by James P. Delgado, 250–51. London: British Museum Press, 1997.

Stevenson, P. "Comparative Study of the Garthneill and Enterprise Hulks." Unpublished wreck inspection report, Flinders University, Adelaide, Aus., 1999.

Still, W. N., Jr. "Confederate Naval Strategy." *Journal of Southern History* 27 (1961): 330–43.

———. *Iron Afloat: The Story of Confederate Ironclads.* New York: Vanderbilt University Press, 1971.

Stone, P., and J. K. Loney. *High and Dry: Visible Wrecks and Wreckage in Australian Waters.* Newtown, Aus.: Neptune Press, 1983.

Strachan, S. *The History and Archaeology of the Sydney Cove Shipwreck (1797): A Resource for Future Site Work.* Canberra: Department of Prehistory, Research School of Pacific Studies, Australian National University, 1986.

Sullivan, C. *Legacy of the Machault: A Collection of 18th-Century Artifacts.* Quebec: Environment Canada, 1986.

Sunday Times. Western Australian Maritime Museum, Fremantle, 1996.

Switzer, D. C. "Interpretation of the Stern Area of the Privateer Defence." In *Underwater archaeology: The challenge before Us: The proceedings of the Twelfth Conference on Underwater Archaeology,* edited by Gordon P. Watts, 144–50. San Marino, Calif.: Society for Historical Archaeology, 1981.

———. "Nautical Archaeology in Penobscot Bay: The Revolutionary War Privateer Defence." In *New Aspects of Naval History: Selected Papers Presented at the Fourth Naval History Symposium, United States Naval Academy, 25–26 October 1979,* edited by C. L. Symonds, 90–101. Annapolis: Naval Institute Press, 1981.

———. "Recovery and Initial Interpretation of the Shot Locker and Bilge Pump Well from the Privateer Defense." *In the Realms of Gold: The Proceedings of the Tenth Conference on Underwater Archaeology,* edited by William A. Cockrell, 76–94. San Marino, Calif.: Fathom Eight, 1981.

———. "The Defence Project: 1975–1981." In *Proceedings of the Second Southern Hemisphere Conference on Maritime Archaeology,* edited by W. Jeffery and J. Amess, 205–35. Adelaide: South Australian Department of Environment and Planning and the Commonwealth Department of Home Affairs and Environment, 1983.

———. "Maritime Archaeology in the United States." In *Proceedings of the Second Southern Hemisphere Conference on Maritime Archaeology,* edited by W. Jeffery and J. Amess, 133–42. Adelaide: South Australian Department of Environment and Planning and the Commonwealth Department of Home Affairs and Environment, 1983.

———. Privateers, Not Pirates." In *History from Beneath the Sea: Shipwrecks and Archaeology,* edited by Peter Throckmorton, 194–98. Melbourne: RD Press, 1987.

———. "Defence." In *Encyclopedia of Underwater and Maritime Archaeology*, edited by James P. Delgado, 128–29. London: British Museum Press, 1997.

———. "The Defence." In *Excavating Ships of War*, edited by Mensun Bound, 182–93. Oswestry, UK: Anthony Nelson, 1998.

Tann, J., and M. J. Breckin. "The International Diffusion of the Watt Engine, 1775–1825." *Economic History Review* 31, no. 4 (1978): 541–64.

Tatton-Brown, T. "Excavations at the Customs House Site, City of London—Part 2." *Transactions of the Middlesex Archaeological Society, London* 26 (1975): 103–70.

Thomas, D. "Clarence River." *Australian Sea Heritage* 14 (Spring 1987): 3.

Thompson, W. R. "Some Mild and Radical Observations on Desiderata in Comparative Naval History." In *Doing Naval History: Essays Toward Improvement*, edited by John B. Hattendorf, 93–116. Newport, R.I.: Naval War College Press, 1995.

Thomson, D. *England in the Nineteenth Century: 1815–1914*. London: Penguin Books, 1978.

Throckmorton, P. *Shipwrecks and Archaeology: The Unharvested Sea*. London: Victor Gollancz, 1970.

———. "The American Heritage in the Falklands." *Sea History* 4 (1976): 36–71.

———. "Bones on a Beach." In *History from Beneath the Sea: Shipwrecks and Archaeology*, edited by Peter Throckmorton, 210–14. Melbourne: RD Press, 1987.

———. "The Shipwright's Art." In *History from Beneath the Sea: Shipwrecks and Archaeology*, edited by Peter Throckmorton, 92–100. Melbourne: RD Press, 1987.

Times-Colonist. (Fremantle, Western Australia) 1992.

Tregenza, J. *Le Messuriers of Port Adelaide: Five Generations of Enterprise in Transport and Timber*. Adelaide: Le Messurier Timber, 1991.

Trigger, B. G. *A History of Archaeological Thought*. Cambridge: Cambridge University Press, 1995.

Tull, M. T. "Shipping, Ports and the Marketing of Australia's Wheat, 1900–1970." In *Land and Sea: The Role of Shipping in Australasian Economic Development*, edited by G. D. Snooks and J. J. Pincus, 33–59. Melbourne: Oxford University Press and the Economic History Society of Australia and New Zealand, 1992.

———. *A Community Enterprise: The History of the Port of Fremantle, 1897 to 1997*. St. John's, Canada: International Maritime Economic History Association, 1997.

Valdaliso, J. M. "The Diffusion of Technological Change in the Spanish Merchant Fleet During the Twentieth Century: Available Alternatives and Conditioning Factors." *Journal of Transport History*, 3rd ser., 17, no. 2 (1996): 95–115.

Vancouver Sun. (Fremantle, Western Australia) 1992.

Van Der Vat, D. *The Grand Scuttle: The Sinking of the German Fleet at Scapa Flow In 1919*. Edinburgh: Birlinn, 1998.

Varns, P. E. J. *Blue Peter: Australian Maritime Journal* 1, no. 2 (1969).

Veth, P., and M. McCarthy. "Types of Explanation in Maritime Archeology: The Case of the SS XANTHO." *Australian Archaeology* 48 (June 1999): 12–15.

Volti, R. *Society and Technological Change*. 3rd ed. New York: Tom Doherty Associates, 1995.

Wachsmann, S. "The Galilee Boat." In *History from Beneath the Sea: Shipwrecks and Archaeology*, edited by Peter Throckmorton, 81–83. RD Press: Melbourne, 1987.

———. "Sea of Galilee Wreck." In *Encyclopedia of Underwater and Maritime Archaeology*, edited by James P. Delgado, 364–65. London: British Museum Press, 1997.

Walter, R. D. "70 Years of Progress: A History of Walter & Morris." *Portonian*, June 1999, 8–16.

Wanklyn, N. "Floating Circus—Use for Redundant Ship?" *Australasian Ships and Ports Magazine* 1, no. 2 (1988): 31.

Ward, I. A. K., P. Larcombe, and P. Veth. "Towards New Process-Oriented Models for Describing Wreck Disintegration—an Example Using the Pandora Wreck." *Bulletin of the Australian Institute for Maritime Archaeology* 22 (1998): 109–14.

———. "A New Process-Based Model for Wreck Site Formation." *Journal of Archaeological Science* 26 (1999): 561–70.

Ward, J. M. *Empire in the Antipodes: The British in Australasia 1850–1860*. London: Edward Arnold, 1966.

Ward, R. *Australia*. North Sydney: Ure Smith, 1969.

Ward-Haldane, C. "Boat Timbers from El-Lisht: A New Method of Ancient Egyptian Hull Construction. Preliminary Report." *Mariner's Mirror* 74 (1988): 141–52.

Warne, I. "Marmion Beach Wreck." *Bulletin of the Australian Institute for Maritime Archaeology* 10, no. 1 (1986): 46–47.

Warner, O. *The Navy*. Harmondsworth, UK: Penguin Books, 1968.

Watson, K. "Wreck Rescue: Nautical Archaeology in the River Medway." *Nautical Archaeology: Society Newsletter for the World of Underwater, Foreshore, Ship and Boat Archaeology* August (1993): 7–8.

Watson, P. J. "Method and Theory in Shipwreck Archaeology." In *Shipwreck Anthropology*, edited by Richard A. Gould, 23–36. Albuquerque: University of New Mexico Press, 1983.

Watt, J. P. C. *Stewart Island's Kaipipi Shipyard and the Ross Sea Whalers*. Havelock North, N.Z.: Published by the author, 1989.

Watts, G. P., Jr. "The Civil War at Sea: Dawn of an Age of Iron and Engineering." In *Ships and Shipwrecks of the Americas: A History Based on Underwater Archaeology*, edited by George F. Bass, 207–30. London: Thames and Hudson, 1996.

Weaver, P. "HMAS Perth Decommissioned." *Quarterly Newsletter of the Australian Association for Maritime History* 77 (December 1999): 3–4.

Webb, W. J. "The United States Wooden Steamship Program During World War 1." *American Neptune* 35, no. 4 (1975): 275–88.

Wehausen, J. V., A. Mansour, M. C. Ximenes, and F. Stross. "The Colossi of Memnon and Egyptian Barges." *International Journal of Nautical Archaeology and Underwater Exploration* 17, no. 4 (1988): 295–310.

Weisgall, J. M. *Operation Crossroads: The Atomic Tests at Bikini Atoll*. Annapolis: Naval Institute Press, 1994.

Weski, T. "German Windships at the Beginning of the 20th Century—Modern or Outdated?" *Great Circle* 20, no. 1 (1998): 19–45.

West Australian. (Perth, Western Australia) 1938–1996.

Western Australian Maritime Museum. File 193/79/2: Richard McKenna Notes. Fremantle, Western Australia.

White, C. "Putting People Back into Ships: The Use of Archaeological Evidence in the Interpretation of Preserved Ships." *Bulletin of the Australian Institute for Maritime Archaeology* 19, no. 1 (1995): 1–4.

Wilson, R. A. "Wreck of the 'Lady Elizabeth.'" *Sea Breezes: The Magazine of Ships and the Sea* 57, no. 446 (1983): 85–88.

Wood, A. "Hulk Survey, Kidwelly, Dyfed." *Nautical Archaeology: Society Newsletter for the World of Underwater, Foreshore, Ship and Boat Archaeology,* Spring 1996, 6–7.

Wood, J. T. "The Battle Was a Drawn One." In *Battles and Leaders of the Civil War,* edited by R. V. Johnson and C. C. Buel, 97–109. New York: Appleton-Century-Crofts, 1956.

Wyman, D. 1981. "Developing the Plans for the Revolutionary War Privateer Defence." *In the Realms of Gold : the Proceedings of the Tenth Conference on Underwater Archaeology,* edited by William A. Cockrell, 85–94. San Marino, Calif.: Fathom Eight, 1981.

Zacharchuk, W., and P. J. A. Waddell. *The Excavation of the Machault: An 18th-Century French Frigate.* Quebec: Environment Canada, 1984.

Zarzynski, J. "Wiawaka Bateaux Cluster." In *Encyclopedia of Underwater and Maritime Archaeology,* edited by James P. Delgado, 463–64. London: British Museum Press, 1997.

Index

Page numbers in italics refer to illustrations.

Nathan Richards is assistant professor in the Program in Maritime Studies at East Carolina University in Greenville, North Carolina. He is editor of the *Newsletter of the Australasian Institute for Maritime Archaeology*, the author of numerous chapters, articles, and reports, and coauthor of *The Garden Island Ships' Graveyard Maritime Heritage Trail* (2001) with Robyn Hartell. His academic interests include archaeological method and theory and the history of technology.